MW00985514

More Than
Beans and Cornbread

Traditional West Virginia Cooking

More Than Beans and Cornbread

Traditional West Virginia Cooking

Barbara Beury McCallum

Red Sumac Tea,
a West Virginia summertime favorite

Quarrier Press
Charleston, West Virginia

© 1993 by Barbara McCallum

All rights reserved. No portion of this book
may be used of reproduced
without permission of the publisher.

LIBRARY OF CONGRESS
CATALOG CARD NO. 93-86404

ISBN 1-891852-10-8
(Formerly ISBN 0-929521-81-1)

10   9   8   7   6

Photographs courtesy of the West Virginia Department of Agriculture

Original Watercolor Cover Illustration: Sarah Burgess
Cover Design: Mark Phillips, Marketing+Design Group
Typography: Leslie Maricelli
Layout: Stan Cohen

Distributed by
Pictorial Histories Distribution • 1416 Quarrier Street • Charleston, West Virginia 25301

Printed in Canada

TABLE OF CONTENTS

INTRODUCTION

— MORE THAN BEANS AND CORNBREAD —

Texas Chili, New England Clam Chowder, New York Strip Steak, Florida Gulf Shrimp, Virginia Smoked Ham, California Avocado Salad, Boston Baked Beans, Alaskan King Crab...all these mouth-watering foods come to mind when you think of regional specialities.

So what do food fanciers associate with West Virginia? If anything, probably pinto beans and cornbread. A truth, but not the whole truth.

First of all, you must take into account that after the Indians, the State's earliest settlers were chiefly Anglo-Saxon (some say Celts), and Northern European. Later, immigrants came from Middle and South Europe, from Asia, and Africa. Economic opportunity for unskilled labor in the coal fields brought an influx of Southern Negroes after the Civil War (West Virginia is the only State born of this war, separating from Virginia in 1863). Mining also attracted people of Irish, Italian and Hungarian extraction, and later industrial progress in chemicals and other fields brought highly skilled people from all over the globe.

According to the 1990 census, the State's largest ethnic single ancestry groups were still: English, German, Irish, and Italian, followed by Dutch, Polish, French, Hungarian, Greek, Russian, Norwegian, and Portuguese.

Often touted as the "most eastern of the western, western of the eastern, northern of the southern, and southern of the northern" states, West Virginia's food reflects this diversity. Visitors to West Virginia's northern panhandle or western counties may think they're in Pennsylvania or Ohio; the southern counties are more like Kentucky, Tennessee or North Carolina's mountain regions; our eastern panhandle cannot be distinguished from Virginia; while the central counties remind one of the mid-western farm states.

Needless to say, this diversity brings a diversity in "native dishes." Ethnic specialities were often adapted to nature's bounty of wild game and plants; or new dishes were created by necessity because of limited food supplies due to the State's isolation from major markets.

Most people are not aware of West Virginia's large production of apples (10th in the nation), peaches, poultry...even watercress. Or that we celebrate with festivals such agricultural products as buckwheat, black walnuts, strawberries, molasses, and pota- toes. Ewell Gibbons, the late natural foods guru, stated that West Virginia was "nature's supermarket." All these factors add up to some "mighty fine eatin.'"

Preserved here are typical downhome recipes (some converted to use with modern appliances and/or convenience products) which is not to say that West Virginia doesn't have its share of sophisticated cooks and dining places. After all, The

Greenbrier, is internationally known for its cuisine, and many culinary school graduates are chefs at various West Virginia restaurants.

As a collector of West Virginia recipes for some 25 years, I often wondered why most of the cookbooks had few vegetable, salad, or main dish entrees, but huge sections on cakes, pies, and breads. But it makes sense. First of all our pioneer ladies assumed that everyone knew how to make a good stew, roast a haunch of venison, or cook a turnip. Salads (not even introduced until later) were nothing more than lettuce, tomatoes, and cucumbers from the garden, or perhaps native greens with hot bacon dressing. Their real accomplishments in the kitchen were measured by the tantalizing treats they shared at church socials, weddings, funerals, or entered in the county fair. So as a recipe was written down, it was one for Mama's Jam Cake or Aunt Sophie's Pickle Relish that was treasured, and survived.

This cookbook will keep your family eating well, using simple ingredients. If you are mostly into microwave zapping, fast foods, or obsessed with low salt, fat, cholesterol, and have not much interest in how foods "taste," just put this book down now. But if you still like to eat, and believe the enjoyment of same is not the 8th Deadly Sin (as long as you practice Terence's "moderation in all things") then take it home with you.

I promise you "old West Virginia family recipes" to leave to your children, and their children. The kind that celebrate a time when cooking and eating were ends in themselves...not just the joyless science it is becoming.

So, let's break bread —West, By God, Virginia style — you'll discover it is more than pinto beans and cornbread.

THIS BOOK IS DEDICATED TO MY FATHER,
LAWTON H. BEURY,
WHO STILL MAKES THE BEST SCRAMBLED EGGS I'VE EVER TASTED
(IN A WELL-SEASONED IRON SKILLET, OF COURSE);
AND ALL THE WONDERFUL COOKS THROUGHOUT THE
HILLS AND VALLEYS OF WEST VIRGINIA.

Beans and corn bread still a W.Va. favorite

by Delmer Robinson

And how did you survive the Blizzard of '93? I imagine there were quite a few cases of cabin fever before it was all over.

It is traditional that Jewish mothers consider chicken soup the sovereign remedy for all ills, both personal and those of Mother Nature.

But here in West Virginia the big favorite "comfort" food is the magical combination of pinto beans and corn bread. Who am I to fly in the face of tradition? Never mind that the combination of beans and grain is something highly recommended by nutritionists as being good for you, it is sufficient that they simply taste good together. Let the diet experts point out that it is a combination in which 2 and 2 make more than 4 (they complement each other to make a complete protein).

So when the storm hit, my first thought (about food, anyway) was to get a package of cooked pinto beans out of the freezer, and whip up a skillet full of corn bread to go with them. I have some cast-iron skillets that get plenty of use, but never to greater advantage than in making corn bread.

It is nutritional heresy to use bacon drippings (that's a fancy term meaning "grease"). But when the thermometer plunges to below 10 degrees it's easy for me to be heretical.

Using bacon drippings in the skillet in a hot oven produces a crisp, crunchy crust that contrasts well with the light and creamy interior. Even the color is inviting. Split and slathered with butter (another heresy), that's real food on a wintry day. Besides, there's something comforting in using homemade jam or jelly "to make the corn bread come out even." Not exactly a fancy dessert, but a joy nevertheless.

So a skillet-size recipe makes a lot for one person. Just freeze the leftovers for turkey dressing or some other use. Individual slices can be defrosted when needed. I wrap them in slightly dampened paper towels to heat up in the microwave. Don't get them too hot or they will toughen.

Here's the recipe I use for the corn bread.

Ann's Skillet Corn Bread

1 cup cornmeal	1 teaspoon sugar
1/2 cup flour	1 egg
2 teaspoons baking powder	3/4 cup milk
1 teaspoon salt	5 tablespoons bacon drippings or oleo

Preheat oven to 450 degrees. Place 2 tablespoons drippings in 8-inch cast-iron skillet and heat in oven while preparing batter.

Combine dry ingredients well. Mix the egg and milk together. Add the 3 tablespoons melted drippings or oleo. Combine with dry mixture thoroughly but do not overbeat. Pour batter in hot skillet. Bake 20 to 25 minutes until done.

There is a controversy on how much sugar is to be used, if any at all. My mother, who was from Boone County, added just a smidgen to her corn bread, and to this day I do not like corn bread that could pass as dessert it is so sweet. Moderation in all things, I say, to coin a phrase. *Reprinted with permission of Chef Robinson and The Charleston Gazette*

Soups and Stews

Like busy women today, soups and stews were simple ways for pioneer West Virginia women to provide hearty meals for their families while they hoed corn, did the laundry in the wash tub outside, or made their family's clothing. It was also an excellent way to use many garden vegetables, native plants, wild game, or the odds and ends from butchering (and often conceal a meat's rather rancid smell and taste). Many old recipes are found for soups using calf's head, ox tails, pig snouts, or chicken's feet.

Soups would stretch to feed the family, any extra farm help, and wayfaring strangers — a mountain tradition. Even the much-feared "Devil Anse" Hatfield, patriarch of the famed clan who feuded with the McCoys, never turned away a stranger without supper.

Turkey Bone Soup

Bones of one turkey or chicken
2 stalks celery
1 medium onion, sliced thick
1/4 green bell pepper, cut in pieces
1 teasp. paprika

1 teasp. Worcestershire sauce
Salt to taste
6 peppercorns
2 quarts water

Combine all ingredients in a large pot. Bring to SLOW boil, and cook over low heat for 2-3 hours. Strain and freeze in ice cube trays, which after frozen may be put in freezer bags for easy use in recipes calling for chicken stock.

Garden Tomato Soup

4 large tomatoes
1 cup canned chicken broth
4 small spring onions, thinly sliced with tops
1 small cucumber, sliced
1/2 cup diced green pepper

1 cup canned tomato (or V-8) juice
Juice of one lemon
2 teasp. sugar
1 tbsp. seasoned salt
1/4 teasp. seasoned pepper

Prepare this cold soup the day before planning to serve so flavors blend well. Peel tomatoes and cut into chunks. In large saucepan, simmer onions, cucumber, green pepper and tomatoes in the chicken broth for 5 mins. Add tomato (V-8) juice, lemon juice, sugar, salt and pepper. Simmer, covered, for 10 mins. Transfer to large bowl and refrigerate overnight. Makes 6 servings.

Settlers Beans

1/2 lb. ground beef
1/2 lb. bacon, chopped
1 onion, chopped
1 can kidney beans (15 oz.)
1 can pork n' beans (15 oz.)

1 can butter beans (15 oz.)
3/4 cup brown sugar
1 cup catsup
1/2 teasp. dry mustard
Dash Worcestershire sauce

Brown bacon slightly in skillet, remove some of the grease, add onion, then ground beef and continue to cook until beef is brown. Drain well. Drain beans and add to meat mixture, then pour into baking dish. Add remaining ingredients and mix well. Cover and bake at 350 degrees for one hour. Good picnic fare.

Vegetable Soup with Meatballs

3 TBSP. BUTTER

5 CARROTS, SLICED

2 MEDIUM ONIONS, CHOPPED

1 CUP CELERY, DICED

1/2 CUP CHOPPED PARSLEY

1 CUP CORN

1/2 CUP GREEN BELL PEPPER, CHOPPED

2 CUPS CANNED TOMATOES

4 CUPS HOT WATER

2 BEEF BOUILLON CUBES

2 TEASP. SALT

1/4 TEASP. PEPPER

1 SMALL BAY LEAF

1/2 TEASP. BASIL

DISSOLVE BOUILLON CUBES IN HOT WATER IN LARGE SAUCEPAN AND ADD ALL INGREDIENTS. SIMMER FOR 30 MINS., BUT DO NOT BOIL. DROP IN SMALL MEATBALLS AND SIMMER ANOTHER 15 MINS. MAKES 6 SERVINGS.

Small Meatballs

1/2 LB. GROUND BEEF

1/4 CUP DRY BREAD CRUMBS

1/4-1/2 CUP MILK

1 EGG

1/2 TEASP. SALT

1/8 TEASP. PEPPER

1/2 TEASP. NUTMEG

2 TBSP. MINCED ONION

1/2 CLOVE GARLIC, CHOPPED

COMBINE INGREDIENTS AND MIX THOROUGHLY. SHAPE INTO VERY TINY BALLS. BROWN QUICKLY ON ALL SIDES IN SMALL AMOUNT OF VEGETABLE OIL IN HEAVY SKILLET. ADD MEATBALLS TO SOUP.

Game Soup

SKIN GAME BIRDS, RABBIT, HARE OR VENISON. CUT MEAT INTO SMALL PIECES AND BROWN IN BACON DRIPPINGS WITH PIECES OF HAM, ONION, CARROT AND PARSNIP. DRAIN OFF ANY EXCESS FAT, ADD BEEF STOCK TO COVER. ADD ANY BONES AND SEASONINGS (BLACK PEPPER, SALT, CLOVES). STEW FOR TWO HOURS. REMOVE BONES, SKIM FAT AND SERVE HOT.

Potato Soup I

1 LB. POTATOES

1 LARGE SOUP BONE

1 ONION

1/2 LB. OF CARROTS

2 PINTS OF WATER

SALT AND PEPPER

WASH BONE, PEEL ONION AND PUT IN STOCKPOT WITH WATER AND SEASONINGS. BRING TO A BOIL, THEN SIMMER FOR ONE HOUR. PEEL AND DICE POTATOES AND GRATE CARROTS. ADD TO SOUP, THEN SIMMER FOR ONE HOUR. REMOVE SOUP BONE, ONION, CORRECT SEASONINGS.

CREAM OF CHICKEN/CHEESE

4 TBSP. BUTTER
1/4 CUP CHOPPED ONIONS
1/2 CUP CHOPPED CARROTS
1/2 CUP CHOPPED CELERY
SALT, PEPPER, PARSLEY

1 QUART CHICKEN BROTH
1 CUP HEAVY CREAM
1 LB. AMERICAN PROCESSED CHEESE
3 CUPS CHOPPED, COOKED CHICKEN
BREASTS

SAUTÉ THE VEGETABLES IN BUTTER FOR 10 MINS. ADD THE BROTH AND SIMMER 15 MINS. UNTIL VEGETABLES ARE TENDER. ADD CREAM, CHICKEN AND CHEESE THAT HAS BEEN CUT INTO CHUNKS. HEAT UNTIL CHEESE IS MELTED AND SOUP HOT (DO NOT BOIL) AND SEASON WITH SALT AND PEPPER. GARNISH WITH PARSLEY. SERVES 6-8.

LENTIL

4 QUARTS WATER
1 HAMBONE
2 BAY LEAVES
2 CUPS LENTILS

3/4 CUP CHOPPED CELERY
1 CUP SLICED CARROTS
1 LARGE ONION

TO WATER, ADD HAMBONE, BAY LEAVES, SLICED ONION AND SALT AND PEPPER TO TASTE. SIMMER 3 HOURS. REFRIGERATE OVERNIGHT. REMOVE FAT FROM TOP OF STOCK AND DISCARD, ALONG WITH HAMBONE AND BAY LEAVES (REMOVE ANY BITS OF HAM FROM BONE AND ADD TO SOUP). ADD LENTILS (WASHED), CELERY AND CARROTS, SIMMER FOR 1-1/2 HOURS. CORRECT THE SALT AND PEPPER AND ADD A SUGGESTION OF GARLIC, IF DESIRED. SERVES 6-8. *ALISON BERNARD*

CHICKEN VEGETABLE SOUP

3 LBS. CHICKEN
2 QUARTS OF COLD WATER
1 CUP GREEN LIMA BEANS (PARBOILED)
1 CUP DICED CELERY
PEPPER AND SALT TO TASTE

3 TBSP. BUTTER
1 TEASP. SALT
1 CUP SWEET CORN
1/2 CUP STEWED TOMATOES
1 CUP CREAM

DISJOINT CHICKEN AND BROWN CAREFULLY IN BUTTER. PLACE IN SOUP KETTLE WITH WATER AND SALT AND SIMMER UNTIL TENDER. REMOVE CHICKEN, CAREFULLY SKIM GREASE FROM BROTH, THEN ADD LIMA BEANS, SWEET CORN, CELERY AND TOMATO TO BROTH, WITH SALT AND PEPPER. SIMMER UNTIL THE VEGETABLES ARE TENDER, THEN ADD CHICKEN MEAT CUT INTO SMALL PIECES AND STIR IN THE CUP OF CREAM.

Pasta and Bean Soup

2 slices lean salt pork
1 clove garlic
3 tbsp. olive oil
2 quarts hot water
2 cups shell or kidney beans,
(fresh, dried or canned)
3-4 tbsp. Romano cheese, grated

1 small onion
1 rib celery
3-4 plum tomatoes, peeled and
chopped
2 teasp. salt
2 cups pasta (small elbow, squares
or broken spaghetti/linguine).

Chop salt pork, onion, garlic and celery together until mixture has turned into a paste. Heat olive oil in soup kettle. Add salt pork mixture and sauté until golden. Add tomatoes and cook about 3 mins. Add hot water, salt and beans. If using fresh beans, bring to boiling. If using dried beans follow package instructions. If using canned beans, use ones without sugar and add liquid in can plus 1-1/2 quarts water. Once water, salt and beans are boiling, reduce heat and cook until beans are tender (if fresh) or heated through (if canned). Crush a few beans against the side of the pot, add pasta and continue cooking until well done. If soup is too thick, add more water. Taste and add more salt, if needed. Serve with sprinkling of Romano cheese. 8 servings.

Irish Stew

2 lbs. neck or shoulder of lamb
4 cups water
8 small onions

4 small carrots
8 medium potatoes
salt and pepper

Cut meat into servings pieces, discarding excess fat. Place in saucepan with water almost to boiling point and simmer one hour. Add vegetables, coarsely chopped. Season and cook one hour longer without stirring. Serves 4.

Mock Turtle Soup

3 lbs. lean beef cubes
1 pint milk
1 tbsp. flour
1/2 teasp. mace
salt and pepper to taste

1/2 teasp. dry mustard
1-1/2 quarts water
1/4 lb. butter
1/2 pint cream

Boil meat in water until one quart of liquid remains. Add 1 pint milk and 1/4 lb. butter. Remove meat, allow to cool, grind, and return to stock. Let it cook down a little more. Add flour which has been dissolved in cream. Add seasonings. 8 servings.

Mountain Goulash

1 LB. GROUND BEEF
1 LARGE ONION, CHOPPED
1 TBSP. SALAD OIL
1 (12 OZ.) CAN MIXED VEGETABLE JUICE (V-8)
1 CAN TOMATO SAUCE
6 CARROTS, SCRAPED AND SLICED

1 BAY LEAF, CRUMBLED
3 WHOLE ALLSPICE
1 TEASP. SALT
1/2 TEASP. SUGAR
1/8 TEASP. PEPPER

BROWN BEEF AND ONIONS IN SALAD OIL IN LARGE SAUCEPAN. BREAK MEAT WITH A FORK AS IT COOKS. STIR IN REMAINING INGREDIENTS. SIMMER, COVERED, STIRRING OCCASIONALLY UNTIL CARROTS ARE TENDER, ABOUT 30 MINS. SERVE OVER HOT BUTTERED NOODLES OR MASHED POTATOES. 4-6 SERVINGS.

Scotch Broth

1 LB. NECK OF LAMB, OR LEAN BEEF
1 LB. DICED VEGETABLES
 (CARROTS, TURNIPS, LEEKS)
1 GRATED CARROT
1 TEASP. SALT
1 TBSP. CHOPPED PARSLEY

3 PINTS COLD WATER
1 OZ. PEARL BARLEY
2 OZ. DRIED PEAS, SOAKED
1/4 TEASP. PEPPER
4 TBSP. CHOPPED KALE

PUT MEAT, WATER, SALT, PEPPER, WASHED PEARL BARLEY AND PEAS IN A POT. BRING TO A BOIL AND SKIM. ADD DICED VEGETABLES AND SIMMER 3-4 HOURS. REMOVE BONES, CHOP MEAT, REMOVE EXCESS GREASE AND ADD GRATED CARROT AND KALE. COOK 10 MINS. MORE. ADD CHOPPED PARSLEY AND REHEAT.

Spinach Soup

1 PACKAGE FROZEN SPINACH
2 CUPS CLEAR CHICKEN BROTH OR
 1 CAN (13-3/4 OZ.)
1 SMALL ONION
3 TBSP. BUTTER
3 TBSP. FLOUR

2 CUPS MILK
1/3 CUP HEAVY CREAM
SALT AND PEPPER TO TASTE
1/4 TEASP. GRATED NUTMEG OR MACE
1 CUP SOUR CREAM

COOK THE SPINACH ACCORDING TO PACKAGE DIRECTIONS, AND CHOP FINE. PEEL ONION AND FINELY CHOP. MELT THE BUTTER, ADD ONION AND COOK GENTLY WITHOUT BROWNING, STIRRING WITH A WOODEN SPOON UNTIL SOFT. ADD FLOUR, COOK FOR A MINUTE OR TWO, THEN STIR IN THE HOT CLEAR CHICKEN BROTH. WHEN THIS COMES TO A LIVELY BOIL, ADD COOKED SPINACH AND ANY JUICE IT MAY HAVE. ADD MILK AND CONTINUE COOKING UNTIL MIXTURE COMES TO A BOIL. REMOVE FROM HEAT AND SEASON TO TASTE WITH SALT, PEPPER AND NUTMEG OR MACE. STIR IN HEAVY CREAM. SERVE AT ONCE, GARNISH WITH SOUR CREAM.

Potato Soup II

6 CUPS CUBED POTATOES	2 CHICKEN BOUILLON CUBES
2 CUPS WATER	1 TEASP. SALT
1 CUP DICED CELERY	1/8 TEASP. PEPPER
1 CUP CARROTS, SLICED THIN	3 CUPS MILK, DIVIDED
1/2 CUP CHOPPED ONION	1/4 CUP FLOUR
2 TEASP. PARSLEY FLAKES	1/2 TO 3/4 LB. VELVEETA CHEESE

COMBINE FIRST NINE INGREDIENTS. BRING TO BOIL. COVER, REDUCE HEAT AND SIMMER 7 TO 8 MINS. OR UNTIL VEGETABLES ARE DONE. STIR 1/4 CUP MILK INTO FLOUR (MAKING A SMOOTH PASTE). STIR INTO SOUP. ADD 2-3/4 CUPS MILK AND CHEESE. COOK OVER MEDIUM HEAT, STIRRING CONSTANTLY, UNTIL SOUP IS THICKENED. YIELDS 9 CUPS.

Split Pea Soup

1 (16-OZ.) PACKAGE DRIED GREEN SPLIT PEAS	2 BAY LEAVES
2-3/4 QUARTS WATER	1 LARGE HAM HOCK
4 SMALL HOT PEPPERS	1/4 CUP CHOPPED CELERY LEAVES
3 MEDIUM ONIONS, CHOPPED	2 TBSP. CHOPPED PARSLEY
2 MEDIUM CARROTS, DICED	

SORT AND WASH PEAS; PLACE IN A DUTCH OVEN. ADD WATER, COVER AND BRING TO A BOIL. COOK 2 MINS. REMOVE FROM HEAT, AND LET STAND 1 HOUR. ADD REMAINING INGREDIENTS TO PEAS. BRING TO A BOIL AGAIN, COVER, REDUCE HEAT AND SIMMER 1 HOUR. REMOVE HAM HOCK, PEPPERS AND BAY LEAVES. CUT HAM FROM HOCK, AND CHOP; ADD TO PEAS. IF DESIRED, SPOON MIXTURE INTO CONTAINER OF AN ELECTRIC BLENDER, AND PROCESS UNTIL SMOOTH. YIELDS ABOUT 2-1/2 QUARTS.

Leek Soup

3 QUARTS BOILING WATER	2 CUPS FINELY CHOPPED LEEKS*
4 CUPS POTATOES, DICED	2 TBSP. BUTTER
3 TEASP. SALT	1/2 TEASP. PEPPER
4 SLICES STALE BREAD, CUT IN CUBES	4 TBSP. MINCED ONION

WASH LEEKS AND CUT OFF ROOTS. CUT WHITE PARTS INTO THIN SLICES. PARE THE POTATOES AND DICE, PLACE IN BOWL OF COLD WATER UNTIL READY TO USE. PUT THE BUTTER, LEEKS AND ONION IN THE SOUP POT AND COOK SLOWLY ABOUT 20 MINS., STIRRING FREQUENTLY, THEN ADD HOT WATER, POTATOES AND SEASONINGS AND COOK AT LEAST HALF AN HOUR LONGER. ADD BREAD CUBES BEFORE SERVING.

* MAY USE WILD GREEN ONIONS AND/OR RAMPS, OR MIXTURE OF BOTH, OMITTING ONION.

Onion-Vermicelli Soup

3 LBS. LEAN STEW BEEF, CUBED
2 CUPS VERMICELLI

1-1/2 QUARTS WATER
2 CUPS CRISP, FRIED ONIONS

COVER BEEF WITH WATER AND COOK UNTIL MEAT IS VERY WELL DONE AND TENDER. ADD VERMICELLI AND LET BOIL UNTIL TENDER (8-10 MINS.); ADD ONIONS. STIR SWIFTLY UNTIL SOUP THICKENS, THEN SEASON WITH SALT AND PEPPER TO TASTE. 8 SERVINGS.

Vegetable Stew

1/2 LB. DRIED WHITE KIDNEY BEANS*
1-1/2 LBS. FRESH ZUCCHINI
3 MEDIUM TURNIPS
2 RIBS CELERY WITH LEAVES
4 WHOLE CLOVES
1 BAY LEAF
1 TBSP. DRIED BASIL
1-1/2 TBSP. SALT

1 LARGE POTATO
6 MEDIUM CARROTS
3 RED ONIONS
6 CUPS BEEF STOCK
1 CAN (1 LB.) WHOLE TOMATOES
1/8 TEASP. DRIED HOT RED PEPPER
2 TBSP. OLIVE OIL

DRAIN BEANS AND RINSE THEM WELL UNDER COLD WATER. DICE ZUCCHINI; PARE AND DICE TURNIPS AND POTATO; PARE CARROTS AND SLICE THIN; SLICE CELERY IN 1-INCH PIECES. CHOP 2 ONIONS COARSELY AND STUD THIRD ONION WITH 4 WHOLE CLOVES. PLACE BEANS IN 6 QUART DUTCH OVEN WITH STOCK. BRING TO BOIL OVER MEDIUM HEAT. ADD ZUCCHINI, TURNIPS, POTATO, CARROTS, CELERY, ONIONS AND REMAINDER OF INGREDIENTS, EXCEPT OLIVE OIL. RETURN TO BOILING; REDUCE HEAT AND SIMMER, COVERED, 2-1/2 HOURS, OR UNTIL BEANS ARE TENDER. BEFORE SERVING, REMOVE AND DISCARD CLOVE-STUDDED ONION AND BAY LEAF. STIR IN OIL JUST BEFORE SERVING. 6-8 SERVINGS.

* SOAK BEANS OVERNIGHT IN COLD WATER EVEN IF PACKAGE DIRECTIONS SAY NOT TO DO THIS.

Old-Fashioned Bean Soup

HEAT 7 CUPS OF WATER TO BOILING IN A LARGE SOUP POT. SORT AND WASH 2-1/3 CUPS (ABOUT 1 LB.) NAVY BEANS. ADD GRADUALLY TO THE WATER SO BOILING DOES NOT STOP. BOIL TWO MINUTES AND REMOVE FROM HEAT. COVER AND SET ASIDE 1 HOUR. THEN ADD: 5 CUPS OF WATER, 1 LARGE HAM BONE, 2 TEASP. SALT, 1/2 TEASP. PEPPER. COVER POT AND SIMMER 2 HOURS, STIRRING OCCASIONALLY. WASH, PARE AND COOK 3 MEDIUM POTATOES ABOUT 20 MINS. DRAIN AND MASH, SET ASIDE. CLEAN AND CHOP 3 MEDIUM ONIONS, 2 STALKS CELERY, 3 SPRIGS PARSLEY AND 1 CLOVE GARLIC. BLEND POTATOES AND THESE VEGETABLES INTO BEANS AND SIMMER FOR ONE MORE HOUR. REMOVE MEAT FROM HAM BONE AND RETURN TO SOUP. 8-10 SERVINGS.

Asparagus Soup*

1 LB. FRESH ASPARAGUS
1 SMALL ONION
1 CUP CHICKEN BROTH
1/2 TEASP. SALT

1/4 TEASP. PEPPER
1/2 TEASP. SWEET BASIL
1-1/2 CUPS MILK
1/2 CUP CREAM

DISCARD COARSE WHITE ENDS OF ASPARAGUS. COMBINE IN SAUCEPAN WITH ONION, CHICKEN BROTH, SALT AND BASIL. BRING TO A BOIL AND SIMMER FOR 20 MINS. POUR INTO A BLENDER AND BLEND AT HIGH SPEED. WITH MOTOR RUNNING, ADD 1/2 CUP MILK. BLEND UNTIL SMOOTH. RETURN TO SAUCEPAN AND STIR IN REMAINING MILK AND CREAM. HEAT TO SERVING TEMPERATURE, STIRRING TO BLEND.

* WE HAVE WILD ASPARAGUS GROWING IN WEST VIRGINIA.

Corn Chowder

2 SLICES SALT PORK OR 2 TBSP. BUTTER
1/4 CUP PEELED, SLICED ONION
4 CUPS SLICED POTATOES
2 CUPS BOILING WATER
1-1/2 TEASP. SALT
1 CAN KERNEL CORN

1 QUART MILK
2 TBSP. BUTTER, BACON OR HAM FAT
3 TBSP. FLOUR
1/4 TEASP. PEPPER
2 TBSP. MINCED PARSLEY

CUT PORK INTO SMALL PIECES AND ADD ONION. COOK UNTIL SOFT, BUT NOT BROWN. STRAIN OFF FAT INTO POT IN WHICH CHOWDER IS TO BE MADE. ADD POTATOES AND WATER. COVER AND BOIL 15 MINS. ADD CORN AND MILK AND BRING TO BOILING POINT. STIR TOGETHER FAT, FLOUR AND SEASONINGS UNTIL WELL BLENDED AND STIR INTO CHOWDER. HEAT TO BOILING POINT, STIRRING OCCASIONALLY SO IT DOES NOT BURN. SERVE WITH MINCED PARSLEY.

Carrot and Beef Soup

1-1/2 LBS. BEEF BONES
2 QUARTS COLD WATER
6 MEDIUM CARROTS, CUT IN LARGE PIECES
2 TBSP. FRESH CHOPPED PARSLEY

1 MEDIUM ONION, MINCED
1-1/2 TEASP. SALT
1/3 TEASP. PEPPER

CRACK THE BEEF BONES AND PUT INTO COLD WATER WITH CARROTS, ONION AND SEASONINGS. BRING SLOWLY TO BOILING POINT, THEN REDUCE HEAT AND SIMMER UNTIL LIQUID IS REDUCED BY HALF. STRAIN. REMOVE ANY MEAT PIECES AND ADD WITH CARROTS (SLICED) WITH PARSLEY TO SOUP. REHEAT.

Fresh Tomato Soup

2 TBSP. BUTTER

1/4 CUP MINCED CELERY

6 LARGE, RIPE TOMATOES,
   PEELED AND COARSELY CHOPPED

1/2 TEASP. DRIED THYME

SALT AND PEPPER

LARGE ONION, THINLY SLICED

2 TBSP. MINCED CARROT

6 CUPS CHICKEN BROTH OR WATER

2 TBSP. UNCOOKED RICE

1/4 CUP MINCED PARSLEY

IN HEAVY SAUCEPAN COMBINE BUTTER, ONION, CELERY, CARROT AND 2 TBSP. CHICKEN BROTH OR WATER. SIMMER, COVERED OVER LOW HEAT, STIRRING FREQUENTLY, FOR ABOUT 10-15 MINS., OR UNTIL VEGETABLES ARE SOFT. DO NOT BROWN. ADD TOMATOES AND THE REST OF THE BROTH OR WATER. COOK, COVERED OVER LOW HEAT, STIRRING OCCASIONALLY FOR 15 MINS. OR UNTIL TOMATOES HAVE COOKED INTO PULP. REMOVE FROM HEAT AND PUREE IN A BLENDER OR FOOD PROCESSOR. RETURN TO SAUCEPAN AND ADD THYME AND RICE. COOK COVERED OVER MEDIUM HEAT ABOUT 10 MINS. OR UNTIL RICE IS SOFT. CHECK SEASONING, ADDING SALT, IF NECESSARY, AND PEPPER. SPRINKLE WITH PARSLEY AND SERVE. (AMOUNT OF JUICE FROM FRESH TOMATOES IS UNPREDICTABLE. IF SOUP LOOKS TOO THICK, ADD MORE WATER, 2 TBSP. AT A TIME. IF TO BE SERVED CHILLED, OMIT RICE.) 4-6 SERVINGS.

French Onion

3 CUPS SLICED ONIONS

1/2 CUP BUTTER

1-1/2 QUARTS BEEF BROTH

1/2 CUP GRATED PARMESAN CHEESE

SALT AND PEPPER

4 SLICES THIN RYE BREAD, TOASTED

SAUTÉ ONIONS IN BUTTER UNTIL GOLDEN, OVER LOW HEAT, STIRRING FREQUENTLY. ADD BEEF BROTH AND SIMMER 30 MINS. SEASON TO TASTE WITH SALT AND PEPPER. BUTTER RYE TOAST AND SPRINKLE WITH PARMESAN CHEESE. SLIDE UNDER BROILER 2-3 MINS. OR UNTIL CHEESE MELTS. CUT TOAST INTO SQUARES AND FLOAT ON TOP OF SOUP. SERVES 4-6. *ALISON BERNARD.*

Dried Pinto Beans

2 CUPS PINTO BEANS, SOAKED OVERNIGHT

1 HAMBONE WITH SOME MEAT LEFT ON IT

3 QUARTS WATER

1/2 CUP MASHED POTATOES (OPTIONAL)

3 ONIONS, CHOPPED FINE

1 CLOVE GARLIC, MINCED

SIMMER SOAKED BEANS AND HAMBONE FOR 2 HOURS IN 3 QUARTS WATER. ADD THE POTATOES AND STIR, THEN ADD CHOPPED ONION AND GARLIC AND SIMMER 1 HOUR LONGER. REMOVE HAMBONE AND CHOP ALL MEAT. RETURN MEAT TO SOUP AND SERVE WITH SQUARES OF CORNBREAD OR CRACKERS.

Cabbage-Bean Soup

8 OZ. KIELBASA, SLICED 1/4-INCH THICK
1 TBSP. VEGETABLE OIL
1 TEASP. SALT
1/4 TEASP. PEPPER
1 CAN TOMATOES (16 OZ.)
2 CUPS WATER

1 MEDIUM ONION, CHOPPED
1/2 TEASP. THYME
1 SMALL CABBAGE (ABOUT 1-1/2 LBS.)
  COARSELY SHREDDED
1 CAN (20 OZ.) WHITE KIDNEY (GREAT
  NORTHERN) BEANS, DRAINED

IN DUTCH OVEN BROWN SAUSAGE IN OIL, REMOVE SAUSAGE; POUR OFF ALL BUT 1 TBSP. FAT. ADD ONION AND SAUTÉ UNTIL TENDER. STIR IN SALT, THYME AND PEPPER, THEN CABBAGE, TOMATOES, SAUSAGE AND WATER. BRING TO A BOIL, REDUCE HEAT, COVER AND SIMMER 15 MINS. STIR IN BEANS; COOK 5 MINS. OR UNTIL CABBAGE IS DONE AS DESIRED AND BEANS ARE HEATED. 4 SERVINGS.

Hamburger Soup

1 LB. GROUND BEEF
1 (16 OZ.) CAN WHOLE TOMATOES, UNDRAINED
4 CUPS WATER
1 TEASP. SALT
1 BAY LEAF
1 TEASP. WORCESTERSHIRE SAUCE
1 CUP MEDIUM EGG NOODLES, UNCOOKED

1/2 TEASP. DRIED WHOLE THYME
1 MEDIUM ONION, CHOPPED
2 BEEF BOUILLON CUBES
1/2-1 TEASP. PEPPER
3/4 CUP SLICED CELERY
1 (10 OZ.) PACKAGE FROZEN MIXED
  VEGETABLES

COOK GROUND BEEF AND ONION OVER MEDIUM HEAT UNTIL BROWNED. DRAIN ON PAPER TOWEL. DISCARD PAN DRIPPINGS. ADD REST OF INGREDIENTS EXCEPT VEGETABLES, NOODLES AND THYME. BRING TO A BOIL, COVER AND SIMMER 30 MINS. ADD VEGETABLES, NOODLES AND THYME. BRING TO A SECOND BOIL, SIMMER, UNCOVERED, ABOUT 20 MINS., STIRRING OCCASIONALLY. 6-8 SERVINGS.

Beef Stew

2 LBS. BEEF STEW MEAT, CUBED
SALT AND PEPPER TO TASTE
1 CAN (12 OZ.) STRONG ALE
3 ONIONS, CUT IN PIECES
6 CARROTS, CUT IN CHUNKS

1/4 TEASP. THYME
1/4 TEASP. MARJORAM
1/4 TEASP. SAVORY
2-3 LARGE POTATOES, IN CHUNKS

PLACE BEEF, SALT, PEPPER AND 1 CUP WATER IN DUTCH OVEN. ADD ALE, ONION, POTATOES. BRING TO BOIL. LOWER HEAT, COVER AND SIMMER ABOUT 2 HOURS, OR UNTIL BEEF IS ALMOST TENDER. ADD THYME, MARJORAM, SAVORY AND CARROTS. COVER AND COOK ABOUT 30 MINS., OR UNTIL CARROTS AND MEAT ARE VERY TENDER. 4-6 SERVINGS.

Turkey Soup

Turkey bones and leftover skin from roasted turkey
3 onion or chicken bouillon cubes
dash powdered ginger
1/8 teasp. white pepper
1 teasp. poultry seasoning
leftover gravy, if any
1 onion
1 teasp. sugar
1 tbsp. salt
10 cups cold water
3 large carrots, chopped
5 stalks celery with leaves, chopped

Crush turkey carcass, if large, and place in large kettle with remaining bones and skin. Cover with cold water. Add the onion (without removing outer dark leaves as they add color), carrots, celery, sugar, ginger, pepper, salt and poultry seasoning. Bring to boil, reduce heat and simmer 2 hours. Add bouillon cubes and any leftover gravy. Adjust seasonings, adding more salt, if needed. Simmer an additional 30 mins. Strain through a sieve and serve with rice or noodles. For a thicker soup, strain through a colander. Add any bits of meat. Makes about 2-1/2 quarts.

Railroad Stew

2 lbs. ground venison or lean beef
1 green pepper, chopped
4 carrots, diced
2 large turnips, peeled, cubed
1/2 cup shelled green peas
4 teasp. salt
3 large onions, peeled, chopped
4 stalks celery, diced
6 medium potatoes, cubed
1/2 small cabbage, shredded
2 quarts cold water
1/4 teasp. pepper

Brown venison or beef in heavy 2-gallon kettle over fairly high heat, adding about 1 tbsp. bacon drippings or butter, if needed, to keep meat from sticking. Add all remaining ingredients, cover and reduce heat, simmer for 1-1/2 hours. Uncover and simmer very low about 1 hour longer, stirring occasionally. Add more salt and pepper, if needed. Leftover stew freezes well. 6 quarts (16-20 servings.)

Fish Chowder

1 can cream of potato soup
1 can water (or 1-1/2 cans of milk)
1 small onion, grated
As much boneless fish as you like
2 tbsp. butter
salt and pepper to taste

Boil or steam fish. Then combine all ingredients. Bring to boil, lower heat and simmer, stirring occasionally.

Okra Soup

8 CUPS CHICKEN STOCK

4 MEDIUM ONIONS, PEELED AND CHOPPED

2 GREEN PEPPERS, CORED, SEEDED AND CHOPPED

6 LARGE RIPE TOMATOES, PEELED, CORED AND CHOPPED (RESERVE JUICE)

SALT AND CAYENNE PEPPER TO TASTE

4 CUPS SLICED FRESH OKRA (USE TENDER YOUNG PODS AND SLICE ABOUT 1/2-INCH THICK)

3 CUPS COOKED LONG-GRAIN RICE

1 TBSP. SUGAR

2 CUPS MINCED, COOKED CHICKEN

PUT CHICKEN STOCK, MEAT, ONIONS, PEPPERS, TOMATOES AND THEIR JUICE IN LARGE KETTLE AND LET SIMMER AT MEDIUM HEAT, COVERED, ABOUT 1-1/2 HOURS, THEN UNCOVER AND LET COOK ABOUT 1 TO 1-1\2 HOURS LONGER. ADD THE OKRA, COVER AND COOK ABOUT 10 MINS., OR UNTIL OKRA IS JUST TENDER (DO NOT OVERCOOK). ADD COOKED RICE, SUGAR AND SALT. JUST BEFORE SERVING ADD CAYENNE PEPPER (1/4 TEASP. MAKES IT ZIPPY). SERVE WITH CORNBREAD. 12 SERVINGS.

Watercress Soup*

2 TBSP. UNSALTED BUTTER

2 MEDIUM ONIONS, SLICED

2 LBS. POTATOES, PEELED (IF PREFERRED) AND SLICED

3 CUPS MILK

SALT AND PEPPER TO TASTE

2 BUNCHES WATERCRESS

GARNISH: WATERCRESS LEAVES

MELT BUTTER IN LARGE SAUCEPAN. ADD ONIONS, POTATOES, COVER AND SIMMER 10 MINS. ON VERY LOW HEAT. CUT WATERCRESS IN 1-INCH LENGTHS AND ADD TO SAUCEPAN. CONTINUE TO SIMMER FOR ANOTHER 5 MINS. ADD MILK, SALT AND PEPPER. SIMMER 30 MINS., UNTIL POTATOES ARE SOFT AND BREAKING UP. SERVE HOT OR COLD, GARNISHED WITH LEAVES OF WATERCRESS.

* WATERCRESS GROWS WILD IN MANY WEST VIRGINIA STREAMS.

Fresh Corn Soup

6 EARS SWEET CORN (2 CUPS RAW PULP)

1/8 TEASP. WHITE PEPPER

2 CUPS MILK OR CREAM, HEATED

1 TEASP. FLOUR

1 TEASP. SALT

1 TEASP. SUGAR

1 TBSP. BUTTER

GRATE CORN. COVER THE COBS WITH COLD WATER, AND BOIL 30 MINS., THEN STRAIN. TO 1 PINT OF THIS CORN LIQUID ADD THE RAW CORN PULP AND COOK 15 MINS. ADD THE SEASONINGS AND HOT MILK. HEAT THE BUTTER, ADD THE FLOUR AND GRADUALLY ADD THE CORN MIXTURE; COOK 5 MINS. LONGER. 4-6 SERVINGS.

Savory Potato–Cheese Soup

2 CUPS DICED, PEELED POTATOES
1/2 CUP DICED CELERY
2 TEASP. SALT
1-1/4 TEASP. PEPPER
1-1/2 TEASP. STEAK SAUCE
8 OZ. SHARP CHEDDAR CHEESE, GRATED
1 CUP CANNED STEWED TOMATOES
1/4 CUP BUTTER/MARGARINE

1 CUP CHOPPED ONION
2-1/2 CUPS BOILING WATER
1/4 CUP ALL-PURPOSE FLOUR
1/2 TEASP. DRY MUSTARD
2 CUPS MILK
1 TEASP. MINCED PARSLEY
PINCH OF DILLWEED

PUT POTATOES, CELERY, ONION, 1 TEASP. SALT AND PEPPER, AND WATER IN HEAVY KETTLE. BRING TO BOIL AND COVER. SIMMER FOR ABOUT 15 MINS. IN A SAUCEPAN, MELT BUTTER AND BLEND IN FLOUR. ADD REMAINING SALT AND PEPPER, MUSTARD, STEAK SAUCE AND MILK. COOK, STIRRING CONSTANTLY, UNTIL SMOOTH AND THICKENED. ADD REMAINING INGREDIENTS AND POTATO MIXTURE. SIMMER FOR A FEW MINUTES. ABOUT 1-1/2 QUARTS.

Pea and Hambone Soup

3 CUPS DRIED SPLIT PEAS
1 LARGE ONION, CHOPPED
2 TBSP. BACON FAT

SALT AND PEPPER TO TASTE
1-1/2 CUPS MILK
4 CUPS CHICKEN STOCK

GARNISH: 4 TEASP. CHOPPED FRESH MINT

PUT PEAS IN A BOWL, COVER WITH WATER AND SOAK OVERNIGHT. NEXT DAY, DRAIN PEAS AND DISCARD WATER. COARSELY CHOP ONION. PUT BACON FAT IN LARGE SAUCEPAN AND FRY ONION ONLY UNTIL SOFT. ADD HAM BONE AND STOCK. BRING TO A BOIL AND REDUCE HEAT TO SIMMER. ADD PEAS, BRING TO BOIL AGAIN, AND REDUCE TO SIMMER. COOK 1-1/2 TO 2 HOURS, STIRRING OCCASIONALLY. STIR IN SALT, PEPPER AND MILK, AND SIMMER ANOTHER 10 MINS. GARNISH WITH MINT. 6-8 SERVINGS.

Baked Bean Soup

1 QUART BAKED BEANS OR 2 CANS
 (1 LB. EACH) BAKED BEANS
1 MEDIUM ONION, CHOPPED
3 TBSP. BUTTER

SALT AND PEPPER TO TASTE
2 QUARTS WATER
3 TBSP. FLOUR

COOK BEANS, WATER AND ONION UNTIL BEANS ARE VERY SOFT. PUT THROUGH A STRAINER. MELT BUTTER, ADD FLOUR AND WHEN BUBBLING, ADD 2/3 CUPS OF THE BEAN LIQUID. STIR WELL; ADD THE REST OF THE SOUP. SEASON WITH SALT AND PEPPER, REHEAT TO BOILING POINT AND SERVE. 1 CUP STRAINED TOMATOES MAY BE ADDED. SERVES 4-6.

14

Fruit Soup*

2 TBSP. TAPIOCA
1 QUART OF FRUIT (PITTED CHERRIES, PLUMS, STRAWBERRIES, RASPBERRIES, CURRANTS, ETC.)
3 OR 4 STICKS OF CINNAMON

2 EGG YOLKS, WELL-BEATEN
1 CUP BOILING WATER
1/4 CUP SUGAR
1/2 LEMON, SLICED FINE

COOK TAPIOCA IN 1 CUP BOILING WATER UNTIL TENDER, ADDING MORE WATER, IF NECESSARY. BOIL REST OF INGREDIENTS, EXCEPT EGGS, FOR 15 MINS., ADD THE COOKED TAPIOCA, BRING TO A BOIL. POUR VERY GRADUALLY OVER THE 2 WELL-BEATEN EGG YOLKS. SERVE CHILLED.

*ALTHOUGH FRUIT SOUPS ARE CONSIDERED "NOUVELLE CUISINE," THEY ARE, IN FACT, AN OLD-FASHIONED FAVORITE FOR SUMMER.

Chicken Soup

1 STEWING CHICKEN (WHOLE OR CUT UP)
FEW SPRIGS OF PARSLEY
1 WHOLE ONION
6 CARROTS, CUBED
5-6 STALKS CELERY (PIECES WITH SOME TOPS)

4 QUARTS OF WATER
1 BAY LEAF
2 CLOVES (OPTIONAL)
1 TBSP. SALT
WHITE PEPPER

PLACE CHICKEN IN COLD WATER; BRING TO BOIL AND SKIM. COOK ABOUT AN HOUR, ADD ONION, CARROTS, CELERY, SALT AND PEPPER. COOK FOR ANOTHER HOUR OR TWO UNTIL CHICKEN AND VEGETABLES ARE TENDER. REMOVE CHICKEN TO PLATE AND STRAIN SOUP. CHILL AND SKIM OFF FAT BEFORE REHEATING TO SERVE. 8-10 SERVINGS.

**EXTRA CHICKEN BACKS MAKE SOUP STRONGER IN FLAVOR AND ADDING A SWEET POTATO WILL MAKE IT GOLDEN IN COLOR.

Parmesan Herb Soup

HANDFUL OF EACH OF THE FOLLOWING HERBS, MINCED:
CHERVIL, CHIVES, SORREL
1 BUNCH CELERY, MINUS LEAVES, MINCED
1 SPRIG TARRAGON

6 SPRIGS OF PARSLEY
6 CUPS BEEF OR CHICKEN BROTH
GRATED PARMESAN CHEESE

WASH AND DICE CHERVIL, CHIVES, SORREL AND CELERY. ADD TO HEATED BROTH AND SIMMER. ADD TARRAGON AND PARSLEY AND CONTINUE SIMMERING UNTIL ALL HERBS ARE TENDER. BEFORE SERVING SPRINKLE TOP WITH GRATED PARMESAN CHEESE. 6 SERVINGS.

Squash Soup*

1 CUP COLD BOILED SQUASH, MASHED	1 TEASP. SALT
1 TEASP. SUGAR	PINCH PEPPER
PINCH OF MACE	1 TBSP. ONION JUICE
2 TBSP. MINCED CELERY	1 QUART MILK
2 TBSP. BUTTER	1 TBSP. FLOUR

BEAT INTO THE MASHED SQUASH THE SALT, SUGAR, PEPPER, MACE, ONION JUICE AND MINCED CELERY. PLACE ON HEAT STIRRING CONSTANTLY UNTIL HOT. SET ASIDE WHILE HEATING MILK IN SEPARATE SAUCEPAN TO WHICH YOU GRADUALLY ADD BUTTER AND FLOUR STIRRING CONSTANTLY. COMBINE INGREDIENTS AND MIX WELL UNTIL HOT. 4-6 SERVINGS.

* MAY USE TURNIPS OR OTHER ROOT VEGETABLES.

Nut and Tomato Soup

2 CUPS COOKED, FRESH OR CANNED, TOMATOES, STRAINED*	2 TBSP. PEANUT BUTTER OR 1 CUP ROASTED, UNSALTED PEANUTS,
2 CUPS WATER PLUS A LITTLE MORE (*USE STRAINED TOMATO JUICE THEN ADD WATER TO MAKE 2+ CUPS)	GROUND INTO PASTE SALT TO TASTE
2 CUPS MILK	PINCH OF CAYENNE

TAKE THE PEANUT BUTTER OR PEANUT PASTE AND ADD ENOUGH WATER TO MAKE A THICK CREAMY PASTE. ADD TO TOMATOES, WATER AND BOIL 10 MINS. WHEN READY TO TAKE OFF THE HEAT, ADD THE MILK, SALT AND CAYENNE.

Sweet and Sour Cabbage Soup

2 LBS. STEW MEAT AND BONES	1 LARGE ONION
1 CAN TOMATO SAUCE	1/2 TEASP. SALT
1 CAN TOMATO PASTE	1 CARROT
COLD WATER TO COVER	2 LEMONS
HEAD OF CABBAGE	1/2 CUP SUGAR
1 PIECE CELERY	1 APPLE, GRATED

COOK BONES AND ONION SLOWLY IN ABOUT 3 QUARTS OF WATER. WHEN IT COMES TO A BOIL, ADD THE STEW MEAT, SALT, CARROT AND CELERY THEN SIMMER FOR ANOTHER HOUR. STRAIN AND WASH POT REMOVING ANY SCUM THAT MAY HAVE ADHERED TO SIDES. RETURN TO PAN ADDING TOMATO SAUCE, TOMATO PASTE, GRATED APPLE AND SHREDDED CABBAGE. ALLOW TO COOK ANOTHER HOUR. SEASON WITH JUICE FROM 2 LEMONS, ADD SUGAR (WHITE OR BROWN). LET SIMMER UNTIL FLAVORS BLENDED WELL. ABOUT 8 SERVINGS.

OLD-FASHIONED VEGETABLE SOUP

3-4 LBS. MARROW BONES
3 LBS. SHORT RIBS
6 QUARTS COLD WATER
6-7 CARROTS, SLICED
2 EARS CORN (SCRAPE CORN OFF COB, BUT
COOK COB FOR A FEW HOURS AND DISCARD)
2 CANS TOMATOES, CHOPPED, WITH JUICE
1/2 CUP SPLIT YELLOW PEAS
1/2 CUP MACARONI OR 1/4 CUP RICE (OPTIONAL)

1/2 HEAD CABBAGE, CHOPPED
1/2 CUP BARLEY
1 ONION, DICED
2 TEASP. SALT
PEPPER TO TASTE
2 CUPS GREEN BEANS
1 TURNIP, DICED
2 CUPS DICED POTATO
1 CUP CHOPPED CELERY

COOK BONES AND MEAT IN WATER FOR AN HOUR, SKIMMING EVERY 10 MINS. AFTER IT BOILS. ADD ONION, SALT, TOMATOES, CELERY, GREEN BEANS, CABBAGE, BARLEY, CARROTS, CORN AND COBS, AND SPLIT PEAS. COOK SLOWLY 2 HOURS OR MORE. ADD POTATOES (MACARONI/RICE IF USED) AND CONTINUE COOKING UNTIL ALL VEGETABLES ARE DONE. DISCARD CORN COBS. 10 SERVINGS OR MORE. FREEZES WELL.

HEARTY BEEF SOUP

1/4 CUP BUTTER
2 CUPS SHREDDED POTATOES
2 TBSP. CHOPPED ONION
1 TBSP. ALL-PURPOSE FLOUR
4 CUPS MILK

1 PACKAGE (3-1/2 OZ.) DRIED BEEF
1 CAN (8-3/4 OZ.) WHOLE KERNEL CORN
1/4 TEASP. CELERY SEED
SALT AND PEPPER TO TASTE

MELT BUTTER IN 3-QUART SAUCEPAN. ADD POTATOES, ONION AND 1 CUP WATER. COVER ADN BRING TO BOIL; LOWER HEAT AND SIMMER ABOUT 15 MINS. OR UNTIL POTATOES ARE COOKED. STIR FLOUR INTO MIXTURE AND SIMMER 1 MIN. GRADUALLY ADD MILK, STIRRING CONSTANTLY. BREAK DRIED BEEF INTO SMALL PIECES AND STIR IN. ADD UNDRAINED CORN AND CELERY SEED. HEAT, BUT DO NOT BOIL. SEASON TO TASTE WITH SALT AND PEPPER AND SERVE HOT. 6 SERVINGS.

WATERCRESS AND CORN SOUP

2 TEASP. MINCED PARSLEY
PINCH MARJORAM
1 QUART BEEF STOCK
2 CUPS FRESH CORN CUT FROM COB OR 1 CAN
(16 OZ.) WHOLE KERNEL CORN

1/2 CUP CHOPPED WATERCRESS
3 TBSP. BUTTER
SALT AND FRESHLY GROUND PEPPER
TO TASTE
2 HARD COOKED EGGS, SLICED, (OPT.)

COMBINE PARSLEY, MARJORAM, BEEF STOCK IN SAUCEPAN. BRING TO BOIL AND SIMMER 5 MINS. ADD CORN AND SIMMER 25 MINS. OR UNTIL CORN IS WELL-COOKED. PURÉE IN BLENDER. STIR IN WATERCRESS AND BUTTER. SEASON TO TASTE. SERVE HOT GARNISHED WITH EGG SLICES, IF DESIRED. 6-8 SERVINGS.

Pumpkin Soup

1 SMALL PUMPKIN
1/3 CUP BUTTER, DIVIDED
1 QUART CHICKEN OR BEEF STOCK
1 TBSP. SUGAR

SALT AND PEPPER TO TASTE
PINCH OF GROUND ALLSPICE
MILK OR LIGHT CREAM

PEEL, SEED AND CUT PUMPKIN IN SMALL CHUNKS (SHOULD BE ABOUT 1 QUART OF PUMPKIN PIECES.) PLACE IN SAUCEPAN WITH HALF THE BUTTER, STOCK, SUGAR AND 1 TEASP. SALT. BRING TO BOIL, LOWER HEAT AND SIMMER ABOUT 35 MINS. OR UNTIL PUMPKIN IS TENDER. PURÉE IN BLENDER AND RETURN TO SAUCEPAN. SEASON WITH PEPPER AND ALLSPICE AND ADDITIONAL SALT, IF NECESSARY. ADD REMAINING BUTTER AND ENOUGH MILK TO MAKE SOUP OF DESIRED CONSISTENCY. HEAT BUT DO NOT BOIL SERVE WITH FRIED BREAD, IF DESIRED. 6 SERVINGS.

Cucumber Soup

3 POTATOES, PEELED AND CUBED
2 LEEKS, WHITE PART ONLY, SLICED
1 SPRIG PARSLEY
1 TEASP. SALT
1/2 TEASP. PEPPER

1/2 CUP BUTTER
2 ONIONS, FINELY CHOPPED
2 CUPS LIGHT CREAM
1 LARGE CUCUMBER, PEELED AND
   FINELY CHOPPED

PLACE POTATOES, LEEKS, PARSLEY, SALT, PEPPER AND 1 QUART WATER IN LARGE SAUCEPAN. COVER AND SIMMER GENTLY ABOUT 1 HOUR, OR UNTIL VEGETABLES ARE VERY WELL DONE. MELT BUTTER IN A SKILLET, ADD ONION AND COOK UNTIL SOFT BUT NOT BROWN. COMBINE ONION WITH COOKED POTATO MIXTURE AND PURÉE IN BLENDER. COOL THOROUGHLY IN REFRIGERATOR. WHEN MIXTURE IS COLD, STIR IN CREAM AND CHOPPED CUCUMBER. SERVE WELL-CHILLED. SERVES 4-6.

Hearty Ham Soup

1/2 WHOLE HAM BONE OR 1-1/2 LBS.
   SMOKED HAM HOCKS
1/2 HEAD CABBAGE, DICED
1/2 CUP ONION, DICED
3 LARGE CARROTS, DICED
GRATED PARMESAN CHEESE

8 CUPS WATER
1 CLOVE GARLIC
3 LARGE POTATOES, DICED
8 SLICES RYE BREAD, TOASTED
8 SLICES SWISS CHEESE

COMBINE ALL INGREDIENTS EXCEPT CABBAGE IN DUTCH OVEN. COOK UNTIL VEGETABLES ARE TENDER. TAKE HAM FROM BONE AND CUT INTO CHUNKS. RETURN HAM TO SOUP, ADD CABBAGE AND BRING TO BOIL. REDUCE HEAT, COVER AND SIMMER 10 MINS. LADLE SOUP INTO BOWL, TOAST RYE BREAD AND PLACE OVER SOUP IN BOWL. ADD GRATED AND SWISS CHEESE AND BROIL 2-3 MINS. UNTIL CHEESE MELTS.

Parsnip Chowder

5 STRIPS BACON
1 LARGE ONION, THINLY SLICED
1-1/2 LBS. PARSNIPS, PEELED, CORED AND
CUT IN SMALL CUBES
1-1/2 LBS. POTATOES, PEELED AND CUT INTO
SMALL CUBES

3 CUPS MILK
3 TBSP. BUTTER
1 CUP HEAVY CREAM
SALT AND FRESHLY GROUND PEPPER
TO TASTE
CHOPPED PARSLEY

CUT BACON IN SMALL PIECES. COOK UNTIL CRISP AND LIGHTLY BROWNED. REMOVE FROM PAN AND DRAIN ON ABSORBENT PAPER. COOK ONION IN BACON FAT UNTIL SOFT AND LIGHTLY BROWNED. REMOVE ONION AND PLACE IN HEAVY DUTCH OVEN; RESERVE BACON FAT. ADD PARSNIPS, POTATOES, 2 CUPS BOILING WATER TO DUTCH OVEN. COVER TIGHTLY AND COOK ABOUT 30 MINS. OR UNTIL VEGETABLES ARE TENDER. ADD MILK AND HEAT, BUT DO NOT BOIL. STIR IN BUTTER, CREAM AND RESERVED BACON FAT AND SEASON TO TASTE WITH SALT AND PEPPER. POUR HOT SOUP INTO HEATED TUREEN AND SPRINKLE WITH BACON BITS AND CHOPPED PARSLEY. SERVES 6-8.

Cream of Chicken/Cucumber/Onion Soup

2 CUCUMBERS, PEELED, DICED
2 SMALL ONIONS, PEELED, DICED
1/2 CUP BUTTER
2 CUPS WATER
SALT AND WHITE PEPPER TO TASTE

2 CANS (10 OZ.) CREAM OF CHICKEN
SOUP
2 CUPS MILK
1 TEASP. CURRY POWDER

IN A HEAVY 3-4 QUART SAUCEPAN COOK CUCUMBERS, ONIONS AND BUTTER IN WATER UNTIL SOFT. ADD SOUP, MILK, CURRY POWDER, SALT AND WHITE PEPPER TO TASTE. HEAT TO A STRONG SIMMER, STIRRING FREQUENTLY. SERVES 8. *THE COUNTRY INN, BERKELEY SPRINGS, WV*

Old-Fashioned Split-Pea Soup with Ham

2 CUPS SPLIT PEAS (YELLOW OR GREEN)
10 CUPS BOILING WATER
1 (12-16 OZ.) HAM HOCK
1 LARGE ONION, CHOPPED

1 CARROT, DICED
1/4 TEASP. FRESHLY GROUND BLACK
PEPPER
SALT TO TASTE

WASH AND PICK OVER PEAS. PLACE IN A DEEP POT WITH BOILING WATER. ADD HAM HOCK, ONION, CARROT AND PEPPER. SIMMER, COVERED, 1 TO 1-1/2 HOURS OR UNTIL PEAS ARE CREAMY AND ONIONS AND CARROTS VERY SOFT. REMOVE HAM HOCK. DICE MEAT; DISCARD BONE. RETURN MEAT TO POT. SKIM OFF ANY EXCESS FAT. TASTE AND ADD SALT, IF NECESSARY. MAKES 8 SERVINGS.

Oxtail Vegetable

1 PACKAGE OXTAILS
4 QUARTS WATER
2 LARGE ONIONS
2 CUPS SLICED CARROTS
1 CUP CHOPPED CELERY
2 CUPS BARLEY

2 CUPS TOMATOES
2 CUPS DICED POTATOES
1 TEASP. BASIL
1 BAY LEAF
SALT AND PEPPER

SIMMER THE OXTAILS IN WATER WITH SALT, PEPPER, BAY LEAF, AND BASIL FOR 3 HOURS. REFRIGERATE OVERNIGHT. REMOVE FAT AND DISCARD WITH BONES (FROM WHICH MEAT HAS BEEN REMOVED AND ADDED TO SOUP), AND BAY LEAF. ADD THE REMAINING INGREDIENTS AND SIMMER FOR 2 HOURS. ADJUST SEASONINGS AND SERVE. 8-10 SERVINGS. *ALISON BERNARD*

Short Cut Chowder

1 LB. GROUND BEEF
1 (14-1/2 OZ.) CAN TOMATOES
1 (6 OZ.) CAN TOMATO PASTE
1 CAN WATER
1/2 LB. THIN SPAGHETTI (RAW)

1 TEASP. CELERY SALT
1 ONION, DICED
1 (NO. 2) CAN PEAS (DO NOT DRAIN)
1/2 LBS. LONGHORN CHEESE, GRATED

SAUTÉ ONION; BROWN BEEF, SPRINKLE WITH CELERY SALT. ADD TOMATOES, TOMATO PASTE, WATER AND PEAS WITH LIQUID; MIX WELL. ADD RAW SPAGHETTI. COVER AND COOK ABOUT 20 MINS., UNTIL SPAGHETTI IS DONE. ADD CHEESE AND MELT JUST BEFORE SERVING.

Minestrone

1/4 LB. DRIED BEANS, LENTILS AND SPLIT PEAS
  TOGETHER
2 QUARTS WATER
3/4 CUP DICED FRESH VEGETABLES
2 TBSP. RICE
3 TBSP. TUBETTI MACARONI (TINY TUBES)

1/2 CUP RIGATONI
1/4 LARGE ONION, MINCED
1 TSBP. OIL
1/2 CUP FRESH TOMATO, CHOPPED
BASIL AND SALT
1 TBSP. HONEY

WASH BEANS IN COLD WATER AND LET SOAK OVERNIGHT. DRAIN AND PUT INTO 2 QUARTS FRESH WATER ALONG WITH THE 3/4 CUP DICED FRESH VEGETABLES. COOK 1 HOUR. IN THE LAST 15 MINS. OF COOKING ADD THE RICE, TUBETTI AND RIGATONI. SIMMER. SAUTÉ THE ONION IN THE OIL UNTIL LIGHTLY BROWNED. (DO NOT LET IT GET TOO BROWN OR IT WILL BE BITTER.) ADD THE CHOPPED TOMATOES AND COOK WITH THE ONION UNTIL THE TOMATOES BEGIN TO "MELT." ADD BASIL, SALT AND HONEY AND LET COOK A FEW MINS. LONGER. STIR SAUCE INTO SOUP. SERVE VERY HOT. 8 SERVINGS.

Beef Gumbo

1-1/2 LBS. STEWING BEEF
1/2 LB. RAW HAM
3 TBSP. FAT
1 QUART SLICED FRESH OKRA OR
  1 PINT CANNED OKRA
1 MEDIUM ONION, MINCED
1 RED PEPPER POD

3 SWEET PEPPERS, CHOPPED
3 RAW TOMATOES, SLICED OR 1 CUP
  CANNED TOMATOES
2 QUARTS COLD WATER
2 TEASP. SALT
WHITE OR BROWN RICE, COOKED

DICE BEEF AND HAM IN 1-INCH CUBES AND FRY UNTIL WELL-BROWNED IN FAT, USING A HEAVY DEEP KETTLE. ADD THE OKRA, IF FRESH OKRA IS USED, THE ONION, SWEET PEPPERS, TOMATOES, WATER, SALT AND RED PEPPER POD. COVER AND SIMMER FOR 2 HOURS. ADD MORE WATER IF THE LIQUID BOILS AWAY OR THE GUMBO WILL BE TOO THICK. IF CANNED OKRA IS USED, ADD IT DURING THE LAST 30 MINS. BEFORE SERVING REMOVE THE RED PEPPER. SERVE IN DEEP SOUP BOWL CONTAINING A SMALL MOUND OF THE RICE. 6-8 SERVINGS.

Pigs' Knuckles Chowder

3 LBS. PIGS' KNUCKLES
3 QUARTS COLD WATER
1 TBSP. SALT
1/4 TEASP. PEPPER
BLACK BREAD

3/4 CUP SPLIT PEAS, LENTILS OR
BLACK-EYED PEAS (SOAKED TO SOFTEN)
1 MEDIUM ONION, CHOPPED
1 BUNCH SOUP GREENS (CREASY,
  COLLARD, ETC.)

WASH THE PIGS' KNUCKLES, PLACE IN A DEEP KETTLE. COVER WITH THE COLD WATER, ADD SALT AND PEPPER, BOIL FOR 1 HOUR. THEN ADD THE SPLIT PEAS, LENTILS, OR BLACK-EYED PEAS, WHICH SHOULD HAVE BEEN SOAKED 2-3 HOURS IN BOILING WATER TO SOFTEN. ADD ONION AND SOUP GREENS AND TAKE OUT PIGS' KNUCKLES; CUT OFF THE MEAT, LEAVING IT IN GOOD-SIZED PIECES. RETURN TO SOUP AND SERVE WITH BLACK BREAD.

Spanish Bean

1 BEEF SOUP BONE
4 MEDIUM POTATOES, CUBED
2 GREEN PEPPERS, CHOPPED
1 CUP RICE
1 PACKAGE SLICED PEPPERONI

1 CAN CHICK PEAS
1/4 TEASP. GARLIC POWDER
1 TBSP. COOK'S MAGIC YELLOW
  RICE SEASONING

SIMMER THE SOUP BONE IN WATER 3 HOURS. CHILL AND REMOVE THE FAT AND BONE. ADD CUBED POTATOES, CHOPPED GREEN PEPPERS, SLICED PEPPERONI, RICE AND SEASONINGS. COOK 45 MINS. OR UNTIL RICE AND POTATOES ARE DONE. ADD CHICK PEAS AND COOK 15 MINS. LONGER. 6-8 SERVINGS. *ALISON BERNARD*

GOULASH

1-1/2 LBS. GROUND BEEF
3 CUPS EGG NOODLES
2 QUARTS STEWED TOMATOES
2 CANS WHOLE KERNEL CORN

2 CANS PEAS
2 CANS KIDNEY BEANS
1 CUP PARTLY COOKED CELERY
2 CANS STRING BEANS

BROWN BEEF IN FRY PAN. COOK ABOUT 3 CUPS EGG NOODLES; DRAIN. IN LARGE ROASTER COMBINE BEEF, TOMATOES, CORN, PEAS, BEANS AND CELERY. DO NOT DRAIN CANS BEFORE COMBINING. BAKE 1 HOUR AT 350 DEGREES.

JUNE'S TEXAS-STYLE BEAN SOUP

4 CUPS PINTO BEANS
1/4 LB. SALT PORK OR BACON, DICED
1 CUP DICED GREEN PEPPER
2 TEASP. SALT AND PEPPER TO TASTE
6 TEASP. HOT PEPPER SAUCE (LESS IF DESIRED)

1 CUP CHOPPED ONION
1 CLOVE GARLIC
1 TBSP. SUGAR
4 CUPS CANNED TOMATOES OR
  1 LARGE CAN TOMATO SAUCE

COVER BEANS WITH WATER AND SOAK OVERNIGHT. TO WATER AND BEANS, ADD ONION, PORK AND GARLIC. COOK OVER LOW HEAT, COVERED FOR 2 HOURS. ADD TOMATOES, GREEN PEPPER, HOT SAUCE AND SUGAR, COVER, AND COOK FOR 3 MORE HOURS. ADD SALT AND PEPPER TO TASTE BEFORE SERVING. 10-12 SERVINGS. *ALISON BERNARD*

SWISS POTATO SOUP

1 CUP CHICKEN BROTH
3 CUPS CHOPPED POTATOES
1/2 CUP CHOPPED CELERY
1/4 CUP CHOPPED ONION
1 TEASP. PARSLEY FLAKES
1 TEASP. SALT

2-1/2 CUPS MILK
2 TBSP. FLOUR
1 6 OZ. PACKAGE SHREDDED SWISS
  CHEESE
6 SLICES BACON, COOKED, CRUMBLED

COOK VEGETABLES AND SEASONINGS IN CHICKEN BROTH OVER MEDIUM HEAT 10 MINS. OR UNTIL POTATOES ARE TENDER. ADD SMALL AMOUNT OF MILK TO FLOUR, STIRRING UNTIL WELL-BLENDED. GRADUALLY ADD FLOUR MIXTURE TO HOT VEGETABLES. ADD REMAINING MILK; COOK UNTIL MIXTURE BOILS AND THICKENS. ADD CHEESE AND BACON, STIRRING UNTIL CHEESE MELTS. 6-8 SERVINGS.

Tomato-Cabbage Soup with Meatballs

Soup

3 VEGETABLE BOUILLON CUBES
1 CAN (6 OZ.) TOMATO PASTE
1 TBSP. BUTTER OR MARGARINE
1 TEASP. SALT
1/4 TEASP. PEPPER

1-1/2 TEASP. SUGAR
DASH OF CRUSHED RED PEPPER
1 LARGE ONION, CHOPPED
4 CUPS SHREDDED CABBAGE

Meatballs

1-1/2 SLICES WHITE BREAD
1/2 CUP STOCK OR WATER
1 LB. GROUND BEEF
1 MEDIUM ONION, GRATED
1 CLOVE GARLIC, CRUSHED
1 EGG

1/2 TEASP. SALT
DASH CRUSHED RED PEPPER
DASH SAGE
DASH THYME
2-1/2 TEASP. SHORTENING OR
    VEGETABLE OIL

PREPARE MEATBALL MIXTURE FIRST. PUT BREAD IN A LARGE BOWL. POUR IN STOCK AND LET SOAK A FEW MINS. THEN MASH WITH FORK. ADD BEEF, ONION, GARLIC, EGG, SALT, RED PEPPER, SAGE AND THYME. MIX THOROUGHLY AND KEEP REFRIGERATED UNTIL NEEDED. TO MAKE SOUP, POUR 1-1/2 QUARTS WATER INTO A LARGE POT, STIR IN BOUILLON CUBES AND TOMATO PASTE. ADD BUTTER, SALT, PEPPER, SUGAR, RED PEPPER AND ONION. COOK TO A BOIL, THEN LOWER HEAT, COVER AND COOK SLOWLY 15 MINS. ADD CABBAGE AND COOK 15 MINS. LONGER. WHILE CABBAGE COOKS, MAKE ABOUT 24 LITTLE MEATBALLS. HEAT SHORTENING IN SKILLET AND BROWN MEATBALLS. ADD TO SOUP AND COOK 10 MINS. MAKES 6 SERVINGS.

West Virginia's senior U.S. Senator, the Honorable Robert C. Byrd,
toasts a 1950's Dairy Princess.

MEATS AND ENTREÉS

When the first settlers came into what is now West Virginia, they were overwhelmed with its pristine beauty, and the abundance of wild game. There were wild turkeys, ducks, pigeons, woodcock and grouse as well as deer, bear, squirrel, rabbit, raccoon and possum filling the woods and meadows. All manner of fish inhabited its streams, rivers and lakes. They brought with them cows, although they were kept more for milk, butter and cheese, than eating. Sheep were raised for wool, chickens for eggs, although old chickens often found their way into the cookpot where a long, slow cooking tenderized the meat. Pigs were the easiest livestock to raise for meat as they were allowed to roam free to eat berries, nuts and roots (the beginning of the Hatfield-McCoy feud was over just such a roamin' hog). So many older recipes use very little meat, often just as a seasoning for the vegetable ingredients, which would gather applause from the nutritionists of today.

STUFFED CABBAGE I

2 LARGE HEADS CABBAGE
2 LBS. GROUND CHUCK OR LEAN BEEF
1/4 CUP RICE, RINSED BUT NOT DRY
1/2 CUP KARO SYRUP (LIGHT)
SALT AND PEPPER TO TASTE

JUICE OF 1-1/2 LEMONS
6 TBSP. MINCED ONIONS
2 CANS TOMATO SOUP
2 CANS COLD WATER
1 CUP BROWN SUGAR

SOFTEN CABBAGE LEAVES IN BOILING WATER. USE ONLY LARGE OUTER LEAVES TO MAKE
ROLLS. COMBINE MEAT, RICE, SEASONINGS AND ONION. SPREAD MIXTURE ON INDIVIDUAL
CABBAGE LEAVES AND ROLL UP, FOLDING OR TUCKING ENDS IN. PLACE IN LARGE ROASTING
PAN. MIX TOMATO SOUP, WATER, SYRUP, SUGAR AND LEMON JUICE. POUR OVER CABBAGE
ROLLS, COVER AND BAKE AT 300 DEGREES FOR 1 TO 1-1/2 HOURS.

SAUSAGE LASAGNA WRAPS

1 LB. SMOKED SAUSAGE
3 SLICES MOZZARELLA CHEESE
6 LASAGNA NOODLES

1 16 OZ. JAR SPAGHETTI SAUCE
PARMESAN CHEESE

COOK AND DRAIN LASAGNA NOODLES. DIVIDE SAUSAGE INTO 6 PIECES. SPLIT LENGTHWISE
AND STUFF WITH 1/2 SLICE OF MOZZARELLA CHEESE. WRAP EACH SAUSAGE IN A LASAGNA
NOODLE. PLACE IN A BAKING DISH AND COVER WITH SPAGHETTI SAUCE. BAKE AT 350
DEGREES FOR 30 MINS. SPRINKLE WITH PARMESAN CHEESE BEFORE SERVING. SERVES 6.

BEER BATTER FRIED CHICKEN
THIS BATTER MAY BE USED FOR ANY FRIED FOODS THAT YOU USE MILK BATTER
FOR FRYING, BUT MAKES LIGHTER, FLUFFIER BATTER.

1 12 OZ. CAN LIGHT BEER
2 TEASP. SALT
1/2 TEASP. PEPPER
2 BROILER/FRYERS ABOUT 2 TO 2-1/2 LBS.
  EACH, CUT INTO PIECES

LARD, SALAD OIL OR VEGETABLE
  SHORTENING FOR FRYING
1-1/2 CUPS ALL-PURPOSE FLOUR
2 TEASP. PAPRIKA (OPTIONAL)

POUR BEER INTO LARGE BOWL. SIFT FLOUR, SALT, PEPPER AND PAPRIKA INTO BEER,
STIRRING WITH WIRE WHIP OR ROTARY BEATER UNTIL LIGHT, FROTHY AND SMOOTH. LET
STAND AT ROOM TEMPERATURE FOR 15 MINS. TO 2 HOURS, STIRRING OCCASIONALLY TO
KEEP BATTER MIXED. PUT FAT TO MEASURE 1-INCH IN HEAVY FRYING PAN. HEAT TO 375
DEGREES OR UNTIL BREAD CUBE DROPPED IN TURNS BROWN IN 60 SECS. DIP CHICKEN PIECES
INTO BATTER AND ALLOW EXCESS TO DRIP BACK INTO BOWL. DROP INTO HOT FAT, A FEW
AT A TIME, NOT ALLOWING TO TOUCH. COOK FOR 15 MINS. ON ONE SIDE, THEN TURN AND
COOK 15 MINS. MORE. DRAIN ON PAPER TOWELS AND BLOT OFF EXCESS OIL. KEEP WARM
IN 200 DEGREE OVEN UNTIL ALL CHICKEN IS READY TO SERVE.

Oven Barbecued Pork Chops

6 LEAN PORK CHOPS
1 TEASP. SALT
1/3 CUP VINEGAR
1 CUP WATER

1/2 CUP KETCHUP
1 TEASP. CELERY SALT
1/2 TEASP. NUTMEG
1 BAY LEAF

BROWN PORK CHOPS. COMBINE REMAINING INGREDIENTS, POUR OVER CHOPS. BAKE IN SLOW OVEN 300 DEGREES FOR 1-1/2 HOURS, TURNING ONCE DURING COOKING TIME.

Chicken Croquettes I

5 TBSP. BUTTER
4 TBSP. FLOUR
1/2 TEASP. GROUND MUSTARD
1/4 LB. MUSHROOMS, MINCED
SALT AND PEPPER TO TASTE

2 TBSP. MINCED ONION
1 CUP WELL-SEASONED STRONG
   CHICKEN BOUILLON
2 CUPS COOKED, MINCED CHICKEN OR
   TURKEY

Breading

1/2 CUP FLOUR
1 EGG SLIGHTLY STIRRED, NOT BEATEN
1/2 CUP DRY BREADCRUMBS, FINELY CRUSHED

3 TBSP. GRATED PARMESAN CHEESE
OIL OR SHORTENING FOR FRYING

PLACE MINCED MUSHROOMS IN A HEAVY FRYING PAN AND COOK, STIRRING CONSTANTLY, UNTIL NO LIQUID REMAINS. STIR IN 1 TBSP. BUTTER AND REMOVE FROM HEAT. COOL BEFORE ADDING TO CROQUETTE MIXTURE AND REFRIGERATE FOR ABOUT 30 MINS., OR UNTIL FIRM ENOUGH TO SHAPE. WITH LIGHTLY FLOURED HANDS SHAPE CROQUETTES INTO 1x1x2-1/2 SIZE. DIP INTO FLOUR, THEN EGG, THEN BREADCRUMBS WITH PARMESAN CHEESE. LET STAND AT ROOM TEMPERATURE UNTIL SOMEWHAT DRIED OUT (ABOUT 1 HOUR). HEAT OIL AND FRY ABOUT 3-4 MINS. ON EACH SIDE. DRAIN AND KEEP WARM UNTIL ALL CROQUETTES ARE FRIED.

Stewed Mutton*

REMOVE THE PINK SKIN AND EXTRA FAT. CUT INTO PIECES, SEASON WITH SALT AND PEPPER, AND COVER WITH BOILING WATER. ADD A DICED CARROT, AND A SLICED ONION. COOK SLOWLY UNTIL TENDER, ABOUT 2-1/2 HOURS. SERVE WITH BISCUITS AND BROWN GRAVY.

*MUTTON COMES FROM SHEEP OVER ONE YEAR OF AGE, AND ITS FLAVOR IS DISTINCTLY STRONGER THAN THAT OF LAMB WHICH COMES FROM SHEEP LESS THAN ONE YEAR OLD.

Brisket and Carrot Stew

2 LBS. BRISKET OF BEEF
2 BUNCHES OF CARROTS
2 TBSP. FLOUR

SALT AND PEPPER TO TASTE
2 TBSP. FAT

SEASON THE MEAT AND LET STAND SEVERAL HOURS. PEEL AND DICE THE CARROTS. PLACE IN A PAN WITH THE MEAT, COVER WITH BOILING WATER AND COOK, COVERED, ABOUT 1 HOUR, OR UNTIL TENDER. HEAT THE FAT IN A SKILLET, BROWN SLIGHTLY, ADD FLOUR, AND GRADUALLY ADD 1 CUP OF STOCK FROM COOKED MEAT/CARROTS. ADD TO MEAT AND CARROTS AND SIMMER UNTIL CARROTS BECOME BROWNED, ABOUT 1 MORE HOUR. 8 SERVINGS.

Southern Spaghetti for a Crowd

2 LBS. SPAGHETTI
3 ONIONS, SLICED
2 GREEN PEPPERS, CHOPPED
1 CUP COOKED KIDNEY BEANS
1 CAN (10-1/2 OZ.) TOMATOES
SALT AND PEPPER TO TASTE

1/2 LB. BACON, DICED
1-1/2 LBS. CHOPPED RAW BEEF
2 TBSP. CHOPPED PARSLEY
1 CUP COOKED PEAS
1/2 LB. MUSHROOMS, SLICED
1/2 LB. GRATED CHEDDAR CHEESE

BOIL SPAGHETTI AND RINSE IN COLD WATER; DRAIN. PLACE BACON IN SKILLET AND FRY OUT FAT; ADD ONIONS, AND FRY TO GOLDEN BROWN. ADD MEAT AND VEGETABLES AND SIMMER A FEW MINS. SEASON TO TASTE. IN A LARGE BAKING DISH, ALTERNATE LAYERS OF SPAGHETTI, MEAT MIXTURE. SPRINKLE THE LAST LAYER OF SPAGHETTI WITH THE GRATED CHEESE. BAKE AT 300 DEGREES ABOUT 2 HOURS. SERVES 15.

Mock Duck

2 THIN SLICES RUMP OR FLANK STEAK
1/8 TEASP. PEPPER
3 TBSP. FAT DRIPPINGS
1 TBSP. GRATED ONION
1 SLICE CHOPPED BOILED HAM

1 TEASP. SALT
1/8 TEASP. GINGER
1 CUP BREADCRUMBS
1 TEASP. CHOPPED PARSLEY

SEASON STEAK WITH SALT, PEPPER AND GINGER. MELT FAT, ADD BREADCRUMBS AND THE REST OF THE INGREDIENTS AND SPREAD EVENLY OVER HALF THE STEAK. COVER WITH REMAINING STEAK AND SEW THE EDGES TOGETHER WITH COARSE THREAD. TIE A STRING AROUND THE END OF THE MEAT TO RESEMBLE THE HEAD OF A DUCK. PLACE THE "DUCK" IN A HEAVY SKILLET WITH A LITTLE FAT. BROWN, ADD 1 CUP BOILING WATER, COVER, AND LET SIMMER SEVERAL HOURS UNTIL TENDER. REMOVE STRINGS, PLACE "DUCK" IN HOT 450-475 DEGREE OVEN AND BROWN, BASTING OFTEN. SERVE WITH ITS OWN SAUCE. SERVES 4.

Corn and Swiss Cheese Bake

3 cups fresh corn, cut from cob*
1 egg, well-beaten
1/2 teasp. salt
4 oz. (approx. 1 cup) Swiss cheese, shredded

1 cup sour cream
2 tbsp. onion, finely chopped
dash of white pepper
1/2 cup soft breadcrumbs
1 tbsp. butter

Preheat oven to 350. Place 1/4 teasp. salt and 1 cup water in saucepan. Bring water to boil and cook fresh corn 2-3 mins., just until tender. Drain corn well. Combine corn, sour cream, egg, onion, salt, pepper and 3/4 of cheese in a mixing bowl. Turn corn mixture into 10x6x1-1/2-inch baking dish. Melt butter in small pan. Remove from heat and toss breadcrumbs and remaining cheese in butter. Sprinkle over corn mixture. Bake for 25-30 mins. 4-6 servings.

*May substitute two 9 oz. packages frozen corn or two 1 lb. cans whole kernel corn.

Boiled Sweetbreads*

1 lb. sweetbreads
1/2 teasp. salt

1 pint boiling water
1 tbsp. vinegar or lemon juice

Soak the sweetbreads in cold water for 20 mins. Cook in boiling, salted water with vinegar or lemon juice for 20 mins. Plunge into cold water, remove and discard tubes and membranes. Slice meat in medium white sauce and serve on toast, or with chicken, mushrooms or peas in patty shells. 4 servings.

Medium White Sauce: 1 cup hot milk, 2 tbsp. butter, 2 tbsp. flour, 1/4 teasp. salt, 1/8 teasp. pepper. Scald milk. Melt butter in saucepan over low heat or in double boiler. Add flour, stirring constantly. Stir in the hot milk gradually, and cook, stirring constantly, until mixture thickens. If lumpy, beat well with electric beater. Season with salt and pepper to taste.

*Sweetbreads are the thymus glands of calf, steer or lamb.

Spareribs and Sauerkraut I

2-1/2 to 3 lbs. of spareribs

1 (1 lb. 13 oz.) can sauerkraut

Brown spareribs in a skillet. Transfer to a large Dutch oven, add sauerkraut, and cook, covered 1 hour, or until ribs are tender and very well done. May also be baked in 375 degree oven about 1 hour. If desired, add 1/2 teasp. caraway seeds and one apple, pared, cored and grated. 4 servings.

Chicken Fricassee

1 STEWING CHICKEN
SALT, PEPPER AND GINGER TO TASTE
4 TBSP. FLOUR

1/2 CUP EACH, DICED ONION AND
   CELERY
3 TBSP. FAT

COVER CHICKEN WITH WATER, ADD VEGETABLES AND SEASONINGS, AND SIMMER UNTIL TENDER (ABOUT 1 HOUR). REMOVE FROM BROTH. MELT FAT IN A DOUBLE BOILER, ADD FLOUR, STIR WELL, AND GRADUALLY ADD 2 CUPS OF CHICKEN BROTH, STIRRING TO PREVENT LUMPS. ADD CHICKEN, REHEAT. 6-8 SERVINGS.

Swiss Cream Steak

2 LBS. ROUND STEAK
SALT, PEPPER
1/2 TEASP. DRIED MARJORAM
FLOUR
1/2 CUP SOUR CREAM

2 TBSP. GRATED PARMESAN CHEESE
2 MEDIUM ONIONS, THINLY SLICED
1/2 CUP BEEF BROTH OR 1 BEEF
   BOUILLON CUBE DISSOLVED IN
    1 CUP WATER

SPRINKLE BOTH SIDES OF STEAK WITH SALT, PEPPER, MARJORAM AND FLOUR. POUND INTO MEAT. HEAT BUTTER IN LARGE SKILLET (WITH LID), TOSS IN ONION SLICES AND COOK UNTIL TRANSLUCENT. LIFT OUT ONIONS WITH SLOTTED SPOON AND SET ASIDE. ADD STEAK TO HOT FAT AND FRY ON BOTH SIDES, OVER BRISK HEAT, UNTIL WELL-BROWNED. ADD BEEF BROTH MIXED WITH SOUR CREAM, GRATED CHEESE AND COOKED ONIONS. COVER TIGHTLY AND COOK OVER LOW HEAT FOR ABOUT 1 TO 1-1/2 HOURS OR UNTIL MEAT IS FORK TENDER.

Stuffed Cabbage II

1 HEAD GREEN CABBAGE
3 EGGS
1 MEDIUM ONION, CHOPPED
2 TEASP. SALT, 1/4 TEASP. PEPPER
1 CUP TOMATO JUICE
1/4 CUP CIDER VINEGAR

8 OZ. GROUND SIRLOIN
12 OZ. GROUND PORK
1/2 CUP COOKED WHITE RICE
ABOUT 1/3 CUP MILK
1 CUP BEEF STOCK
1 BAY LEAF

CORE CABBAGE. PLACE IN DEEP POT ADDING BOILING WATER TO COVER. SIMMER ABOUT 10 MINS. DRAIN CAREFULLY. PULL OFF 16-18 LARGEST OUTER LEAVES. TRIM DOWN THE THICK CENTER RIBS. COMBINE SIRLOIN, PORK, EGGS, ONION, RICE, SALT, PEPPER AND JUST ENOUGH MILK TO MAKE LOOSE MIXTURE. PUT 1/4 CUP FILLING IN CENTER OF EACH CABBAGE LEAF, ROLL UP AND TUCK IN THE ENDS, MAKING A NEAT PACKAGE. PREHEAT OVEN TO 350 DEGREES. PLACE CABBAGE ROLLS SIDE BY SIDE IN A SHALLOW, WELL-GREASED BAKING DISH. COMBINE THE TOMATO JUICE, STOCK, VINEGAR, AND BAY LEAF AND POUR OVER CABBAGE ROLLS. COVER AND BAKE FOR 1 HOUR. SERVES 6.

Red Flannel Hash

3 MEDIUM BEETS, COOKED	PEPPER
1 LARGE POTATO, COOKED	1/2 CUP (1 STICK) BUTTER
1 LB. CHUCK STEAK, GROUND	1 MEDIUM ONION, CHOPPED
SALT	1 TBSP. CREAM

CHOP BEETS AND POTATO, MIX WITH GROUND CHUCK, ADD SALT AND PEPPER. MELT 4 TBSP. OF THE BUTTER IN LARGE SKILLET, ADD CHOPPED ONION, AND COOK UNTIL LIMP. STIR IN MEAT/VEGETABLE MIXTURE AND COOK OVER LOW HEAT FOR 10 MINS., STIRRING OCCASIONALLY. PUT MIXTURE INTO MEDIUM BAKING DISH. MELT REMAINING BUTTER AND COMBINE WITH CREAM. SPOON OVER HASH. PLACE UNDER PREHEATED BROILER, 3 INCHES FROM UNIT FOR 5 MINS. OR UNTIL HASH HAS A RICH, BROWN CRUST. MAY BE SERVED WITH POACHED EGGS ON TOP. SERVES 4.

Baked Chicken Salad

3 CUPS CHOPPED, COOKED CHICKEN	1-1/2 CUPS CELERY SLICES
1 CUP (4 OZ.) SHREDDED CHEDDAR CHEESE	1 TBSP. CHOPPED ONION
1 TBSP. LEMON JUICE	DASH OF PEPPER
6 TOMATO SLICES	2 CUPS CRUSHED POTATO CHIPS
MAYONNAISE	

PREHEAT OVEN TO 350 DEGREES. COMBINE CHICKEN, CELERY, 1/2 CUP CHEESE, ONION, LEMON JUICE, SEASONINGS AND ENOUGH MAYONNAISE TO MOISTEN, MIX LIGHTLY. PLACE IN 1-1/2 QUART CASSEROLE, TOP WITH TOMATO SLICES. BAKE FOR 35 MINS. COMBINE REMAINING CHEESE AND POTATO CHIPS; SPRINKLE OVER CASSEROLE, RETURN TO OVEN UNTIL CHEESE MELTS, 5-10 MINS. 4 SERVINGS.

Chicken-Fried Steak

1 CUP DRY BREADCRUMBS	1 LARGE EGG, BEATEN
1/2 TEASP. SALT	1/4 CUP VEGETABLE OIL
1/4 TEASP. FRESHLY GROUND BLACK PEPPER	2 TBSP. FLOUR
8 THIN SLICES ROUND STEAK OR MINUTE	1 CUP WATER OR MILK
STEAK (APPROX. 1 LB.)	ADDITIONAL SALT/PEPPER TO TASTE

ON A PLATE, MIX BREADCRUMBS WITH 1/2 TEASP. SALT AND 1/4 TEASP. PEPPER. DIP BEEF INTO BEATEN EGG, THEN BREADCRUMBS. HEAT OIL IN HEAVY SKILLET AND ADD MEAT. BROWN OVER LOW HEAT 10-15 MINS. ON EACH SIDE. PLACE ON A WARM PLATTER AND KEEP HOT. MAKE A GRAVY BY ADDING FLOUR TO PAN DRIPPINGS. STIR OVER MEDIUM HEAT UNTIL LIGHT BROWN. WITH A WHISK, STIR IN WATER OR MILK UNTIL THICKENED. ADD MORE LIQUID IF TOO THICK. ADD SALT/PEPPER TO TASTE. RETURN STEAKS TO PAN. SIMMER UNTIL READY TO SERVE. 4 SERVINGS.

Reuben Casserole

1 6 oz. package noodles, cooked, drained
1 11-oz. can sauerkraut, drained
2 medium tomatoes, thinly sliced
2 tbsp. Thousand Island dressing
2 tbsp. melted butter

1 8 oz. can corned beef, shredded
1 8 oz. package shredded Swiss cheese
3 rye crackers, crumbled
1/4 teasp. caraway seeds

Layer noodles, sauerkraut and tomatoes in 7x11 baking dish. Top with salad dressing, drizzle with butter. Then layer corned beef and cheese, topping with crackers and caraway seeds. Bake, covered, in 350 degree oven for 45 mins. to 1 hour, or until bubbly. Serves 4.

Chicken à la King

2 tbsp. chopped celery
1/3 cup chopped green pepper
3 tbsp. butter
1 tbsp. flour
1 can condensed cream of chicken soup
salt and pepper to taste

1-1/2 cups sliced mushrooms (two 3-oz. cans)
3/4 cup diced chicken (one 5-1/2 oz. can, if using canned)
1/4 cup chopped pimiento

Sauté celery and pepper in butter until tender. Stir in flour, soup and mushrooms. Cook until thick, stirring fairly often. Add pimiento, chicken, salt and pepper. Heat. Serve over rice or biscuits. Serves 4-6.

Baked Stuffed Pork Chops

4 (1-1/2 inch thick) pork loin chops
1/4 cup butter
2 garlic cloves, minced
1 medium onion, chopped
1/2 cup chopped celery

1/2 cup chopped green pepper
2 cups soft breadcrumbs
about 1 cup beef or chicken broth
salt and black pepper to taste
1/4 cup all-purpose flour

Preheat oven to 325 degrees. With a sharp knife, cut a slit in each pork chop for stuffing. In a large, heavy, ovenproof skillet or casserole, heat 2 tbsp. butter. Add garlic, onion, celery and green pepper. Sauté over low heat about 10 mins. or until soft. Mix with breadcrumbs. Add about 1/2 cup broth to moisten so mixture will stay together. Add salt and black pepper. Stuff each pork chop with 1/4 mixture. Close chop with wooden pick. Sprinkle with salt, pepper and flour. Melt remaining butter in skillet. Add stuffed chops. Brown quickly on both sides. Add 1/2 cup broth. Cover with lid or foil, place in oven, and bake 30-40 mins. or until chops are thoroughly cooked.

CHICKEN & DUMPLINGS

1 (3-1/2 LB.) CHICKEN, CUT UP
1-1/2 QUARTS WATER
SALT AND FRESHLY GROUND PEPPER TO TASTE
1 SMALL ONION, QUARTERED
1 SMALL CARROT, CUT INTO CHUNKS
2 CELERY STALKS WITH LEAVES, CUT INTO CHUNKS

3 TBSP. BUTTER OR CHICKEN FAT
1/4 CUP ALL-PURPOSE FLOUR
1/8 TEASP. PAPRIKA
1/2 CUP HALF AND HALF
WHITE PEPPER TO TASTE

WASH CHICKEN AND PAT DRY WITH PAPER TOWELS. PLACE CHICKEN IN LARGE POT. ADD WATER, SALT, PEPPER, ONION, CARROT AND CELERY, AND SIMMER, COVERED, 45 MINS. TO 1 HOUR OR UNTIL CHICKEN IS TENDER. REMOVE FROM BROTH, STRAIN AND RESERVE BROTH. COOL CHICKEN UNTIL ABLE TO HANDLE THEN DISCARD SKIN AND BONES, DICING MEAT, REFRIGERATE. IN A LARGE HEAVY SAUCEPAN HEAT BUTTER OR CHICKEN FAT. STIR IN FLOUR AND PAPRIKA. GRADUALLY ADD 3 CUPS RESERVED CHICKEN BROTH, STIRRING UNTIL THICKENED AND SMOOTH. COOK 2 MINUTES. ADD HALF AND HALF, AND WHITE PEPPER. TASTE AND ADJUST SEASONINGS. RETURN DICED CHICKEN TO BROTH. PREPARE DUMPLINGS (SEE BELOW). DIP A TEASPOON INTO COLD WATER, SPOON TEASPOONFULS OF BATTER ON TOP OF SIMMERING CHICKEN MIXTURE. COOK, COVERED, 15 MINS., WITHOUT LIFTING LID. SPRINKLE WITH PARLSEY AND SERVE IMMEDIATELY. 6 SERVINGS.

DUMPLINGS

1-1/2 CUPS ALL-PURPOSE FLOUR
1/2 TEASP. SALT
3 TEASP. BAKING POWDER

1 TBSP. MELTED SHORTENING
1/3 CUP MILK

IN A MEDIUM BOWL, COMBINE FLOUR, SALT AND BAKING POWDER. BLEND IN SHORTENING AND MILK; MIX WELL.

COUNTRY SAUSAGE

COMBINE 2 LBS. OF FRESH LEAN PORK, COARSELY GROUND, WITH 1/2 TBSP. DRIED THYME OR SAGE, DASH OF CAYENNE, 3/4 TEASP. FRESHLY GROUND BLACK PEPPER AND 1 TEASP. SALT. MIX WELL WITH YOUR HANDS. DIVIDE IN HALF AND SHAPE INTO TWO ROLLS, WRAPPING EACH ROLL SECURELY IN FOIL. SAUSAGE WILL KEEP SEVERAL WEEKS UNDER REFRIGERATION.

TO FRY: CUT OFF SLICES ABOUT 3/4-INCH THICK. PLACE IN COLD SKILLET AND FRY OVER LOW HEAT UNTIL WELL-BROWNED ON BOTH SIDES AND THOROUGHLY COOKED. SERVE WITH APPLESAUCE OR CUT UNPARED APPLES INTO RINGS ABOUT 1/2-INCH THICK AND FILL SKILLET. SPRINKLE LIGHTLY WITH BROWN SUGAR AND CINNAMON AND FRY IN SAUSAGE GREASE, TURNING FREQUENTLY. COVER PAN A FEW MINS. TO SOFTEN APPLES, THEN REMOVE COVER AND COOK UNTIL RINGS HAVE RICH GLAZE.

Country Ham with Red-Eye Gravy I

6 slices (1/4-inch thick) well-smoked country ham
1/4 cup packed brown sugar

1/2 cup double-strength black coffee or water

Trim fat off ham. Sauté fat in a heavy skillet until enough fat is rendered to coat bottom of skillet. Add ham. Cook, turning several times until heated through. Remove ham and keep warm. Stir brown sugar into drippings. Cook over low heat, stirring constantly until sugar melts. Add coffee or water. Stir 5 mins. or until mixture is a rich red-brown color. Spoon gravy onto a warm serving platter and top with ham slices. Serves 6.

Chicken Pot Pie I

4 lbs. chicken
1 stalk celery
1 carrot
1 onion, stuck with 2 cloves
1 tbsp. salt
2 cups sifted all-purpose flour

1/2 teasp. salt
2 eggs
2-3 tbsp. water
4 medium potatoes, sliced
6-7 sprigs parsley, chopped

Cut chicken into serving pieces, place in kettle with celery, carrot, onion, salt and enough cold water to cover. Bring to boil, reduce heat, cover and cook over low heat for about 40 mins. or until tender. Remove vegetables and discard. DOUGH: Sift flour and salt into bowl. Dig a small well in center, drop in eggs, blend mixture to make a stiff dough. Add 2-3 tbsp. water, if needed. Roll as thin as possible on lightly floured board and cut into 1-inch squares with sharp knife. Drop potato slices and pastry into the boiling broth, cover, and cook over moderate heat for 20 mins. Sprinkle in the chopped parsley and serve in hot soup plates. Serves 6.

Garlic Sauce for Pasta

Cook slowly and serve over any type pasta.

1/2 cup garlic, minced
1/4 cup butter
1/2 cup Parmesan cheese, freshly grated

1 cup parsley, minced
1/4 cup olive oil

Cook garlic in butter and oil over low heat until soft to the fork. DO NOT BROWN. Slowly add parsley, stirring for 3 mins. Remove from heat until mixture cools; reheat over low flame and spoon over pasta. Sprinkle cheese over top.

Fried Chicken

3 TO 3-1/2 LB. FRYING CHICKEN, CUT UP
SALT
2 TBSP. CIDER VINEGAR

2/3 CUP ALL-PURPOSE FLOUR
4 HEAPING TBSP. BUTTER
4 HEAPING TBSP. LARD/SHORTENING

AT LEAST 1 HOUR BEFORE FRYING, PUT CHICKEN PIECES IN LARGE BOWL. SPRINKLE WITH 1 TBSP. SALT AND THE VINEGAR AND COVER WITH VERY COLD WATER. LET STAND AT LEAST 30 MINS., THEN DRAIN CHICKEN AND FLOUR. IN LARGE SKILLET HEAT BLENDED BUTTER AND LARD/SHORTENING UNTIL VERY HOT, BUT NOT SMOKING. OVER MEDIUM HEAT BROWN CHICKEN ON EACH SIDE (ABOUT 5 MINS.). REDUCE HEAT TO MEDIUM-LOW AND COOK 10-15 MINS. LONGER OR PLACE IN 350 DEGREE OVEN UNTIL FORK TENDER. SERVES 6.

Southern Fried Chicken

SOAK CHICKEN PARTS IN SALTED WATER OVERNIGHT OR AT LEAST 2 HOURS. DRAIN AND ROLL PIECES IN FLOUR AND SPRINKLE WITH PEPPER. HEAT LARD TO SMOKING POINT IN HEAVY SKILLET, ABOUT 2-INCHES DEEP. FRY, COVERED, ON EACH SIDE (DON'T PEEK) FOR ABOUT 15 MINS. KEEP HEAT HIGH AND COOK FAST.

Baked Steak

USE ROUND STEAK. POUND UNTIL THIN AND ROLL IN FLOUR AND SALT. BROWN IN HOT FAT IN SKILLET. POUR WATER AROUND STEAK, COVER AND SIMMER UNTIL TENDER. FOR TOMATO/ONION STEAK, POUR 1 CUP STEWED TOMATOES AND A SLICED ONION OVER TOP OF MEAT BEFORE PLACING IN OVEN. BAKE AT 325 DEGREES FOR ABOUT 1 HOUR.

Chicken Pot Pie II

4 CUPS COOKED CHICKEN, TURKEY OR BEEF,
  CUT IN SMALL PIECES
1 TBSP. FRESH, CHOPPED PARSLEY,
  (1-1/2 TBSP. DRY FLAKES)
1 CUP EACH CHOPPED ONION, CELERY
2 CUPS SLICED CARROTS

1 CUP PEAS
1/2 CUP WATER
4 CUPS CHICKEN (BEEF) STOCK
1 CUP GREEN BEANS
1/2 CUP FLOUR
BISCUITS

PUT STOCK IN LARGE SAUCEPAN AND ADD ALL VEGETABLES, EXCEPT PEAS AND COOK UNTIL TENDER. ADD PEAS. BLEND FLOUR WITH WATER AND ADD TO PAN, STIRRING UNTIL BROTH THICKENS (ABOUT 5 MINS.). ADD MEAT AND REMOVE FROM HEAT. PUT CHICKEN MIXTURE IN 2-3 QUART CASSEROLE AND TOP WITH HOMEMADE OR CANNED BISCUITS. BAKE AT 450 DEGREES FOR 15 MINS., THEN REDUCE HEAT TO 350 DEGREES AND BAKE UNTIL BISCUITS ARE DONE. MAY OMIT BISCUITS AND TOP WITH PIE CRUST. SERVES 4-6.

SAVORY GRILLED FISH

1/4 CUP SALAD OIL
1 TBSP. ONION POWDER
1 TEASP. SALT
1/8 TEASP. GARLIC POWDER

2-1/2 TBSP. WORCESTERSHIRE SAUCE
4 TEASP. LEMON JUICE
4 SMALL FISH, CLEANED (10 OZ. EACH)

COMBINE OIL, ONION POWDER, SALT, GARLIC POWDER, WORCESTERSHIRE SAUCE AND LEMON JUICE. BRUSH FISH INSIDE AND OUT. PLACE ON OILED GRILL 6 INCHES FROM COALS. GRILL 5 MINS. TURN OVER AND BRUSH WITH REMAINING OIL MIXTURE. GRILL ABOUT 3 MORE MINS. (UNTIL FLAKES WHEN TESTED WITH FORK.)

BEER BATTER

1 CUP PREPARED BAKING MIX
1/3 CUP CORN MEAL
1 TEASP. SALT

1/4 TEASP. PEPPER
4-6 OZ. BEER

COMBINE DRY INGREDIENTS AND ADD BEER TO GET PROPER CONSISTENCY FOR DIPPING FISH FILLETS. SALT FISH LIGHTLY, THEN DIP IN BATTER. DEEP FAT FRY AT 375 DEGREES UNTIL GOLDEN BROWN ON EACH SIDE.

HAM CROQUETTES

1 CUP MINCED LEFTOVER HAM
2 CUPS COOKED, CHOPPED COLD POTATOES
1 EGG

1 CUP STALE BREADCRUMBS
1 TBSP. BUTTER
FLOUR, FINE CRUMBS FOR COATING

MIX HAM, CRUMBS, POTATOES WITH THE BUTTER AND EGG AND MAKE INTO SMALL BALLS. FLOUR, DIP IN EGG, THEN COAT WITH FINE CRUMBS AND FRY IN HOT FAT. GOOD WAY OF USING LEFTOVER HAM, POTATOES AND STALE BREAD.

FRIED CATFISH

6 FRESH CATFISH, CLEANED. (FILLET IF DESIRED)
1 TEASP. SALT
1/4 CUP LARD, BACON GREASE OR SHORTENING
1 CUP YELLOW CORNMEAL

1/4 CUP MILK
1 TEASP. GROUND PEPPER
2 EGGS, BEATEN

CLEAN AND DRAIN FISH. SPRINKLE WITH SALT AND PEPPER ON BOTH SIDES. IN LARGE CAST IRON SKILLET MELT FAT UNTIL SIZZLING. MIX THE BEATEN EGGS WITH MILK. DIP FISH, THEN ROLL IN CORNMEAL. FRY, NO LONGER THAN 3 MINS. ON EACH SIDE. SERVES 6.

SPAGHETTI PIE

CRUST
6 OZ. SPAGHETTI, COOKED; 2 TBSP. BUTTER AND 2 EGGS BEATEN. COMBINE ALL INGREDIENTS AND LINE A 10-INCH PIE PLATE WITH MIXTURE AND SET ASIDE.

FILLING

1 LB. GROUND BEEF
1/2 CUP ONIONS, CHOPPED
1/4 CUP GREEN PEPPER, CHOPPED
1 8-OZ. CAN TOMATOES
1 8-OZ. CAN TOMATO PASTE
1 TEASP. SUGAR

1/4 TEASP. GARLIC POWDER
1/2 TEASP. SALT
1 CUP COTTAGE CHEESE
1/2 CUP MOZZARELLA CHEESE, SHREDDED

BROWN BEEF, ONIONS AND PEPPER TOGETHER UNTIL ONIONS ARE TENDER. DRAIN. ADD TOMATOES, TOMATO PASTE, SUGAR, GARLIC POWDER AND SALT, SIMMER 30 MINS. SPREAD COTTAGE CHEESE OVER SPAGHETTI. ADD MEAT MIXTURE. TOP WITH SHREDDED MOZZARELLA CHEESE. BAKE, UNCOVERED AT 350 DEGREES FOR 20 MINS. SERVES 4-6.

SALMON CROQUETTES

2 EGGS
1/4 TEASP. BAKING POWDER
1/4 CUP FLOUR

1/4 CUP CORNMEAL
8 OZ. CAN SALMON, UNDRAINED

MIX INGREDIENTS THOROUGHLY AND DROP FROM TEASPOON INTO HOT FAT TO FRY. WATCH CLOSELY AND TURN TO BROWN. FRY ABOUT 2-3 MINS. EACH SIDE. YIELD 8-12 CROQUETTES. *MARY ELLEN MEANS*

COUNTRY POTATO PIE

2 LARGE POTATOES, GRATED
1/2 TEASP. SALT
1 CUP MILK
1 CUP GRATED CHEDDAR OR SWISS CHEESE
1/2 TEASP. EACH: DRY MUSTARD, SALT, PEPPER

1 TEASP. PAPRIKA
1 MEDIUM ONION
2 EGGS
2 TBSP. BUTTER
2 TBSP. CHOPPED FRESH PARSLEY

GREASE BOTTOM OF 9-INCH PIE PAN WITH 1 TBSP. BUTTER. PRESS IN GRATED POTATOES TO MAKE A CRUST. SPRINKLE WITH CHEESE. SAUTÉ ONION IN REMAINING BUTTER AND SPREAD OVER CHEESE. BEAT REST OF INGREDIENTS TOGETHER AND POUR OVER PIE. BAKE AT 375 DEGREES FOR 45 MINS., UNTIL CRUST IS GOLDEN BROWN AND KNIFE INSERTED IN PIE COMES OUT CLEAN. COOL 10 MINS. BEFORE SLICING. 4-6 SERVINGS.

Escalloped Chicken and Ham

1-1/2 TBSP. BUTTER	SALT AND PAPRIKA
1-1/2 TBSP. FLOUR	2 CUPS DICED, COOKED CHICKEN
1 CUP STOCK, GRAVY OR MILK	1 CUP DICED, COOKED HAM
1/2 TEASP. GRATED LEMON RIND	1/2 CUP BUTTERED CRUMBS

BLEND BUTTER AND FLOUR UNTIL SMOOTH, GRADUALLY ADD LIQUID BRINGING TO A BOIL. COOK 3 MINS. ADD LEMON RIND, SALT AND PAPRIKA. COMBINE CHICKEN AND HAM, AND PLACE IN BAKING DISH IN LAYERS, ALTERNATELY WITH BREAD CRUMBS AND SAUCE, UNTIL ALL INGREDIENTS ARE USED. SPRINKLE WITH BUTTERED CRUMBS AND BAKE IN MODERATELY HOT OVEN (375 DEGREES) FOR ABOUT 20 MINS. SERVES 4.

Shrimp & Crab ala Marsala

1/2 STICK BUTTER	1 LB. LUMP CRAB MEAT
3 TBSP. GREEN PEPPER, MINCED	1/4 CUP MARSALA WINE
1 TBSP. PIMIENTO, MINCED	3 WHOLE EGGS
1 TEASP. TABASCO	2 OZ. PARMESAN CHEESE
1 TEASP. WORCESTERSHIRE	1 DOZEN LARGE SHRIMP, CLEANED

MELT BUTTER IN SKILLET AND SAUTÉ GREEN PEPPER UNTIL TRANSPARENT. ADD PIMIENTO, TABASCO, WORCESTERSHIRE SAUCE. BLEND WELL. ADD SHRIMP AND COOK FOR 10 MINS. REMOVE SHRIMP AND SET ASIDE. ADD CRAB MEAT TO SKILLET DRIPPINGS, ADD WINE AND SIMMER FOR 10 MINS. PLACE CRAB MEAT MIXTURE IN BUTTERED BAKING DISH AND ARRANGE SHRIMP ON THE TOP. WHIP EGGS AND MILK THOROUGHLY. POUR OVER CASSEROLE AND SPRINKLE WITH PARMESAN CHEESE. BAKE AT 350 DEGREES FOR 25-30 MINS. SERVES 4. *SAM OLIVERIO, GOURMETS' DELITE*

Ham and Red-Eye Gravy II

2 (1/2-INCH THICK) HAM STEAKS	1 CUP STRONG BLACK COFFEE
(ABOUT 1 LB. EACH)	1/4 TEASP. PEPPER
1-1/2 CUPS MILK	HOT BISCUITS
2 TBSP. VEGETABLE OIL, DIVIDED	

PLACE HAM IN A LARGE SHALLOW CONTAINER; POUR IN MILK. COVER AND REFRIGERATE 8 HOURS. REMOVE HAM FROM MILK. CUT GASHES IN FAT TO KEEP HAM FROM CURLING. COOK 1 SLICE OF HAM IN 1 TBSP. OIL IN A HEAVY SKILLET OVER LOW HEAT UNTIL LIGHT BROWN, TURNING ONCE. REMOVE FROM SKILLET AND KEEP WARM. DRAIN OFF PAN DRIPPINGS, RESERVING FOR GRAVY. REPEAT PROCEDURE WITH REMAINING OIL AND HAM. ADD PAN DRIPPINGS, COFFEE AND PEPPER TO SKILLET; BRING TO A BOIL, STIRRING CONSTANTLY. REDUCE HEAT, AND SIMMER 3 MINS. SERVE GRAVY WITH HAM AND HOT BISCUITS. SERVES 4.

BARBECUE

1 TO 1-1/2 LBS. GROUND BEEF	1 TBSP. MUSTARD
1 ONION, DICED FINE	1 TBSP. SUGAR
1/3 CUP KETCHUP	1/2 TEASP. ONION SALT
1/3 CUP BARBECUE SAUCE	1/2 TEASP. GARLIC SALT
1 TBSP. VINEGAR	1/2 TEASP. HOT SAUCE

COOK BEEF AND ONION UNTIL ALL REDNESS HAS DISAPPEARED. DRAIN GREASE. ADD REMAINING INGREDIENTS. A LITTLE MORE KETCHUP OR BARBECUE SAUCE CAN BE USED DEPENDING ON THE AMOUNT OF HAMBURGER. MAY BE USED AS HOT DOG SAUCE OR ON HAMBURGER BUNS.

CHEESE AND TURNIP GREENS QUICHE

1 UNBAKED 9-INCH PIE SHELL	1/4 TEASP. SALT
1 TEASP. DIJON MUSTARD	1/8 TEASP. PEPPER
1/2 CUP 1%-FAT COTTAGE CHEESE	1/8 TEASP. GROUND NUTMEG
1/2 CUP BUTTERMILK OR PLAIN YOGURT	1 PACKAGE (10 OZ.) FROZEN, CHOPPED
2 LARGE EGGS	TURNIP GREENS, THAWED AND
WHITE OF 1 LARGE EGG	SQUEEZED DRY
1 TBSP. INSTANT NONFAT DRY MILK	1 CUP SHREDDED SWISS CHEESE (4 OZ.)

HEAT OVEN TO 400 DEGREES. BAKE PIE SHELL 10 MINS. OR UNTIL LIGHTLY GOLDEN. REMOVE FROM OVEN TO RACK. BRUSH MUSTARD OVER BOTTOM OF PASTRY; COOL. IN FOOD PROCESSOR OR BLENDER, PROCESS COTTAGE CHEESE, BUTTERMILK, EGGS, EGG WHITE, DRY MILK, SALT, PEPPER AND NUTMEG UNTIL WELL-BLENDED. ADD TO TURNIP GREENS IN A MEDIUM-SIZED BOWL. STIR IN SWISS CHEESE. POUR INTO PARTIALLY BAKED PIE SHELL. RETURN TO OVEN. REDUCE OVEN TEMPERATURE TO 350 DEGREES. BAKE 40 TO 45 MINS. UNTIL KNIFE INSERTED NEAR CENTER COMES OUT CLEAN AND TOP IS FIRM AND BROWNED. COOL ON RACK 5 MINS. CUT IN WEDGES. SERVES 4.

WESTERN SANDWICH

1/4 LB. HAM OR 4 SLICES BACON, DICED	SALT AND PEPPER
1 GREEN PEPPER, CHOPPED	4 EGGS
1 MEDIUM ONION, CHOPPED	

FRY HAM OR BACON IN SKILLET FOR SEVERAL MINUTES. TOSS IN GREEN PEPPER AND ONION AND COOK UNTIL ALMOST TENDER. BEAT EGGS IN BOWL WITH SALT AND PEPPER. POUR OVER MIXTURE IN SKILLET AND COOK UNTIL EGGS ARE SET. TURN WITH BROAD SPATULA AND BROWN ON SECOND SIDE. PLACE ON BUTTERED BREAD OR BUNS. 4 SANDWICHES.

Egg Salad Ring

1-1/2 DOZEN HARD-COOKED EGGS
1/2 CUP CHOPPED GREEN PEPPER
1/4 CUP FINELY CHOPPED CELERY
1 MEDIUM ONION, CHOPPED
SALT AND PEPPER TO TASTE

2 SMALL PACKAGES CREAM CHEESE
(SOFTENED)
1/2 CUP MAYONNAISE
3 TBSP. CHILI SAUCE OR KETCHUP

MASH OR CHOP EGGS. ADD GREEN PEPPER, CELERY AND ONION. MIX SOFTENED CREAM CHEESE, MAYONNAISE AND CHILI SAUCE. COMBINE WITH OTHER INGREDIENTS, SEASON WITH SALT AND PEPPER. SHAPE IN A RING MOLD AND CHILL AT LEAST 4 HOURS. LOOSEN AROUND EDGES WITH A SPATULA AND UNMOLD. FILL CENTER WITH SALAD GREENS TOPPED WITH FRESH DRESSING OF YOUR CHOICE. SERVES 8.

Chicken Scallopini

3 WHOLE CHICKEN BREASTS, SPLIT
3 TBSP. COOKING OIL
1-1/2 TEASP. SALT
1 CUP DRY WHITE WINE

1 GREEN PEPPER, SLICED
1 MEDIUM ONION, SLICED
12 FRESH MUSHROOMS, SLICED

REMOVE SKIN FROM CHICKEN BREASTS. HEAT OIL IN LARGE SKILLET. ADD CHICKEN AND SAUTÉ ON BOTH SIDES UNTIL LIGHTLY BROWNED. SPRINKLE WITH SALT. ADD GREEN PEPPER, ONION AND MUSHROOMS. SAUTÉ LIGHTLY. ADD WINE, COVER AND SIMMER SLOWLY UNTIL TENDER. SERVES 6. *MRS. JARROLL'S COUNTRY ROAD INN, ZELA, WV (MRS. JARROLL SIMMERS THIS DISH IN HER SLOW COOKER.)*

Egg and Asparagus Bake

18 FRESH ASPARAGUS SPEARS
1/4 CUP BUTTER/MARGARINE
1/4 CUP FLOUR
1/2 TEASP. SALT
1-1/2 CUPS MILK

1 CUP SHREDDED CHEDDAR CHEESE
1/8 TEASP. GROUND RED PEPPER
4 HARD COOKED EGGS, SLICED
1/2 CUP CRACKER CRUMBS
1/4 CUP MELTED BUTTER/MARGARINE

COOK ASPARAGUS IN BOILING, SALTED WATER UNTIL JUST TENDER. IN A SAUCEPAN MELT 1/4 CUP BUTTER AND STIR IN FLOUR AND SALT; BLEND IN ENOUGH MILK TO MAKE SMOOTH PASTE. STIR IN REMAINING MILK AND COOK OVER MEDIUM HEAT UNTIL SAUCE IS THICK, STIRRING CONSTANTLY. WHILE SAUCE IS HOT, STIR IN SHREDDED CHEESE AND RED PEPPER. STIR UNTIL ALL THE CHEESE IS MELTED. IN A GREASED 1-1/2 QUART CASSEROLE DISH LAYER HALF OF THE ASPARAGUS, SLICED EGGS AND SAUCE. REPEAT INGREDIENTS TO MAKE A SECOND LAYER. TOP WITH CRACKER CRUMBS MIXED WITH 1/4 CUP BUTTER. BAKE AT 350 DEGREES FOR 30 MINS. OR UNTIL MIXTURE BUBBLES. BROIL 2 MINS. TO BROWN. SERVES 4-5.

Barbecue Fried Chicken

4 LBS. CHICKEN, CUT UP
1 CUP FLOUR
OIL OR FAT FOR FRYING
3/4 CUP WATER
2 TBSP. VINEGAR
1 TEASP. PREPARED MUSTARD
1 TBSP. BROWN SUGAR

2 TEASP. WORCESTERSHIRE SAUCE
1 TBSP. CHOPPED ONION
2 CUPS CANNED TOMATOES
1-1/2 TEASP. SALT
1/2 TEASP. PEPPER
1/4 TEASP. CHOPPED GARLIC

WASH CHICKEN AND PAT DRY WITH PAPER TOWELS. FLOUR, COATING EACH PIECE WELL, AND FRY IN HOT OIL UNTIL GOLDEN BROWN. BLEND TOGETHER SMALL AMOUNT OF WATER WITH 2 TBSP. FLOUR. ADD REMAINING WATER. MIX WITH REST OF INGREDIENTS. DRAIN EXCESS FAT FROM CHICKEN. POUR SAUCE OVER CHICKEN; COVER AND SIMMER ON TOP OF STOVE ABOUT 1 HOUR OR UNTIL TENDER. SERVES 4.

Cheese Baked Fish

2 TBSP. BUTTER/MARGARINE
3 TBSP. FLOUR
3/4 TEASP. SALT
1/8 TEASP. NUTMEG
2 LBS. FISH FILLETS (HADDOCK, PERCH, FLOUNDER OR SOLE)

1 CUP HOT MILK
3/4 TEASP. LEMON JUICE
1/2 CUP SHREDDED CHEDDAR CHEESE
1/2 TEASP. DRY MUSTARD

MELT MARGARINE AND BLEND IN DRY INGREDIENTS. STIR IN MILK AND COOK UNTIL THICKENED, STIRRING CONSTANTLY. ADD LEMON JUICE AND CHEESE. STIR UNTIL CHEESE MELTS. PLACE FISH IN GREASED BAKING DISH AND COVER WITH CHEESE SAUCE. BAKE AT 375 DEGREES FOR 40 MINS. SERVES 6.

Vegetable Stuffed Peppers

6 MEDIUM GREEN PEPPERS
1-1/2 CUPS CANNED OR FRESH CORN
1/2 CUP SOFT BREADCRUMBS
1/4 CUP MINCED CELERY
2 TBSP. MELTED BUTTER/MARGARINE
GRATED CHEESE OR BUTTERED BREADCRUMBS

1 TBSP. MINCED ONION
2 EGGS, SLIGHTLY BEATEN
1/4 TEASP. SALT
DASH OF PEPPER
1 CUP FRESH OR CANNED TOMATOES, DICED

REMOVE TOPS AND SEEDS FROM PEPPERS. PARBOIL FOR 6 MINS. DRAIN. COMBINE REMAINING INGREDIENTS AND STUFF PEPPERS. SPRINKLE WITH CHEESE OR BREADCRUMBS. PLACE UPRIGHT IN A GREASED 10 X 6 X 1-1/2 BAKING DISH. ADD SMALL AMOUNT OF WATER. COVER AND BAKE IN 350 DEGREE OVEN FOR 1 HOUR. 6 SERVINGS.

Chicken Croquettes II

3 tbsp. butter	1-1/2 cups finely chopped chicken
3 tbsp. flour	1/2 teasp. grated lemon rind
1 cup milk	egg and breadcrumbs*
1/3 teasp. salt	1/8 teasp. pepper
fat for frying	

Prepare heavy cream sauce by blending butter and flour, gradually adding milk, stirring until mixture reaches boiling point. Cook 3 mins., stirring constantly. Add seasonings, chicken and lemon rind. Spread on plate to cool (about 3/4-inch thick). Divide into 12 portions, form into cone-shaped croquettes, dip in egg and breadcrumbs and fry until golden in deep hot fat (375-390 degrees). Drain on soft crumbled paper. Makes 12 croquettes.

*Beat one egg on flat plate just until thoroughly beaten, but not frothy. Add 1 tbsp. cold water. Have fine breadcrumbs on another plate. Lay formed croquette in egg and use brush to coat top. Lift with spatula, draining off excess egg and place in breadcrumbs, coating well.

Meat Loaf

1 lb. ground beef	2 teasp. salt
1/2 lb. ground pork	1/4 cup chopped onion
2 eggs, slightly beaten	1/8 teasp. pepper
1/2 cup soft breadcrumbs	1/2 teasp. sage
1 cup milk	

Combine all ingredients, mixing well. Pack lightly in loaf pan. Bake at 350 degrees for 1 hour. Serve with tomato sauce. Serves 4-6.

Stuffed Turkey Loaf

2 lbs. ground turkey	1/2 cup chopped onion
3/4 cup chopped celery	1/4 cup butter
3 cups prepared stuffing mix	2 eggs, slightly beaten
1/2 cup water	1/2 cup tomato juice

Preheat oven to 350 degrees. Brown onion and celery in butter in medium hot skillet. Combine with stuffing mix, eggs and water to make stuffing. Add half of stuffing to ground turkey, mixing well. Pat out half of meat mixture in a two-quart loaf pan, spread with stuffing, then top with remaining meat mixture. Pour tomato juice over loaf and bake for 1-1/4 hours. Serves 8-10.

Applesauce Meat Loaf

Combine:
1 cup soft breadcrumbs (about 1-1/2 slices) and 1/2 cup applesauce
Add:

1 lb. ground beef
1 egg, slightly beaten
1/4 cup celery, minced
2 tbsp. minced onion

1 teasp. Dijon mustard
1/2 teasp. salt
dash pepper

Blend thoroughly. Shape into a round loaf in an 8x8x2 baking dish. With a spoon, make a large depression in top of loaf.

Combine:

1/2 cup applesauce
1 tbsp. brown sugar

1-1/2 teasp. vinegar
1/2 teasp. Dijon mustard

Mix well and pour into depression. Bake at 350 degrees for 1 hour. Serves 4.

Beef Pot Roast I

5 lbs. beef (shoulder or sirloin tip is best)
4 tbsp. Worcestershire sauce
6 whole cloves
pinch of dry mustard
3 small onions, diced
2 slices bacon

1 teasp. celery seed
1 tbsp. vinegar
1/8 teasp. nutmeg
1/2 cup flour
salt and pepper to taste

Sear meat on both sides. Brown the flour and sprinkle over beef. Season with salt and pepper and put in iron pot with vinegar, onions, Worcestershire sauce, cloves, celery seed, nutmeg and dry mustard. Lay bacon across the top, pour cold water to depth covering 2/3 of the meat and cook slowly for 4 hours. Potatoes and carrots may be cooked around the meat.

Pork Loaf

3 lbs. ground pork
2 eggs
1-1/2 cups milk
1-1/2 teasp. sage
1 teasp. salt

1/4 teasp. pepper
1-1/2 cups tomatoes
1-1/2 cups cracker crumbs or
    breadcrumbs

Mix all ingredients well. Bake 45 mins. to 1 hour at 350 degrees, or until well done. Serves 12.

TURKEY PARMESAN

1 LB. TURKEY STEAKS OR CUTLETS
1/4 CUP MILK
1 MEDIUM ONION, DICED
1/2 TEASP. GARLIC SALT
1/2 CUP FRESH MUSHROOMS, SLICED
1 (4 OZ.) CAN TOMATO PUREE
1/2 TO 3/4 CUP GRATED PARMESAN CHEESE

1 EGG
4 TBSP. BUTTER
1/2 CUP GREEN PEPPER, DICED
1/4 TEASP. OREGANO
1 (8 OZ.) CAN TOMATO SAUCE
FLOUR

SEASON TURKEY WITH SALT AND PEPPER TO TASTE. SPRINKLE WITH GARLIC SALT. BEAT EGG AND MILK TOGETHER UNTIL BLENDED. IN A LARGE SKILLET, MELT BUTTER OVER MODERATE HEAT. DIP TURKEY INTO EGG BATTER, FLOUR BOTH SIDES WELL, SHAKING OFF EXCESS, AND FRY TO GOLDEN BROWN IN BUTTER. REMOVE FROM SKILLET AND KEEP WARM. ADD ADDITIONAL BUTTER, IF NECESSARY, SAUTÉ ONION, GREEN PEPPER AND MUSHROOMS. ADD OREGANO, TOMATO SAUCE AND TOMATO PUREE; BLEND WELL. BRING TO SIMMER. RETURN TURKEY TO SKILLET, COVERING WELL WITH MIXTURE. SPRINKLE TOP OF CUTLETS OR STEAKS WITH PARMESAN CHEESE. TURN HEAT TO LOW AND SIMMER FOR 5 TO 15 MINS. DEPENDING ON THICKNESS OF TURKEY. DO NOT OVERCOOK. SERVES 4.

FISH CAKES

1 LB. COOKED FISH, FLAKED WITH
  NO BONES OR SKIN
1 LB. MASHED POTATOES (ABOUT
  2 CUPS, WELL-PACKED)

SALT AND PEPPER TO TASTE
1/2 CUP MILK
1 TBSP. DRIED TARRAGON
2 EGGS, WELL-BEATEN

GARNISH:
CHOPPED FRESH PARSLEY

MIX FLAKED FISH AND POTATOES IN BOWL USING FORK. ADD ENOUGH MILK TO MAKE A SMOOTH MIX. ADD TARRAGON, SALT, PEPPER AND MIX WELL. ADD BEATEN EGGS AND MIX AGAIN. FORM INTO SMALLISH CAKES, ABOUT 3-INCHES IN DIAMETER. ROLL IN FLOUR AND FRY IN LIGHTLY OILED SKILLET UNTIL BROWN. GARNISH WITH PARSLEY. MAKES 8-10 CAKES. SERVES 4.

CARROT MEAT LOAF

1 LB. GROUND BEEF
2 EGGS
2 TBSP. KETCHUP
1 TBSP. PREPARED MUSTARD
2 STALKS CELERY, MINCED

SALT AND PEPPER TO TASTE
2 CUPS GRATED CARROTS
4 SLICES BREAD
1/2 SMALL ONION, MINCED
1 CUP HOT MILK OR BEEF BROTH

POUR HOT LIQUID OVER BREAD TO SOFTEN, THEN MIX WITH OTHER INGREDIENTS AND BAKE IN MEDIUM (325-350 DEGREE) OVEN UNTIL DONE AND BROWN, ABOUT 45 MINS. SERVES 6.

CORN BREAD PIE

2 LBS. GROUND CHUCK	SHORTENING
1 LARGE ONION, CHOPPED	1 GREEN PEPPER, CHOPPED
1 PINT CANNED TOMATOES	1 SMALL CAN TOMATO SAUCE
1 CAN WHOLE KERNEL CORN	1-1/3 TEASP. SALT
1/2 TEASP. PEPPER	1 TEASP. SEASONING SALT
1/4 TEASP. GARLIC SALT	1 TBSP. CELERY FLAKES

BROWN GROUND CHUCK IN A SMALL AMOUNT OF SHORTENING IN SKILLET. PUSH MEAT TO ONE SIDE AND LIGHTLY BROWN ONION AND GREEN PEPPER. ADD TOMATOES, CORN, SALT, PEPPER, SEASONING SALT, GARLIC SALT, CELERY FLAKES AND TOMATO SAUCE. HEAT TO BOILING. POUR INTO A CASSEROLE. COVER WITH THE FOLLOWING CORN BREAD MIXTURE AND BAKE AT 400 DEGREES UNTIL NICELY BROWNED.

CORN BREAD MIXTURE

1/2 CUP FLOUR	1/2 CUP YELLOW CORNMEAL
1/2 TEASP. SALT	2 TEASP. BAKING POWDER
1 TBSP. SUGAR	1 EGG
3/4 CUP MILK	

SIFT TOGETHER ALL DRY INGREDIENTS, ADD EGG AND MILK, BEAT UNTIL SMOOTH AND POUR OVER CASSEROLE MIXTURE.

EGG-ETTI

1-1/4 CUPS SPAGHETTI, BROKEN IN 2-INCH PIECES	1-1/2 CUPS SHREDDED CHEDDAR CHEESE, DIVIDED
2 TBSP. MARGARINE	1/4 CUP CHOPPED ONION
1/4 CUP CHOPPED GREEN PEPPER	6 HARD-COOKED EGGS, CUT IN 6THS
1 (4-1/2 OZ.) CAN MUSHROOMS STEMS AND PIECES	(CUT IN HALF LENGTHWISE, THEN INTO 6 WEDGES)
1 (10-3/4 OZ.) CAN CREAM OF CELERY SOUP	1/2 CUP PINEAPPLE CHUNKS
1/2 CUP MILK	1/2 TEASP. SALT
1/8 TEASP. PEPPER	

COOK SPAGHETTI ACCORDING TO PACKAGE DIRECTIONS; DRAIN AND PLACE IN BUTTERED 1-1/2 QUART CASSEROLE. IN SKILLET OVER MEDIUM HEAT, MELT MARGARINE. COOK ONION AND GREEN PEPPER FOR 3 MINS. OR UNTIL ONION IS TRANSPARENT; SPOON OVER SPAGHETTI. ADD EGGS. PLACE MUSHROOMS AND PINEAPPLE IN CASSEROLE. STIR TOGETHER SOUP, MILK, SALT, PEPPER AND 1 CUP CHEESE; POUR INTO CASSEROLE. TOSS INGREDIENTS LIGHTLY. SPRINKLE REMAINING CHEESE EVENLY OVER TOP. BAKE AT 350 DEGREES FOR 20 MINS. OR UNTIL BUBBLY THROUGHOUT. IF CHEESE ON TOP IS GETTING TOO BROWN BEFORE ENTIRE CASSEROLE IS HEATED THROUGH, COVER WITH FOIL. SERVES 4. (A WEST VIRGINIA EGG COOKING CONTEST WINNER FOR JEAN NAYLOR, CHARLESTON, WV.)

Farmers' Winter Hash

6 SLICES BACON	1 MEDIUM ONION, SLICED
1 CUP CUBED, BOILED POTATOES	1/2 CUP CUBED STALE BREAD
3 BEATEN EGGS	3 TBSP. SHREDDED CHEDDAR CHEESE
SALT AND PEPPER TO TASTE	

FRY BACON UNTIL CRISP, REMOVE FROM PAN. FRY ONION, POTATOES AND BREAD CUBES IN BACON GREASE. WHEN THE ONIONS ARE TENDER, ADD EGGS AND CHEESE, THEN SALT AND PEPPER TO TASTE. WHILE THE EGGS ARE STILL MOIST, CRUMBLE THE BACON AND ADD TO THE MIXTURE, STIRRING WELL. SERVES 4.

Pot Roast II

TAKE 2-3 LB. BONELESS CHUCK ROAST AND DREDGE IN FLOUR TO WHICH HAS BEEN ADDED SALT AND PEPPER. BROWN IN 1/4 CUP BUTTER IN HEAVY DUTCH OVEN. COARSELY CHOP 2-3 POTATOES, CARROTS, ONIONS, CELERY STALKS; AND 1-2 CLOVES OF GARLIC. REMOVE MEAT FROM DUTCH OVEN AND ADD 1/4 CUP MORE BUTTER. ADD VEGETABLES AND LIGHTLY SAUTÉ, TURNING OCCASIONALLY FOR 10-15 MINS. RETURN MEAT TO DUTCH OVEN, ADD BAY LEAF AND 2 CUPS OF BEEF BROTH (OR MIXTURE OF 4 BEEF BOUILLON CUBES TO 2 CUPS WATER). PLACE IN 250 DEGREE OVEN AND COOK FOR 1 HOUR COVERED, THEN RAISE HEAT TO 350 DEGREES AND COOK UNTIL DONE (ABOUT 1 HOUR). SERVES 6-8.

Lemon Chicken

6-8 PIECES OF FRYING CHICKEN	4 TBSP. SALAD OIL OR SHORTENING
(BREASTS, LEGS, THIGHS)	2 TBSP. BROWN SUGAR
1 WHOLE LEMON	1 LEMON, THINLY SLICED
1/3 CUP FLOUR	1 CUP CHICKEN BROTH
1-1/2 TEASP. SALT	2 SPRIGS FRESH MINT
1/2 TEASP. PAPRIKA	

WASH CHICKEN AND DRAIN ON PAPER TOWELS. GRATE THE PEEL FROM THE LEMON AND SET ASIDE; CUT THE LEMON IN HALF AND SQUEEZE THE JUICE OVER THE CHICKEN RUBBING EACH PIECE WITH THE JUICE. MIX THE FLOUR, SALT AND PAPRIKA IN A PAPER BAG AND ADD CHICKEN PIECES (A FEW AT A TIME) AND SHAKE UNTIL WELL-COATED. BROWN CHICKEN SLOWLY IN SALAD OIL. ARRANGE IN A CASSEROLE DISH. SPRINKLE GRATED LEMON PEEL OVER CHICKEN, ADD BROWN SUGAR AND THEN COVER WITH THE THINLY SLICED LEMON. POUR IN THE BROTH AND PLACE FRESH MINT ON TOP. COVER AND BAKE AT 375 DEGREES UNTIL CHICKEN IS TENDER (ABOUT 45 MINS.). REMOVE MINT BEFORE SERVING. 6-8 SERVINGS.

CHARIOT CHICKEN

2 WHOLE CHICKEN BREASTS
2 TEASP. SALT, DIVIDED
2 TBSP. BUTTER
1 ONION, SLICED IN THIN RINGS
1 (8 OZ.) PACKAGE CREAM CHEESE
2 OZ. PIMIENTO, SLICED INTO STRIPS

2 CUPS WATER
1/2 TEASP. PEPPER, DIVIDED
1 ORANGE
1 TEASP. CARAWAY SEEDS
1 (5.3 OZ.) CAN EVAPORATED MILK

IN DEEP SAUCEPAN, PLACE CHICKEN, WATER, 1 TEASP. SALT AND 1/4 TEASP. PEPPER. COVER AND SIMMER ABOUT 1 HOUR OR UNTIL TENDER. COOL. SEPARATE MEAT AND CUT INTO CHUNKS. IN SKILLET PLACE BUTTER AND MELT OVER MEDIUM HEAT. ADD ONION, AND COOK, STIRRING UNTIL TENDER (ABOUT 5 MINS.). ADD CHICKEN, MILK, CARAWAY SEEDS, AND REMAINING SALT AND PEPPER. SIMMER 10 MINS. IN BOWL, MIX JUICE AND PULP FROM ORANGE WITH CREAM CHEESE; ADD TO CHICKEN IN SKILLET AND SIMMER ANOTHER 10 MINS. ADD PIMIENTO AND SIMMER ANOTHER 5 MINS. SERVE OVER RICE OR TOASTED BREAD. SERVES 4. *(1978 WEST VIRGINIA NATIONAL CHICKEN CONTEST WINNER.)*

MAZETTI

2 LBS. GROUND BEEF
2-1/2 CUPS FINELY CHOPPED CELERY
   WITH LEAVES
2 CUPS CHOPPED ONIONS
2 CLOVES GARLIC, FINELY CHOPPED
1 TBSP. WATER
1 (8 OZ.) PACKAGE MEDIUM NOODLES

2 CANS CONDENSED TOMATO SOUP
1 (6 OZ). CAN MUSHROOMS WITH
   LIQUID
2 TEASP. SALT
1/2 TEASP. PEPPER
1/2 LB. GRATED SHARP CHEDDAR
   CHEESE (2 CUPS)

BROWN MEAT IN SKILLET. ADD CELERY, ONIONS, GARLIC AND WATER. COVER AND STEAM UNTIL VEGETABLES ARE TENDER. REMOVE FROM HEAT. COOK NOODLES ACCORDING TO PACKAGE DIRECTIONS; DRAIN. ADD NOODLES TO BEEF MIXTURE; MIX IN SOUP, UNDRAINED MUSHROOMS, SALT AND PEPPER. SPREAD MIXTURE IN 3 QUART CASSEROLE. SPRINKLE CHEESE ON TOP. (DISH MAY BE MADE AHEAD AND REFRIGERATED 24 HOURS). PLACE IN COLD OVEN AND BAKE AT 250 DEGREES FOR ABOUT 1 HOUR, OR UNTIL BUBBLY. 10-12 SERVINGS.

BAKED BEAN SANDWICHES

3 HOT DOG BUNS, HALVED
BUTTER OR MARGARINE
1 (1 LB.) CAN BAKED BEANS OR 2 CUPS
   LEFTOVER BAKED BEANS

3-4 TBSP. KETCHUP
1/3 LB. SHREDDED PROCESSED CHEESE
6 SLICES BACON

TOAST CUT SIDES OF BUN HALVES UNDER BROILER UNTIL LIGHTLY BROWN. SPREAD WITH BUTTER. TOP BUNS WITH BEANS, KETCHUP AND CHEESE, LAY BACON OVER EACH. BROIL ABOUT 3-INCHES FROM HEAT UNTIL CHEESE MELTS AND BACON IS CRISP. SERVE HOT. SERVES 6.

Barbequed Short Ribs

Brown 3 lbs. of spareribs in skillet. Put into deep pan and layer with sliced onions. Pour barbeque sauce over ribs and cook with a tight cover for 1-1/2 hours. Uncover, cook, simmering for another 1/2 hour.

Sauce:

1 cup ketchup
1 teasp. chili powder
1 teasp. Tabasco sauce

2 tbsp. brown sugar
2 teasp. dry mustard
3/4 cup water

Mix well and pour over shortribs to cook.

Stuffed Pork Chops

6 pork chops (at least 1-inch thick) for stuffing
2 tbsp. butter/margarine
2 tbsp. finely chopped onion
1/4 teasp. rubbed sage
1/4 teasp. crushed basil leaves

1 tbsp. parsley flakes or chopped fresh parsley
1-1/2 cups small dry bread cubes
1/4 cup onion soup mix
1/2 cup water

Cut pork chops along bone, about halfway through meat, then cut towards outside to make a pocket (or have butcher do this). Melt butter; add onion, sage, basil and parsley. Sauté until onion is golden. Toss with bread cubes. Stuff mixture into pork chop pockets. Brown chops in small amount of butter/oil. Place in 13x9x2 baking dish. Sprinkle onion soup mix over top and add 1/2 cup water. Bake, covered at 325 degrees for 1 hour or until tender. 6 servings.

Potato Pizza

2 cups mashed warm or reheated potatoes
3/4 cup all-purpose flour
6 tbsp. vegetable oil
1/2 lb. Mozzarella cheese, sliced thin

1/3 cup grated Parmesan cheese
salt and pepper to taste
2 cups tomato sauce
1 tbsp. chopped fresh basil

Preheat oven to 350 degrees. Combine potatoes, flour, salt and pepper with 2 tbsp. oil. Work mixture to a smooth, spreadable dough. Pat dough to 1/2-inch thickness and place in a greased 9-inch pie pan. Spread 2 tbsp. oil over potato shell. Cover with tomato sauce, Mozzarella and Parmesan cheeses in that order. Sprinkle with basil and remaining 2 tbsp. oil. Bake for 20 mins. or until cheese has melted. Brown cheese under broiler for 1 min., if desired. Serves 6.

Hunter's Chicken

1 FRYER, ABOUT 3 LBS.
VEGETABLE OIL FOR FRYING
4 TBSP. CHOPPED ONION
1/2 CLOVE GARLIC, THINLY SLICED
2 TBSP. TOMATO PUREE
SALT AND PEPPER TO TASTE
1 TBSP. BUTTER

1/2 LB. FRESH MUSHROOMS, SLICED
1-1/2 LBS. TOMATOES, PEELED,
  SEEDED AND CHOPPED (OR CANNED)
1/2 TO 3/4 CUP CHICKEN BROTH OR
  DRY WHITE WINE
1 BAY LEAF
1 TBSP. MINCED PARSLEY

DISJOINT FRYER (OR BUY FRYER PARTS) AND BROWN IN HOT OIL (ENOUGH OIL TO COVER BOTTOM OF FRYING PAN). WHEN BROWN, REMOVE FROM PAN AND SAUTÉ ONION, GARLIC AND MUSHROOMS IN THE OIL, ADDING MORE, IF NECESSARY. PUT CHICKEN BACK IN SKILLET AND ADD REMAINING INGREDIENTS, EXCEPT BUTTER AND PARSLEY. COOK COVERED ON SIMMER, UNTIL CHICKEN IS TENDER, ABOUT 35-40 MINS. ARRANGE CHICKEN ON PLATTER AND KEEP WARM. ADD BUTTER AND PARSLEY TO THE SAUCE IN THE SKILLET AND POUR OVER THE CHICKEN BEFORE SERVING. 4-6 SERVINGS.

Swiss Steak

2 LBS. ROUND STEAK
2 TBSP. FLOUR (OPTIONAL)
1/2 TEASP. SALT; DASH PEPPER
1 TBSP. OIL
2-3 STALKS CELERY, CHOPPED

1/4 CUP GREEN PEPPER, CHOPPED
1 CUP PEELED, CHOPPED TOMATOES
1/4 TO 1/2 CUP SLICED MUSHROOMS
  (OPTIONAL)
2 CUPS WATER

POUND FLOUR, SALT AND PEPPER INTO MEAT. CUT INTO SERVING PIECES. BROWN MEAT IN OIL. PUT IN CASSEROLE OR DUTCH OVEN; ADD VEGETABLES AND WATER. COVER AND BAKE AT 300 DEGREES FOR 3-4 HOURS. ADD WATER, IF NEEDED. MAY COOK ON LOW IN SLOW COOKER ALL DAY. SERVES 6.

Stuffed Green Peppers

1 LB. GROUND BEEF
1 MEDIUM ONION, CHOPPED
2 CUPS TOMATO JUICE
1/2 CUP WHITE OR BROWN RICE
4 OZ. GRATED CHEDDAR CHEESE

1/2 TEASP. SALT; DASH PEPPER
DASH OF OREGANO, BASIL, THYME AND
  ROSEMARY
WORCESTERSHIRE SAUCE TO TASTE
6 GREEN PEPPERS

CUT TOPS FROM PEPPERS; REMOVING CORE AND SEEDS. STEAM FOR 5 MINS. BROWN MEAT; DRAIN. SAUTÉ ONION. ADD TOMATO JUICE AND BRING TO A BOIL. ADD RICE; COVER AND SIMMER UNTIL TENDER (ABOUT 40 MINS.). ADD CHEESE AND SPICES. STUFF PEPPERS WITH MIXTURE AND BAKE AT 350 DEGREES FOR 30 MINS. MAY BE MADE AHEAD AND FROZEN. 6 SERVINGS.

Zesty Pork Bake

2 TBSP. BUTTER/MARGARINE, MELTED
6 RIB PORK CHOPS
SALT AND PEPPER TO TASTE
1 (1-3/8 OZ.) PACKAGE DRY ONION SOUP MIX
1 LARGE GREEN PEPPER, CHOPPED
1 CUP UNCOOKED REGULAR RICE

1/2 CUP KETCHUP
1 TEASP. WORCESTERSHIRE SAUCE
2 CUPS BOILING WATER
1 CUP (1/4 LB.) SHREDDED CHEDDAR
   CHEESE

COAT SHALLOW 2 QUART CASSEROLE WITH MELTED BUTTER. SPRINKLE CHOPS WITH SALT AND PEPPER AND ARRANGE IN CASSEROLE. TOP WITH SOUP MIX, GREEN PEPPER AND RICE. COMBINE KETCHUP AND WORCESTERSHIRE SAUCE; SPREAD OVER RICE. POUR IN BOILING WATER, COVER AND BAKE AT 350 DEGREES FOR 55-60 MINS. OR UNTIL DONE. REMOVE FROM OVEN, TOP WITH CHEESE. COVER AND ALLOW TO STAND 10 MINS. SERVES 6.

Honey Chicken

4-1/2 LBS. CHICKEN, BREAST OR THIGHS, WITH SKIN REMOVED.

SAUCE:

3/4 CUP FRESH ORANGE JUICE
2 TBSP. FRESH LEMON JUICE
1/4 CUP SALAD OIL
1/2 CUP HONEY
1 TEASP. SALT

1/2 TEASP. PEPPER
1 TEASP. DRY MUSTARD OR CURRY
   POWDER
1/2 TEASP. PAPRIKA

COMBINE ALL SAUCE INGREDIENTS AND SHAKE OR BLEND WELL. PLACE CHICKEN IN SHALLOW CERAMIC DISH. POUR SAUCE OVER CHICKEN TO COAT IT WELL. COVER AND ALLOW TO SIT IN REFRIGERATOR OVERNIGHT. REMOVE CHICKEN FROM SAUCE AND PUT IN BAKING PAN. BAKE AT 400 DEGREES APPROXIMATELY 30 MINS. TURN AND BASTE WITH SAUCE, THEN BAKE 30 MINS. LONGER OR UNTIL DONE. IF CHICKEN BROWNS TOO FAST, COVER WITH FOIL. SERVES 6-8.

Chicken and Green Corn

1/2 LB. BUTTER (NOT MARGARINE)
1 PACKAGE OF FRYING CHICKEN PARTS

12 EARS SMALL, TENDER, GREEN CORN
SALT AND PEPPER TO TASTE

LIGHTLY FRY CHICKEN WHICH HAS BEEN SEASONED WITH SALT AND PEPPER UNTIL LIGHT BROWN IN OIL OR SHORTENING. PLACE CHICKEN IN GREASED BAKING DISH AND COVER WITH HALF OF BUTTER. GRATE THE CORN OVER THE TOP OF THE CHICKEN AND PUT REST OF BUTTER ON THE TOP WITH ADDITIONAL SALT AND PEPPER. BAKE IN 300 DEGREE OVEN UNTIL DISH IS A NICE BROWN. DO NOT LET IT DRY OUT. ADD MORE BUTTER, IF NECESSARY. SERVES 4-6.

Hominy Pie

2 CUPS HOMINY GRITS
2 TEASP. SALT
1 CUP SLICED ONION
1 LARGE CLOVE GARLIC, MINCED
1/2 LB. GROUND LEAN PORK
2 TBSP. CHILI POWDER
4 OZ. CHEDDAR CHEESE, GRATED

6 CUPS WATER
3 TBSP. BACON DRIPPINGS OR
  VEGETABLE OIL
1/2 CUP GREEN PEPPER, CHOPPED
1 LB. GROUND ROUND
2 CUPS CONDENSED BEEF BOUILLON
12 LARGE RIPE OLIVES, SLICED

BOIL GRITS IN SALTED WATER FOR 30 MINS. MEANWHILE, HEAT BACON DRIPPINGS OR OIL IN LARGE SKILLET. SAUTÉ ONION, GREEN PEPPER AND GARLIC UNTIL ONION BECOMES TRANSLUCENT. ADD GROUND ROUND AND PORK. STIR AND COOK UNTIL RED COLOR DISAPPEARS FROM MEAT. ADD BEEF BOUILLON AND CHILI POWDER. SIMMER 45 MINS. PREHEAT OVEN TO 325 DEGREES. ON THE BOTTOM OF A SHALLOW BAKING DISH, SPREAD 1/2-INCH LAYER OF GRITS. COVER THIS WITH 1-INCH LAYER OF MEAT MIXTURE, LAYER OF SLICED RIPE OLIVES AND A LAYER OF CHEESE. REPEAT LAYERS AND TOP WITH REMAINING GRITS. COVER TIGHTLY AND BAKE FOR 1 HOUR. CUT INTO SQUARES AND SERVE. 8 SERVINGS.

Chicken and Sweet Potato Pot Pie

2 CUPS COOKED CHICKEN, DICED
2 LARGE ONIONS, THINLY SLICED
2 TBSP. BUTTER
2 CUPS CHICKEN BROTH
SALT AND PEPPER TO TASTE

2 GREEN PEPPERS, THINLY SLICED
1/3 CUP MINCED PARSLEY
2 TBSP. FLOUR
1 TEASP. GRATED ORANGE PEEL

Crust:

1 CUP MASHED SWEET POTATOES
1 EGG, BEATEN
2 TBSP. ORANGE JUICE
1 TEASP. BAKING POWDER

1/4 CUP BUTTER, MELTED
1 TBSP. GRATED ORANGE PEEL
1 CUP FLOUR
1/2 TEASP. SALT

GREASE CASSEROLE. ALTERNATE LAYERS OF CHICKEN, PEPPERS, ONIONS AND PARSLEY UNTIL ALL ARE USED. MELT BUTTER, BLEND IN FLOUR, GRADUALLY ADD BROTH, STIRRING CONSTANTLY UNTIL THICKENED. ADD ORANGE PEEL AND SALT AND PEPPER. POUR OVER CONTENTS OF CASSEROLE. FOR CRUST: MIX SWEET POTATOES, BUTTER, EGG, ORANGE PEEL AND ORANGE JUICE. COMBINE FLOUR, BAKING POWDER AND SALT. ADD FLOUR MIXTURE TO POTATOES AND STIR WELL. ROLL CRUST AND FIT TO TOP OF CASSEROLE. BAKE AT 350 DEGREES FOR 35 TO 40 MINS. 6-8 SERVINGS.

ROAST PORK

1 LEG OF PORK, 8-10 LBS. OR SMALLER
1 CUP BROWN SUGAR
1 TBSP. SALT
1 TBSP. BLACK PEPPER
1 CUP WATER

1 QUART CAN TOMATOES
3 SLICED ONIONS
1 TBSP. HOT SAUCE
1 CUP KETCHUP

RUB BROWN SUGAR, SALT AND PEPPER INTO PORK. ADD TO THE PAN FOR BASTING: TOMATOES, ONION, HOT SAUCE, KETCHUP AND WATER. ROAST SLOWLY ABOUT 3-1/2 HOURS, BASTING OFTEN, IN 350 DEGREE OVEN, OR ABOUT 30 MINS. PER POUND. SERVES 8-10.

CREAMY HAM CASSEROLE

1 HEAD CAULIFLOWER (2 LBS. OR 2
   PACKAGES FROZEN)
2 CUPS CUBED COOKED HAM
1 (2 OZ.) CAN SLICED MUSHROOMS, DRAINED
4 TBSP. BUTTER
1/3 CUP FLOUR

1 CUP MILK
1 CUP SHARP CHEDDAR CHEESE CUBES
1/2 CUP SOUR CREAM
1 CUP BREADCRUMBS
1 TBSP. MELTED BUTTER

BREAK CAULIFLOWER INTO BUDS, COOK UNTIL TENDER AND DRAIN. COMBINE HAM AND MUSHROOMS. IN SAUCEPAN ON LOW HEAT, MELT BUTTER, ADD FLOUR THEN MILK. STIR UNTIL THICK AND ADD CHEESE AND SOUR CREAM. STIR UNTIL CHEESE MELTS. COMBINE WITH CAULIFLOWER AND HAM MIXTURE. TURN INTO 2 QUART CASSEROLE. COMBINE CRUMBS AND REMAINING BUTTER AND SPRINKLE OVER TOP. BAKE, UNCOVERED AT 350 DEGREES FOR 20 MINS. OR UNTIL HOT. SERVES 6.

SPARERIBS AND SAUERKRAUT II

3 TO 4 LBS. SPARERIBS
2 ONIONS, SLICED
2 TEASP. VINEGAR
2 TEASP. WORCESTERSHIRE SAUCE
3/4 CUP KETCHUP
3/4 CUP WATER

1 TEASP. PAPRIKA
1/2 TEASP. RED PEPPER
1/2 TEASP. BLACK PEPPER
1 TEASP. CHILI POWDER
1 TEASP. SALT

SELECT MEATY (COUNTRY-STYLE) SPARERIBS. CUT INTO SERVING PIECES. SPRINKLE WITH SALT AND PEPPER. PLACE IN ROASTING PAN AND COVER WITH ONIONS. COMBINE REMAINING INGREDIENTS AND POUR OVER MEAT. COVER AND BAKE AT 350 DEGREES FOR ABOUT 1-1/2 HOURS. BASTE OCCASIONALLY, TURNING RIBS ONCE OR TWICE. REMOVE COVER LAST 15 MINS. SO RIBS WILL BROWN. SERVE WITH WARM SAUERKRAUT. 6 SERVINGS.

HAM OR ROAST BEEF SALAD

2 CUPS LEFTOVER HAM OR ROAST BEEF, CUBED
1/2 CUP CELERY, CHOPPED
1/4 CUP ONION, FINELY CHOPPED
1/2 TO 1 CUP KOSHER DILL PICKLES, DRAINED
  AND CHOPPED

1/2 CUP MAYONNAISE
1 TEASP. PREPARED MUSTARD
1 TEASP. WORCESTERSHIRE SAUCE
1 TEASP. SALT

MIX TOGETHER HAM (BEEF), CELERY, ONION AND PICKLES. COMBINES REMAINING INGREDIENTS AND MIX WITH MEAT MIXTURE. SERVE STUFFED IN TOMATOES ON BED OF LETTUCE OR AS SANDWICH MIXTURE. SERVES 6.

ROAST SPRING LAMB

1-1/4 TEASP. GROUND GINGER
1/4 TEASP. GROUND NUTMEG
1/8 TEASP. PEPPER
1 (11 OZ.) CAN MANDARIN ORANGES,
  UNDRAINED
2/3 CUP MAPLE SYRUP

1/2 TEASP. GROUND CINNAMON
3/4 TEASP. SALT
1 (6 LB.) LEG OF LAMB
2 TEASP. FRESH MINT LEAVES (DRIED
  MAY BE USED)

MIX GINGER, CINNAMON, NUTMEG, SALT AND PEPPER; RUB OVER LAMB. PLACE LAMB ON RACK IN ROASTING PAN; INSERT MEAT THERMOMETER SO THAT TIP IS IN CENTER OF MEAT AWAY FROM FAT OR BONE. ROAST AT 325 DEGREES FOR 2 HOURS. DRAIN ORANGES, RESERVING 2 TBSP. OF JUICE. MIX JUICE, SYRUP AND MINT. ARRANGE ORANGES OVER TOP OF LAMB; BASTE WITH SYRUP MIXTURE. ROAST LAMB FOR 1 HOUR, OR UNTIL THERMO-METER REGISTERS 175 DEGREES, BASTING WITH SYRUP MIXTURE EVERY 15 MINS. REMOVE LAMB TO SERVING PLATTER, COVER LOOSELY WITH FOIL AND LET STAND 15 MINS. BEFORE CARVING. SERVES 6-8.

WEST VIRGINIA HASH

3 TBSP. SHORTENING
2 LARGE ONIONS, SLICED
2 GREEN PEPPERS, CHOPPED
1 LB. GROUND HAMBURGER
1 #2 CAN TOMATOES

1/2 CUP RICE, UNCOOKED
1 TEASP. CHILI POWDER
1 TEASP. SALT
1/4 TEASP. PEPPER

MELT SHORTENING IN A LARGE SKILLET. ADD ONIONS AND GREEN PEPPERS. COOK AND STIR OVER LOW HEAT, UNTIL ONIONS ARE LIGHTLY BROWNED. ADD HAMBURGER AND BROWN WELL, BREAKING UP AS MEAT COOKS. ADD TOMATOES, RICE, CHILI POWDER, SALT AND PEPPER. TURN INTO GREASED 1-1/2 QUART CASSEROLE. BAKE AT 375 DEGREES FOR 45 MINS. 8 SERVINGS.

Lima Bean Casserole

2-1/2 cups home-cooked, or canned
  lima beans
1 tbsp. butter or bacon drippings
1 tbsp. flour
1/2 teasp. salt
2 teasp. dry mustard
1/2 cup buttered crumbs

4-5 frankfurters, bacon strips or
  thin slices of ham
1 tbsp. brown sugar
1/8 teasp. pepper
2 teasp. lemon juice
1/2 cup grated cheese (mild
  Cheddar)

Drain lima beans, reserving liquid. Place limas in greased casserole dish. Heat butter or drippings over low heat; add flour and stir until well-blended. Slowly add 1/2 cup cooking water or liquid from canned limas, stirring until smooth; cook over low heat until thickened. Add brown sugar, salt, pepper, mustard and lemon juice. Pour sauce over lima beans; sprinkle with buttered crumbs and grated cheese. Arrange bacon, frankfurters, or ham on top. Bake in 375 degree oven for 25-35 mins., or until browned. Serves 4-5.

Leftover Ham Patties

3 cups leftover baked ham, ground
1/2 cup maple syrup
1 egg
1 teasp. spicy brown mustard
flour

1-1/2 cups fresh breadcrumbs
2 tbsp. finely chopped onion
1-1/2 teasp. prepared horseradish
1/8 teasp. each: salt and pepper
1/4 cup butter

Mix all ingredients; except flour and butter, in large bowl. Shape mixture into 6 large patties. Cover and refrigerate 30 mins. Coat ham patties with flour. Melt butter in large skillet over medium heat; add patties and sauté until golden brown (about 4 mins. each side). Serves 6.

Beans and Spareribs

1 lb. navy beans
2 teasp. salt
2 lbs. spareribs
1/2 teasp. dry mustard

1 tbsp. sugar
1 tbsp. molasses
1 onion, peeled and chopped
2 tbsp. fat, any kind

Cover the beans with boiling water, soak 50 mins., then boil until the skins wrinkle. Add the salt and spareribs, cut into sections. Stir in the seasonings and onion. Add the fat; cover tightly and continue to boil very slowly until the beans are soft and the spareribs tender, about 2 hours. 4-6 servings.

Roast Goose

12 TO 14 LB. GOOSE	2 TEASP. SALT
1 TEASP. PEPPER	2 TEASP. CARAWAY SEEDS
APPLE PRUNE STUFFING	

WIPE GOOSE INSIDE AND OUT AND SPRINKLE WITH SALT, PEPPER AND CARAWAY SEEDS. STUFF THE CAVITY WITH APPLE PRUNE STUFFING (OR YOUR FAVORITE BREAD STUFFING TO WHICH APPLES HAVE BEEN ADDED). PLACE TRUSSED BIRD ON A RACK IN A SHALLOW PAN. ROAST AT 350 DEGREES FOR ABOUT 3-1/2 HOURS IN ALL, DRAINING OFF THE FAT AS IT ACCUMULATES. BASTE BIRD OCCASIONALLY WITH THE PAN DRIPPINGS MIXED WITH HOT WATER. TEST FOR DONENESS BY PRESSING LEG FLESH. THE SKIN SHOULD BE VERY CRISP AND BROWN.

Apple Prune Stuffing

1/4 LB. STEWED PRUNES (SOAKED FOR AN HOUR IN COLD WATER, AND THEN ADD 1 TO 2 SLICES OF LEMON AND COOK SLOWLY UNTIL TENDER, ADD SUGAR TO TASTE, ABOUT 2 TBSP., AND COOK 5 MINS. LONGER). REMOVE PITS AND QUARTER.
5 SOUR APPLES, PEELED, CORED AND QUARTERED, AND COOKED IN A VERY SMALL AMOUNT OF WATER UNTIL TENDER, BUT STILL FIRM.

MIX PRUNES AND APPLES AND ADD: 1 CUP BREADCRUMBS, 1/2 TEASP. POULTRY SEASONING, 1/2 TEASP. SALT AND A DASH OF PEPPER. MIX WELL.

Corned Beef and Potato Salad

1 CAN CORNED BEEF	2 CUPS GREEN CABBAGE, SHREDDED
2 TEASP. MUSTARD SEED	1/4 CUP GREEN ONIONS, DICED WITH
2 TEASP. CELERY SEED	TOPS
1 TBSP. VINEGAR	3 CUPS DICED WARM POTATOES
1/4 CUP DILL PICKLES, FINELY CHOPPED	1 TEASP. SUGAR
1/2 TEASP. SALT	

SOAK THE CELERY SEED AND MUSTARD SEED IN VINEGAR, THEN DRIZZLE OVER THE POTATOES. SPRINKLE SUGAR AND SALT OVER THE POTATOES AND CHILL. COMBINE THE CORNED BEEF, PICKLES, CABBAGE AND ONION; ADD TO THE POTATOES AND BLEND WITH DRESSING. CHILL BEFORE SERVING. 6-8 SERVINGS.

Dressing

3/4 CUP SALAD OIL	1 TBSP. VINEGAR
3 TBSP. MILK	1/2 TEASP. SALT

Lamb Stew

2 LBS. LAMB SHOULDER CUT INTO 2-INCH
CUBES WITH EXCESS FAT REMOVED
1 TBSP. FAT
2 MEDIUM ONIONS, SLICED

1 LB. STRING BEANS
3 TBSP. SEASONED FLOUR*
3 CUPS BOILING WATER
5 MEDIUM POTATOES

MELT THE FAT IN A HEAVY SKILLET. ROLL EACH PIECE OF LAMB IN THE SEASONED FLOUR; PLACE IN HOT FAT; ADD SLICED ONIONS. BROWN LAMB WELL ON ALL SIDES. POUR OFF FAT; ADD BOILING WATER. COVER AND SIMMER SLOWLY 1-1/2 HOURS. PUSH MEAT TO CENTER OF SKILLET AND PLACE STRING BEANS ON ONE SIDE AND POTATOES ON THE OTHER. COVER AND CONTINUE COOKING OVER LOW HEAT UNTIL VEGETABLES ARE TENDER, ABOUT 30 MINS. SERVES 6.

*SEASONED FLOUR IS PREPARED BY ADDING 1-2 TEASP. SALT AND 1/4 TEASP. PEPPER TO EACH CUP OF FLOUR USED, MIXING THOROUGHLY.

Acorn Squash with Apples and Sausage

2 ACORN SQUASH
1 TEASP. SALT
2 TART COOKING APPLES
2 TEASP. SUGAR

1/2 LB. SAUSAGE MEAT
1/2 TEASP. SALT, ADDITIONAL
1/8 TEASP. PEPPER

CUT THE SQUASH IN HALVES LENGTHWISE AND SCOOP OUT THE SEEDS AND PULP. PLACE SQUASH IN KETTLE. COVER WITH BOILING WATER. ADD 1 TEASP. SALT AND BOIL 10 MINS. DRAIN. PEEL AND CORE APPLES AND CHOP FINE. MIX WITH SAUSAGE. SPRINKLE THE SQUASH WITH THE SALT, PEPPER AND SUGAR. FILL WITH SAUSAGE/APPLE MIXTURE. PLACE IN A PAN AND POUR IN JUST ENOUGH HOT WATER TO KEEP THE SQUASH FROM STICKING. BAKE 30-35 MINS. IN 375 DEGREE OVEN. SERVES 4.

Casserole of Beef

2 TBSP. BUTTER OR MEAT DRIPPINGS
1 CLOVE GARLIC, CRUSHED
2 ONIONS, SLICED
2 GREEN PEPPERS, SHREDDED
1/2 TEASP. PEPPER

1 TEASP. SUGAR
1-1/2 LBS. ROUND STEAK, CUBED
2 TBSP. FLOUR
1-1/2 TEASP. SALT
2 CUPS CANNED TOMATOES

MELT BUTTER; ADD GARLIC, ONIONS, PEPPERS AND SUGAR AND FRY UNTIL BEGINNING TO TURN YELLOW. ROLL THE MEAT IN THE FLOUR WITH SEASONINGS AND ADD TO THE ONION. WHEN BROWNED, TRANSFER TO A CASSEROLE DISH. ADD TOMATO. COVER AND BAKE 2 HOURS IN 350-375 DEGREE OVEN. SERVES 6.

HAM AND APPLE CASSEROLE

3 CUPS GROUND COOKED HAM
1 TBSP. GRATED ONION
1/2 CUP MILK
2 MEDIUM APPLES
2 TBSP. BUTTER

1/2 TEASP. DRY MUSTARD
1 EGG
1 CUP BREADCRUMBS
1/4 CUP BROWN SUGAR

COMBINE HAM, MUSTARD, ONION, EGG, MILK AND CRUMBS. PLACE IN GREASED CASSEROLE DISH. PEEL, CORE AND SLICE APPLES 1/2-INCH THICK. ARRANGE OVERLAPPING SLICES AROUND THE EDGE OF CASSEROLE ON TOP OF HAM MIXTURE. SPRINKLE WITH BROWN SUGAR AND DOT WITH BUTTER. BAKE UNCOVERED AT 375 DEGREES ABOUT 40 MINS. OR UNTIL APPLES ARE BROWN AND TENDER. SERVES 6.

CREAMY CHICKEN HASH

3 TBSP. CHICKEN FAT OR BUTTER
2-1/2 TBSP. FLOUR
1/2 CUP CREAM
SALT AND PEPPER TO TASTE
1/2 CUP GRATED CHEESE (MILD CHEDDAR)

1 TBSP. GRATED ONION
1 CUP CHICKEN STOCK
2-3 CUPS COOKED CHICKEN, CHOPPED
2 EGGS, BEATEN

HEAT FAT, ADD ONION AND COOK OVER LOW HEAT UNTIL SOFT, BUT NOT BROWNED. ADD FLOUR AND STIR UNTIL BLENDED; SLOWLY ADD STOCK AND STIR OVER LOW HEAT UNTIL THICK AND SMOOTH; ADD CREAM AND CHICKEN, SEASONING TO TASTE. SLOWLY ADD A LITTLE OF THE HOT SAUCE TO BEATEN EGGS, ADD TO CHICKEN MIXTURE, STIRRING CONSTANTLY. TURN INTO GREASED SHALLOW CASSEROLE; SPRINKLE WITH GRATED CHEESE AND DASH OF PAPRIKA. HEAT UNDER BROILER UNTIL BROWN AND BUBBLY. 6 SERVINGS.

LIVER AND ONIONS

1 LB. BEEF LIVER, THINLY SLICED INTO
   SERVING PIECES
3 TBSP. FLOUR
1/4 CUP WATER

2 TBSP. VEGETABLE OIL
1 LARGE SPANISH ONION OR 4 MEDIUM
   YELLOW ONIONS, THINLY SLICED
SALT AND PEPPER TO TASTE

LIGHTLY COAT LIVER WITH FLOUR. IN LARGE SKILLET, ADD SMALL AMOUNT OF COOKING OIL (OR SPRAY) AND COOK ONION IN WATER UNTIL SOFT, ABOUT 3 MINS. REMOVE ONION AND RESERVE. SPRAY SKILLET AND HEAT 1 TBSP. OIL OVER MODERATE HEAT. ADD LIVER AND COOK 2-3 MINS. UNTIL BROWN. TURN AND ADD REMAINING OIL, COOKING 2-3 MINS. MORE. WHEN DONE, STIR IN ONION AND COOK MIXTURE, STIRRING UNTIL HEATED THROUGH. SALT AND PEPPER TO TASTE. SERVES 4.

FRESH VEGETABLE LASAGNA

2 TBSP. OIL
3 SMALL ZUCCHINI, SLICED AND QUARTERED
3 LARGE CARROTS, SLICED IN ROUNDS
2 MEDIUM RED SWEET PEPPERS, SLICED
4 GREEN ONIONS, SLICED
15 UNCOOKED LASAGNA NOODLES
1 (28 OZ.) CAN ITALIAN-STYLE TOMATOES, QUARTERED

1 (28-OZ.) CAN TOMATO PUREE
1 LB. SKIMMED RICOTTA CHEESE
1 CUP GRATED PARMESAN CHEESE
1 LB. PART-SKIM MOZZARELLA CHEESE
SALT AND PEPPER TO TASTE
2 CUPS COLD WATER

PREHEAT OVEN TO 350 DEGREES. HEAT OIL IN FRYING PAN. WHEN HOT, ADD VEGETABLES AND STIR-FRY 5 MINS. REMOVE FROM HEAT. COAT A 10-1/2x15-INCH BAKING PAN WITH NON-STICK SPRAY. ARRANGE HALF THE NOODLES IN THE PAN. ADD HALF THE VEGETABLES, TOMATO PIECES, PUREE, RICOTTA, PARMESAN AND MOZZARELLA. ADD ANOTHER LAYER OF NOODLES AND THE REST OF THE OTHER INGREDIENTS. ADD SALT AND PEPPER TO TASTE. ADD 2 CUPS OF WATER. COVER PAN WITH FOIL COATED WITH NON-STICK SPRAY. BAKE FOR 1-1/2 HOURS. LET STAND 1/2 HOUR BEFORE CUTTING. EXCELLENT WHEN SERVED THE NEXT DAY. SERVES 6 TO 8. *TIFFANY'S, FAIRMONT, WV*

MUSHROOM MACARONI AND CHEESE

8 OZ. ELBOW MACARONI
12 OZ. FRESH MUSHROOMS, WIPED CLEAN
2 TBSP. BUTTER
1/8 TEASP. NUTMEG
1/4 CUP BREADCRUMBS
2 TBSP. FRESHLY GRATED PARMESAN CHEESE
2 TBSP. CHOPPED PARSLEY

1 CUP GRATED GRUYERE CHEESE
1 CUP GRATED MOZZARELLA CHEESE
1-1/3 CUPS MILK
2 EGGS
1/2 TEASP. PAPRIKA
PINCH OF CAYENNE
SALT TO TASTE

PREHEAT OVEN TO 350 DEGREES. COOK PASTA IN BOILING WATER UNTIL AL DENTE. DRAIN AND RESERVE. TRIM MUSHROOM STEMS; CUT STEMS AND CAPS INTO SLICES. MELT BUTTER AND COOK MUSHROOMS FOR 3 MINS., OR UNTIL JUST TENDER. SPRINKLE WITH NUTMEG AND SET ASIDE. IN SMALL BOWL, COMBINE BREADCRUMBS, PARMESAN AND PARSLEY. SET ASIDE. LIGHTLY GREASE A 2-1/2 QUART OVENPROOF CASSEROLE. PLACE 1/3 OF PASTA ON BOTTOM. COVER WITH 1/3 OF MUSHROOMS. MIX TOGETHER THE TWO GRATED CHEESES, COVER MUSHROOMS WITH 1/3 MIXTURE. REPEAT LAYERS TWICE, ENDING WITH GRATED CHEESE. WHISK TOGETHER MILK, EGGS, PAPRIKA, CAYENNE AND SALT. POUR OVER CASSEROLE. SPRINKLE TOP WITH BREADCRUMB MIXTURE. BAKE FOR 1 HOUR, OR UNTIL TOP IS GOLDEN AND CHEESES ARE MELTED. 6-8 SERVINGS.

Italian Meatloaf

2 TBSP. OLIVE OIL
1 CUP EACH, FINELY CHOPPED ONION AND
  CELERY
3 CLOVES GARLIC, MINCED
1 TEASP. DRIED ITALIAN HERB SEASONING
1 CUP PREPARED TOMATO SAUCE OR
  MARINARA SAUCE
1/2 CUP CHOPPED ITALIAN OR REGULAR PARSLEY

1/3 CUP CHOPPED FRESH BASIL LEAVES
  (DRIED MAY BE USED)
1/3 CUP BREADCRUMBS
1-1/2 LBS. GROUND BEEF
1/2 LB. GROUND PORK
SALT AND PEPPER TO TASTE
4 STRIPS BACON (OPTIONAL)

HEAT OIL IN SKILLET AND ADD ONION, CELERY, GARLIC AND ITALIAN SEASONING. COOK, COVERED, STIRRING OCCASIONALLY FOR 15 MINS. REMOVE TO BOWL. PREHEAT OVEN TO 350 DEGREES. ADD TOMATO SAUCE, PARSLEY, BASIL AND BREADCRUMBS TO COOKED MIXTURE. BREAK UP GROUND BEEF AND PORK INTO MIXTURE, SEASON WITH SALT AND PEPPER AND GENTLY TOSS TOGETHER. DO NOT OVERMIX. LIGHTLY GREASE A 9x5x3 LOAF PAN. PACK WITH MEAT MIXTURE. LAY BACON LENGTHWISE ACROSS TOP, IF DESIRED. BAKE FOR 45 MINS. DO NOT OVERCOOK. REMOVE FROM OVEN AND LET STAND 5 MINS. DRAIN OFF ANY PAN LIQUID AND PLACE ON PLATE. LET STAND ANOTHER 10 MINS. BEFORE SLICING. SERVES 8.

Homemade Pork & Beans

1-1/2 CUPS SMALL, DRY RED BEANS,
  SOAKED OVERNIGHT IN WATER
2 TBSP. OLIVE OIL
2 TO 2-1/2 LBS. BONELESS PORK SHOULDER,
  CUT INTO 1-1/2 INCH CUBES
1/2 LB. SLAB BACON, RIND REMOVED,
  CUT INTO 1/4 INCH CUBES
2 CUPS CHOPPED YELLOW ONION
2 CUPS CHICKEN BROTH

1 CAN (28 OZ.) PEELED PLUM
  TOMATOES, DRAINED, CRUSHED
4 CLOVES GARLIC, CHOPPED
2 TBSP. WORCESTERSHIRE SAUCE
1 BAY LEAF
DASH TABASCO SAUCE
SALT AND PEPPER TO TASTE
DASH RED WINE VINEGAR

DRAIN BEANS AND SET ASIDE, COVERED, UNTIL READY TO USE. HEAT OLIVE OIL AND BROWN PORK, ADDING MORE OIL, IF NEEDED. REMOVE TO OVENPROOF CASSEROLE DISH. ADD BACON TO SKILLET AND COOK OVER MEDIUM-HIGH HEAT UNTIL LIGHTLY BROWNED. REMOVE TO CASSEROLE. ADD ONION TO SKILLET AND COOK UNTIL WILTED. ADD TO CASSEROLE. IN SEPARATE SAUCEPAN COMBINE BROTH, TOMATOES, GARLIC, WORCESTERSHIRE SAUCE, BAY LEAF, TABASCO, SALT AND PEPPER. BRING TO BOIL AND POUR OVER CASSEROLE. ADD BEANS AND VINEGAR AND STIR WELL. COVER AND BAKE IN PREHEATED 350 DEGREE OVEN FOR 1-1/4 HOURS. REMOVE COVER AND STIR, THEN BAKE 15 MORE MINS., OR UNTIL PORK AND BEANS ARE TENDER. SERVES 6.

Vegetable Noodle Casserole

4 OZ. EGG NOODLES, UNCOOKED
1 STALK CELERY, SLICED
1 SMALL ONION, CHOPPED
1 SMALL GREEN PEPPER, CHOPPED
1 CUP COARSELY CHOPPED FRESH BROCCOLI
2 TBSP. VEGETABLE OIL
1/2 CUP MILK

1/4 TEASP. SALT
1/4 TEASP. PEPPER
1-1/2 CUPS (6 OZ.) SHREDDED
    MONTEREY JACK CHEESE
3 TBSP. FINE, DRY BREADCRUMBS
1 TBSP. BUTTER OR MARGARINE,
    MELTED

COOK NOODLES ACCORDING TO PACKAGE DIRECTIONS; DRAIN AND SET ASIDE. SAUTÉ CELERY, ONION, GREEN PEPPER AND BROCCOLI IN OIL UNTIL TENDER. STIR IN MILK, SALT, PEPPER AND CHEESE. SPOON INTO LIGHTLY GREASED 1-1/2 QUART BAKING DISH. COVER AND BAKE AT 350 DEGREES FOR 15 MINS. SPRINKLE WITH BREADCRUMBS AND DRIZZLE WITH BUTTER. BAKE, UNCOVERED, 10 MINS. 4-6 SERVINGS.

Country Ham

A WELL-CURED HAM SHOULD BE SOAKED A MINIMUM OF 12 HOURS; PREFERABLY 24 WITH WATER CHANGED AT LEAST 3 TIMES. PRIOR TO COOKING, SCRUB WITH A WIRE BRUSH TO REMOVE EXCESS BRINE. IN A LARGE KETTLE COMPLETELY COVER HAM WITH COLD WATER AND ADD 1 PINT OF APPLE CIDER VINEGAR. SIMMER HAM SLOWLY 18 MINS. PER POUND AND MAINTAIN LIQUID LEVEL WHICH COVERS HAM. WHEN SHANK BONE CAN BE LOOSENED AND REMOVED, PREPARE HAM FOR BAKING. CUT AWAY EXCESS FAT AND SKIN HAM, LEAVING 1/4 INCH OF FAT.

MAKE A PASTE OF 1/3 CUP PREPARED MUSTARD, 2/3 CUP BROWN SUGAR AND DRY SHERRY TO MAKE IT SPREADING CONSISTENCY. SPREAD EVENLY OVER HAM FAT, SCORE WITH KNIFE AND SPIKE WITH WHOLE CLOVES. ROAST IN MODERATE OVEN (350 DEGREES) UNTIL CRUST IS BROWN. BASTE WITH DRIPPINGS WHILE ROASTING. SERVE HAM COLD, THINLY SLICED.

Upside-Down Ham Loaf

2 TBSP. BUTTER
8-12 CANNED PINEAPPLE CHUNKS
4 CUPS GROUND COOKED HAM
1/2 TEASP. DRY MUSTARD
1/2 CUP PINEAPPLE JUICE
DASH OF CAYENNE

1/4 CUP BROWN SUGAR
WHOLE CLOVES
2 TBSP. GRATED ONION
1 CUP BREADCRUMBS
2 EGGS, SLIGHTLY BEATEN

MELT BUTTER IN THE BOTTOM OF A GREASED LOAF PAN OR CASSEROLE DISH; SPRINKLE WITH BROWN SUGAR. STUD PINEAPPLE CHUNKS WITH WHOLE CLOVES AND ARRANGE ON TOP OF SUGAR. COMBINE HAM AND REMAINING INGREDIENTS; PACK INTO PAN ON TOP OF PINEAPPLE CHUNKS. BAKE, COVERED IN 375 DEGREE OVEN ABOUT 30 MINS. TURN OUT UPSIDE-DOWN ON HOT PLATTER. 6-8 SERVINGS.

STUFFED CUCUMBERS

3 CUCUMBERS, 7-8 INCHES LONG
1 TEASP. GRATED ONION
1/4 CUP CELERY, FINELY CHOPPED
6 TBSP. MAYONNAISE
1/2 TEASP. SALT
1/2 CUP BUTTERED CRUMBS

1 CUP CANNED TUNA FISH OR
  SALMON, FLAKED
1/2 CUP SOFT BREADCRUMBS
2 TBSP. LEMON JUICE
1/4 TEASP. PEPPER

WASH CUCUMBERS AND CUT IN HALF CROSSWISE; PARE. BOIL ABOUT 5 MINS. OR UNTIL ALMOST TENDER. CUT OFF A THIN SLICE THE LENGTH OF EACH CUCUMBER. SCOOP OUT TO MAKE A SHELL ABOUT 1/2-INCH THICK. SPRINKLE WITH SALT. CHOP THE REMOVED PULP. COMBINE TUNA/SALMON, ONION, CELERY, SOFT BREADCRUMBS, MAYONNAISE, LEMON JUICE AND SEASONINGS; ADD THE CHOPPED CUCUMBER PULP. FILL CUCUMBER SHELLS WITH FISH MIXTURE. SPRINKLE WITH BUTTERED CRUMBS AND DASH OF PAPRIKA. PLACE IN SHALLOW BAKING DISH WITH A LITTLE WATER. BAKE IN 375 DEGREE OVEN ABOUT 30 MINS. OR UNTIL BROWNED. SERVES 6.

MACARONI, LIVER AND MUSHROOMS AU GRATIN

1 PACKAGE (8-9 OZ.) MACARONI
1 CUP CHOPPED CHICKEN LIVERS OR
  CALF'S LIVER
1/2 CLOVE GARLIC, FINELY CHOPPED
2-1/2 CUPS STEWED OR CANNED TOMATOES
2 TEASP. SALT
FEW GRAINS CAYENNE

1/4 CUP BUTTER
1/4 CUP CHOPPED ONION
1/2 LB. SLICED MUSHROOMS
1 CAN TOMATO PASTE
1 TEASP. BROWN SUGAR
3/4 CUP GRATED CHEESE (MILD
  CHEDDAR OR AMERICAN)

COOK MACARONI ACCORDING TO PACKAGE DIRECTIONS; RINSE AND DRAIN. PLACE IN A GREASED CASSEROLE DISH. MELT BUTTER IN SKILLET; ADD CHICKEN LIVERS/CALF'S LIVER, ONIONS, GARLIC AND MUSHROOMS. COOK UNTIL LIGHTLY BROWNED. ADD TOMATOES, TOMATO PASTE AND SEASONINGS. MIX WELL. POUR OVER THE MACARONI, TOPPING WITH GRATED CHEESE. BAKE IN 375 DEGREE OVEN ABOUT 25 MINS. OR UNTIL BROWNED. 6 SERVINGS.

VEGETABLE-STUFFED CHICKEN BREASTS

8 CHICKEN BREAST HALVES, BONED
  AND SKINNED
1 TEASP. SALT
1/2 TEASP. MINCED PARSLEY
4 OZ. FRESH MUSHROOMS, SLICED
1/2 CUP FINELY CHOPPED GREEN PEPPER
2 TBSP. MELTED WHIPPED MARGARINE
1/4 CUP WHIPPED MARGARINE

1/2 TEASP. DRIED CHERVIL LEAVES
1/4 TEASP. PEPPER
1/2 CUP FINELY CHOPPED ONION
1 CLOVE GARLIC, MINCED
2 TBSP. WORCESTERSHIRE SAUCE
MINCED PARSLEY
6 CUPS HOT COOKED RICE

PUT CHICKEN BREASTS BETWEEN 2 SHEETS OF WAXED PAPER AND POUND UNTIL 1/2-INCH THICK. COMBINE SALT, CHERVIL, PARSLEY AND PEPPER. SPRINKLE ON ONE SIDE OF EACH CHICKEN BREAST. SAUTÉ MUSHROOMS, ONION, GREEN PEPPER AND GARLIC IN 1/4 CUP MARGARINE UNTIL ONION IS TENDER. SPREAD MIXTURE OVER SEASONED SURFACE OF CHICKEN TO WITHIN 1/2-INCH OF EDGES. ROLL UP CHICKEN, STARTING AT SHORT END; SECURE WITH TOOTHPICKS AND PLACE IN UNGREASED BAKING DISH. COMBINE WORCESTERSHIRE SAUCE AND 2 TBSP. MARGARINE; BRUSH CHICKEN ROLLS WITH MIXTURE. BAKE AT 375 DEGREES FOR 30-35 MINS., BASTING WITH WORCESTERSHIRE SAUCE MIXTURE SEVERAL TIMES. REMOVE TOOTHPICKS. SPOON PAN JUICE OVER CHICKEN; SPRINKLE WITH PARSLEY. SERVE WITH HOT COOKED RICE. SERVES 8.

OLD-FASHIONED PORK PIE

1-1/2 LBS. SHOULDER OR BLADE PORK
1 SMALL ONION, CHOPPED
1/4 LB. WASHED, SLICED FRESH MUSHROOMS
  OR 1 (4 OZ.) CAN

1 CUP PEELED, SLICED POTATOES
1/2 TEASP. WORCESTERSHIRE SAUCE
SALT AND PEPPER TO TASTE
PIE CRUST

REMOVE THE FAT AND BONES FROM PORK; CUT INTO SERVING-SIZE PIECES. MELT 1 TBSP. FAT OR DRIPPINGS IN A HEAVY SKILLET; ADD PORK, ONION AND MUSHROOMS, FRYING UNTIL BROWN. ADD POTATOES AND WORCESTERSHIRE SAUCE; SEASON TO TASTE WITH SALT AND PEPPER. ADD WATER TO ALMOST SUBMERGE MEAT; COVER AND COOK OVER MODERATE HEAT UNTIL VEGETABLES ARE TENDER. TRANSFER TO A SHALLOW CASSEROLE DISH LINED WITH PIE CRUST. COVER WITH TOP CRUST, SLASHING TOP TO ALLOW STEAM TO ESCAPE. PRESS EDGES TOGETHER AND FLUTE. BAKE IN 425 DEGREE OVEN FOR 30 MINS., OR UNTIL TOP CRUST IS BROWN. 6 SERVINGS.

Pork Chops with Fried Apples

4 PORK LOIN CHOPS
BACON DRIPPINGS OR BUTTER FOR BROWNING
FLOUR, SALT AND PEPPER FOR DREDGING

4-5 TART APPLES
1/2 CUP BROWN SUGAR

MIX FLOUR, SALT AND PEPPER TOGETHER AND DREDGE EACH PORK CHOP IN MIXTURE UNTIL WELL-COATED. MELT FAT IN SKILLET AND BROWN CHOPS ON EACH SIDE. TURN HEAT TO LOW. CUT UNPEELED APPLES INTO QUARTERS AND PLACE AROUND THE CHOPS. SPRINKLE THE 1/2 CUP OF BROWN SUGAR OVER THE CHOPS, COVER AND SIMMER 45 TO 60 MINS. OR UNTIL CHOPS ARE TENDER. SERVES 4.

Homemade Barbecues

2-3 LBS. BEEF OR PORK ROAST
1 TEASP. SALT
1/2 TEASP. PEPPER
2 SMALL ONIONS, CHOPPED
2 TBSP. VINEGAR

2 TBSP. WORCESTERSHIRE SAUCE
1 TEASP. PAPRIKA
1 TEASP. CHILI POWDER
3/4 CUP KETCHUP
3/4 CUP WATER

BOIL ROAST UNTIL TENDER. BREAK UP AND REMOVE ALL BONES AND FAT. PLACE IN LARGE SAUCEPAN AND ADD REMAINING INGREDIENTS. COOK ON LOW HEAT UNTIL ALL LIQUID IS COOKED DOWN. SERVE ON BUNS WITH COLE SLAW.

To Corn or Pickle Beef

10 LB. PIECE OF BEEF, BRISKET OR RUMP
SALT, WHITE PEPPER, GINGER, PAPRIKA

NUTMEG, BAY LEAVES, GARLIC
1 TEASP. SALTPETER

WASH MEAT. RUB WITH SALT, PEPPER, AND OTHER SPICES. IT SHOULD BE WELL SEASONED. PLACE MEAT IN A LARGE STONE JAR. COVER WITH WATER. DISSOLVE SALTPETER IN WATER AND ADD. COVER WITH A PLATE AND WEIGH IT DOWN TO KEEP MEAT SUBMERGED. KEEP IN A COOL PLACE, TURNING AT LEAST ONCE A WEEK. LEAVE IN BRINE FOR 4 WEEKS. ADD MORE SALT DURING THE PROCESS, IF BRINE IS NOT SALTY ENOUGH.

TO PREPARE: RINSE MEAT TO WASH OFF BRINE. IF VERY SALTY, SOAK FOR 1/2 HOUR IN COLD WATER; OR BRING TO A BOIL, THEN DRAIN. PLACE IN A LARGE SAUCEPAN, COVER WITH BOILING WATER, AND SIMMER 3 TO 5 HOURS, OR UNTIL TENDER. REMOVE FROM WATER AND SERVE WITH HORSERADISH SAUCE AND BOILED CABBAGE.

SCRAPPLE I

1 LB. GROUND ROUND STEAK
1 LB. HOT SAUSAGE
1 CUP CORN MEAL
3 CUPS BEEF CONSOMME

1 TBSP. ONION POWDER
1 TEASP. HOT SAUCE
1 TEASP. SAGE
1/2 TEASP. SUMMER SAVORY

COMBINE ALL INGREDIENTS AND MIX WELL. COOK IN HEAVY SKILLET FOR 30 MINS. BROWNING MEAT. PLACE IN OILED BREAD PAN OR MOLD. CHILL. SLICE AND DUST WITH FLOUR THEN LIGHTLY FRY IN A SMALL AMOUNT OF OIL.

SCRAPPLE II

2 CUPS GROUND PORK
2 CUPS GROUND BEEF
3 CUPS MEAT BROTH
1 CUP CORNMEAL

2 TEASP. SALT
1/4 TEASP. PEPPER
1-1/2 TEASP. SAGE
CAYENNE

COMBINE MEATS AND BROTH. HEAT TO BOILING. ADD SEASONINGS. STIR IN CORNMEAL SLOWLY, STIRRING CONSTANTLY. COOK 30 MINS. ADD FEW GRAINS OF CAYENNE. POUR INTO MOLD. CHILL UNTIL FIRM. CUT INTO THIN SLICES. FRY UNTIL WELL-BROWNED.

TASTY SCRAPPLE

1/2 LB. GROUND SAUSAGE
2-1/2 CUPS WATER

1 TEASP. POULTRY SEASONING
1 CUP WHITE CORNMEAL

BROWN SAUSAGE THOROUGHLY IN HEAVY SAUCEPAN. POUR OFF FAT. ADD WATER AND POULTRY SEASONING. BRING TO BOIL AND ADD CORNMEAL SLOWLY UNTIL THICK. POUR IN SMALL OBLONG LOAF PAN. CHILL. SLICE AND BROWN IN LIGHTLY GREASED SKILLET. SERVE WITH, OR WITHOUT SYRUP AND BUTTER.

VEGETABLES AND SIDE DISHES

The Indians gave the settlers the gifts of corn, green beans, limas, kidney beans, black-eyed peas, pumpkins, sweet potatoes and a variety of squash. After the first years the West Virginia homesteaders raised common European vegetables such as carrots, cabbage, turnips and various greens. Root vegetables were popular because they could be stored for the winter. There are not many old recipes for salads since such vegetables were only available during the growing season, unlike today when they are available year-round. Today, gardens in the Mountain State may have cauliflower, broccoli, tomatoes, eggplant, cucumbers, and asparagus but homegrown vegetables are still an important part of West Virginians' diets. Even most city dwellers take pride in a small garden patch or frequent the Farmers' Markets in the larger metropolitan areas.

What can't be eaten fresh is canned, pickled, or today, frozen. Nothing tastes better in the middle of the winter than a big bowl of vegetable soup using these home-canned vegetables in which you can almost feel, and smell, a warm summer day.

CARROT CASSEROLE I

1-1/2 CUPS WATER
1 LB. SHREDDED CARROTS
2/3 CUP BROWN RICE
2 CUPS SHREDDED CHEDDAR CHEESE

1 CUP MILK
2 EGGS, BEATEN
1 TBSP. MINCED ONION
DASH BLACK PEPPER

BRING WATER, CARROTS AND RICE TO A BOIL. COVER AND SIMMER 25 MINS. STIR IN 1-1/2 CUPS SHREDDED CHEESE, MILK, EGGS, ONION AND PEPPER. PLACE ALL IN CASSEROLE. BAKE AT 350 DEGREES, UNCOVERED FOR ONE HOUR. TOP WITH REMAINING CHEESE. BAKE 2 MINS. TO MELT CHEESE. SERVES 6-8.

SAUCY CAULIFLOWER

1 HEAD CAULIFLOWER, STEAMED WHOLE
1 CUP GRATED SHARP CHEDDAR CHEESE
1 CUP MEDIUM WHITE SAUCE*

1 TBSP. MELTED BUTTER
1/2 CUP DRY BREADCRUMBS

PLACE CAULIFLOWER IN GREASED 1-1/2 QUART CASSEROLE. BLEND CHEESE INTO WHITE SAUCE AND POUR OVER CAULIFLOWER. TOP WITH BUTTERED CRUMBS AND BAKE AT 350 DEGREES FOR 30 MINS.

*WHITE SAUCE

2 TBSP. BUTTER
2 TBSP. FLOUR OR 1 TBSP. CORNSTARCH
1 CUP MILK

1/4 TEASP. SALT
DASH PEPPER

MELT BUTTER OVER LOW HEAT. TAKE OFF HEAT AND BLEND IN FLOUR/CORNSTARCH UNTIL SMOOTH. ADD MILK, SALT AND PEPPER. COOK OVER MEDIUM HEAT UNTIL SAUCE THICKENS AND COMES TO BOIL, STIRRING CONSTANTLY. REDUCE HEAT AND SIMMER 2-3 MINS. TO REMOVE FLOURY TASTE.

SWEET AND SOUR CABBAGE

1 CABBAGE (WHITE OR RED)
2 TART APPLES, SLICED
2 TBSP. FLOUR
2 TBSP. VINEGAR

SALT AND PEPPER
2 TBSP. SHORTENING OR FAT
4 TBSP. BROWN SUGAR

SHRED THE CABBAGE FINE, ADD SALT AND PEPPER TO TASTE, AND APPLES. HEAT FAT IN LARGE SKILLET, ADD CABBAGE MIXTURE. ADD BOILING WATER TO COVER AND COOK UNTIL TENDER; SPRINKLE WITH FLOUR ADDING SUGAR AND VINEGAR. SIMMER 10 MINS. SERVE HOT.

FRESH CHOPPED SPINACH

2 LBS. FRESH SPINACH, WASHED WELL
1 TEASP. GRATED ONION
1/2 TEASP. SALT
DASH OF NUTMEG

2 TBSP. BUTTER OR FAT
2 TBSP. BREADCRUMBS
1/8 TEASP. PEPPER
1 CUP BEEF OR CHICKEN STOCK

PUT WASHED SPINACH INTO POT, ADD SMALL AMOUNT OF BOILING WATER, COVER AND COOK UNTIL LEAVES ARE TENDER. DRAIN THOROUGHLY AND CHOP FINE. HEAT BUTTER IN SKILLET, ADD ONION, CRUMBS AND SEASONINGS. BROWN LIGHTLY. ADD STOCK GRADU-ALLY, STIRRING CONSTANTLY. ADD SPINACH, HEAT THROUGH. SERVE GARNISHED WITH LEMON WEDGES AND SLICED HARD-COOKED EGGS. SERVES 8-10.

COTTAGE APPLE RING

2 LBS. COOKING APPLES
1/2 PINT WATER
6 OZ. MAYONNAISE
SUGAR
TOASTED ALMONDS, CHOPPED

1-1/2 OZ. GELATIN
12 OZ. COTTAGE CHEESE
2 TBSP. LEMON JUICE
SALT AND PEPPER
2 EATING APPLES, CORED AND SLICED

PEEL AND CORE 2 LBS. OF COOKING APPLES; CHOP ROUGHLY INTO PIECES AND COOK TO A SOFT PULP IN 1/2 PINT WATER. MASH APPLES. WHEN COOL, BLEND APPLE PURÉE WITH 6 OZ. COTTAGE CHEESE, 6 OZ. MAYONNAISE, LEMON JUICE, AND SUGAR TO TASTE. DISSOLVE GELATIN IN A LITTLE HOT WATER AND ADD TO MIXTURE. POUR INTO A RING MOLD AND ALLOW TO SET. JUST BEFORE SERVING TURN THE APPLE RING OUT ON A SERVING PLATE AND FILL CENTER WITH WATERCRESS, LETTUCE OR A COMBINATION OF BOTH. MOLD REMAINING COTTAGE CHEESE, SEASONED WITH SALT AND PEPPER AND MIXED WITH TOASTED ALMONDS. PLACE ON TOP OF GREENS AND PUT APPLE SLICES (DIPPED IN LEMON JUICE TO PREVENT BROWNING) AROUND EDGES OF PLATE.

TART COLESLAW

1 TEASP. MUSTARD SEED
3 TBSP. VINEGAR
1/2 TEASP. SALT
6 CUPS FINELY SHREDDED CABBAGE

1/2 TO 1 TEASP. CELERY SEED
1 OR 2 TEASP. SUGAR
1 CUP DAIRY SOUR CREAM
3 TBSP. MINCED ONION

COMBINE SEEDS WITH VINEGAR, SOUR CREAM AND OTHER SEASONINGS AND LET STAND IN REFRIGERATOR FOR SEVERAL HOURS TO BLEND FLAVORS. ADJUST SEASONINGS TO TASTE AND COMBINE WITH SHREDDED CABBAGE. CHILL FOR SEVERAL HOURS BEFORE SERVING. SERVES 6.

Minced Ham and Green Bean Salad

1/2 lb. minced ham, cut into
shoestring-size pieces
1 cup celery
1 onion, chopped or sliced
1/4 cup cider vinegar

1/4 teasp. pepper
1 can green beans, drained
1/4 cup salad oil
1/2 teasp. salt

Mix all ingredients, chill. Serves 6. May add: cubed cheese, green peppers, tomatoes, radishes or carrots.

Green Tomato Pie

6 cups sliced green tomatoes
boiling water, as directed
1 cup sugar
1/4 teasp. salt
3 tbsp. flour
pastry for two crust pie

1/4 teasp. nutmeg
1/4 teasp. cinnamon
1/8 teasp. cloves
grated rind and juice of one lemon
2 tbsp. margarine

Wash, but do not peel tomatoes. Slice 1/8-inch thick. Cover with boiling water. Let stand 3 mins. Drain. Combine sugar with salt, flour, nutmeg, cinnamon and cloves. Fill pastry shell with layers of tomato, sprinkling each layer with sugar mixture, dots of butter and lemon mixture. Arrange top pastry in lattice pattern. Bake at 450 degrees for 8-10 mins. Reduce heat to 375 and bake for another 40 mins.

Pickled Beets

7 lbs. 2- to 2-1/2-inch beets
4 cups 5 percent vinegar
2 cups water
2 cinnamon sticks

4-6 onions (2- to 2-1/2-inch)
1/4 cup canning or pickling salt
2 cups sugar
12 whole cloves

Trim off beet tops, leaving 1 inch of stem and roots to prevent bleeding of color. Wash thoroughly. Sort for size. Cover similar sizes together with boiling water; cook 25-30 mins. or until tender. Drain and discard liquid. Cool beets. Trim off roots and stems; slip skins off. Cut into 1/4 inch slices. Peel and thickly slice onions. Combine vinegar, salt, sugar and 2 cups water. Put cinnamon and cloves in cheesecloth bag; add to vinegar mixture. Bring to boil. Add beets and onions; simmer 5 mins. Remove spice bag. Fill jars with beets and onions, leaving 1/2-inch headspace. Add hot vinegar solution, leaving 1/2 inch headspace. Adjust lids and process pints or quarts 40 mins. in boiling water bath. Makes 6 pints. (May "cheat" on this recipe by starting with canned beets).

HEAVEN AND EARTH

4 LARGE POTATOES, PEELED AND   SALT AND SUGAR
    CUT INTO PIECES   1/8 TEASP. GROUND NUTMEG
3 TART APPLES, PEELED, CORED AND   4 TBSP. BUTTER, ROOM TEMP.
    CUT INTO QUARTERS OR EIGHTHS

PLACE POTATOES IN WATER DEEP ENOUGH TO COVER AND COOK FOR ABOUT 10 MINS. OR UNTIL ABOUT 3/4 SOFT. DRAIN OFF ABOUT HALF THE WATER. ADD THE APPLES, MIX AND COOK UNTIL APPLES ARE TENDER. MASH OR RICE THE MIXTURE AND SEASON WITH SALT AND SUGAR TO TASTE. STIR IN NUTMEG AND BUTTER; BEAT UNTIL LIGHT. 4-6 SERVINGS.

GERMAN POTATO SALAD

6 CUPS HOT DICED POTATOES   3/4 CUP BOILING WATER
1/3 CUP FINELY CHOPPED ONION   1 TO 1-1/2 TBSP. PREPARED MUSTARD
9 SLICES BACON, DICED   1 CUP DAIRY SOUR CREAM
3 TBSP. BACON DRIPPINGS   1 TBSP. FINELY CHOPPED PARSLEY
1/3 CUP VINEGAR   1 TBSP. SUGAR
SALT AND PEPPER TO TASTE

COMBINE HOT, COOKED POTATOES AND ONION. FRY BACON UNTIL CRISP; DRAIN ON PAPER TOWELING. POUR OFF ALL BUT 3 TBSP. OF BACON DRIPPINGS. ADD VINEGAR, SUGAR, WATER AND MUSTARD TO BACON DRIPPINGS; STIR UNTIL SUGAR IS DISSOLVED. ADD HOT MIXTURE TO POTATOES AND TOSS GENTLY UNTIL MOST OF THE MOISTURE IS ABSORBED. FOLD IN SOUR CREAM, PARSLEY, BACON, SALT AND PEPPER UNTIL WELL BLENDED. SERVE WARM OR COLD. SERVES 6-8.

WATER CRESS À LA DENNIS*

2 EGGS, RAW   1 TBSP. SALT
2 CUPS SALAD OIL   1/3 CUP VINEGAR
2 TBSP. HORSERADISH   2 TBSP. PAPRIKA
1/4 CUP TOMATO KETCHUP   DASH OF BLACK PEPPER
1/4 LARGE ONION, GRATED   2 TBSP. WORCESTERSHIRE SAUCE
DASH RED PEPPER

MIX ALL INGREDIENTS THOROUGHLY IN LARGE BOWL. SERVE OVER WATER CRESS THAT HAS BEEN TOSSED LIGHTLY WITH CRISP BACON, ALLOWING 1 SLICE BACON FOR EACH SERVING. YIELDS ABOUT 1 QUART DRESSING

*DENNIS WATER CRESS, INC., GROWS CULTIVATED WATER CRESS AND HAS A HOME OFFICE IN MARTINSBURG, W.VA. THIS DRESSING IS GOOD ON ANY FRESH GREENS INCLUDING WILD CRESS, POKE OR DANDELION.

Copper Pennies

2 LBS. CARROTS
1 MEDIUM GREEN PEPPER

2 SMALL ONIONS

COOK CARROTS IN SALTED WATER UNTIL TENDER. DICE PEPPER AND ONION AND ADD TO DRAINED CARROTS, THEN ADD THE FOLLOWING INGREDIENTS WHICH HAVE BEEN WELL MIXED:

1 CAN TOMATO SOUP
3/4 CUP SUGAR
1/2 CUP SALAD OIL

3/4 CUP VINEGAR
1 TEASP. WORCESTERSHIRE SAUCE
1 TEASP. MUSTARD

MARINATE AT LEAST OVERNIGHT, THE LONGER IT MARINATES THE BETTER. SERVES 4-6.

Macaroni and Cheese I

1 CUP MACARONI
4 SLICES WHITE BREAD, CRUMBLED
1 CUP DICED SHARP CHEDDAR CHEESE
1 TBSP. MINCED ONION

3 TEASP. SALT
1/2 TEASP. PAPRIKA
3 EGGS, BEATEN WELL
1 CUP MILK

COOK MACARONI UNTIL TENDER. MIX WITH 1 CUP MILK, CHEESE, ONION, EGGS, SALT, PAPRIKA AND CRUMBLED BREAD. POUR INTO GREASED AND FLOURED RING MOLD OR CASSEROLE. SET IN PAN OF WATER 1 INCH DEEP. COOK UNTIL FIRM AND LIGHTLY BROWNED. ABOUT 35-40 MINS. AT 350 DEGREES. SERVES 6-8.

Fried Potatoes and Tomatoes

4 MEDIUM POTATOES
4 SLICES BACON
1/4 CUP MARGARINE
1 MEDIUM ONION, THINLY SLICED
1 CLOVE GARLIC, MINCED
2 TBSP. PARSLEY, CHOPPED

3/4 TEASP. SALT
1/4 TEASP. PEPPER
1/4 TEASP. THYME
2 MEDIUM TOMATOES, PEELED AND
    DICED

PEEL THE POTATOES AND CUT INTO SLICES ABOUT 1/4-INCH THICK. SET ASIDE. IN LARGE, HEAVY FRYING PAN, FRY BACON SLOWLY UNTIL BROWN AND CRISP. REMOVE BACON FROM PAN. DRAIN AND CRUMBLE. ADD BUTTER TO PAN DRIPPINGS AND SAUTÉ ONION AND GARLIC OVER MEDIUM HEAT UNTIL GOLDEN (ABOUT 5 MINS.). ADD POTATOES, SALT, PEPPER AND THYME. CONTINUE COOKING, TURNING WITH A WIDE SPATULA UNTIL THE POTATOES ARE LIGHTLY BROWNED, ABOUT 10 MINS. SPRINKLE DICED TOMATOES OVER THE POTATOES. REDUCE HEAT TO LOW. COVER AND COOK UNTIL POTATOES ARE TENDER, ABOUT 20 MINS. TURN OCCASIONALLY. SPRINKLE WITH PARSLEY AND CRUMBLED BACON. SERVES 6.

Eggplant Parmesan I

1 peeled eggplant cut in 1/2-inch slices
1/4 cup flour
1/2 cup oil
Homemade spaghetti sauce

1 beaten egg
1/3 cup grated Parmesan cheese
1 6 oz. package sliced Provolone
  cheese

Dip eggplant slices in egg, then flour. Brown in oil. Drain. Place in casserole. Cover with spaghetti sauce and cheeses. Bake at 450 degrees for 20 mins.

Bean Salad I

1 can green beans (drained)
1 can wax beans (drained)
1 can kidney beans (rinsed)
1 green pepper, chopped
1 stalk celery, chopped
1 onion, chopped

1 teasp. salt
1/2 teasp. pepper
3/4 cup sugar
1/2 cup vinegar
1/2 cup salad oil

Mix and chill for several hours. Keeps well in refrigerator.

Potato Salad

6 cubed, boiled potatoes
3 tbsp. each: plain yogurt and mayonnaise
4 teasp. mustard
3 boiled, diced eggs

Diced onion, celery, green
  olives and carrots
Dash of black pepper

Mix all ingredients well and chill.

Old Fashioned Baked Pork and Beans

1 quart dry Northern beans
1 teasp. dry mustard
1/2 lb. salt pork
2 tbsp. molasses

1 tbsp. salt
4 cups cold water
1/2 teasp. pepper

Soak beans overnight, drain. Put in baking dish. Cut pork into small pieces and stir in all other ingredients. Keep covered with water during baking in slow over for at least 12 hours.

Turnip Greens I

2 LBS. FRESH TURNIP GREENS (OR 1 [16 OZ.]
PKG. FROZEN GREENS COOKED ACCORDING
TO DIRECTIONS WITH SEASONINGS ADDED)
5 SLICES BACON
4 CUPS WATER

1 TBSP. WHITE VINEGAR
1 TEASP. SALT
1/4 TO 1/2 TEASP. RED PEPPER FLAKES
1/4 TEASP. PEPPER

WASH GREENS WELL; DRAIN AND TEAR INTO BITE-SIZED PIECES. COMBINE GREENS, BACON
AND WATER IN DUTCH OVEN AND BRING TO BOIL. COVER, REDUCE HEAT AND SIMMER 30
MINS. ADD VINEGAR, PEPPER FLAKES, SALT AND PEPPER. COVER AND COOK ONE HOUR.
REMOVE BACON BEFORE SERVING. SERVES 6.

Corn Oysters

1 CUP GREEN CORN (FRESH FROM COB)
4 TBSP. FLOUR
1/2 TEASP. SALT

1 EGG
1/2 CUP MILK
BUTTER

SCRAPE OR CUT CORN FROM COB. SIFT FLOUR AND SALT AND MIX TO A BATTER WITH EGG
AND MILK. STIR IN CORN AND DROP BY SPOONFULS ONTO HOT, WELL-GREASED GRIDDLE OR
FRYING PAN. BROWN ON BOTH SIDES. 4 SERVINGS.

Glazed Carrots

4 CUPS SLICED CARROTS, COOKED OR
2 (20 OZ.) CANS BABY CARROTS
1/2 CUP BROWN SUGAR

1/4 CUP HOT WATER
4 TBSP. BUTTER

PEEL AND COOK SLICED CARROTS UNTIL TENDER. PLACE SUGAR, WATER AND BUTTER IN
SAUCEPAN. BRING TO BOIL AND ADD THE COOKED (CANNED) CARROTS. SIMMER SLOWLY
AND TURN SO THAT ALL CARROTS ARE GLAZED AND SLIGHTLY BROWNED. SERVES 8.

Celery-Cabbage Salad

2 CUPS DICED CELERY
2 TBSP. PLAIN YOGURT

1 CUP SHREDDED CABBAGE
JUICE OF 1/2 LEMON

MIX ALL INGREDIENTS AND MARINATE AT LEAST ONE HOUR IN REFRIGERATOR.

Baked Stuffed Tomatoes

8 TOMATOES
1/2 CHOPPED ONION
1/4 TEASP. PEPPER
10 DICED MUSHROOMS

3 TBSP. OIL
2 DICED GARLIC CLOVES
2 TBSP. CHOPPED PARSLEY
1 LB. COOKED BROWN RICE

SLICE OFF ROUNDED BOTTOMS OF TOMATOES. SCOOP OUT INSIDES. MIX ONION, GARLIC, MUSHROOMS AND TOMATO PULP. POUR INTO OIL WHICH HAS BEEN PLACED IN 9x12 BAKING DISH AND BAKE AT 375 DEGREES FOR 7 MINS. REMOVE FROM OVEN AND POUR MIXTURE INTO BOWL. BLEND IN RICE AND SEASONINGS. STUFF TOMATOES WITH THIS MIXTURE AND BAKE AT 375 DEGREES FOR 20 MINS.

Carrot Casserole II

1-1/2 CUPS WATER
1 LB. SHREDDED CARROTS
2/3 CUP BROWN RICE
2 CUPS SHREDDED CHEDDAR CHEESE

1 CUP MILK
2 EGGS, BEATEN
1 TBSP. MINCED ONION
DASH BLACK PEPPER

BRING WATER, CARROTS AND RICE TO BOIL. COVER AND SIMMER 25 MINS. STIR IN 1-1/2 CUPS SHREDDED CHEESE, MILK, EGGS, ONION AND PEPPER. PLACE ALL IN CASSEROLE. BAKE AT 350 DEGREES UNCOVERED FOR ONE HOUR. TOP WITH REMAINING CHEESE. BAKE TWO MINS. MORE TO MELT CHEESE.

Broccoli and Celery Casserole

1-1/2 CUPS FRESH COOKED BROCCOLI OR
 1 (10 OZ.) PKG. FROZEN CHOPPED BROCCOLI
2 CUPS 1/2-INCH CELERY CRESCENTS
1/4 CUP BUTTER
1 CUP SHREDDED AMERICAN CHEESE (1/2 LB.)

1/4 CUP FLOUR
1/2 TEASP. SALT
1/4 TEASP. PEPPER
2 CUPS MILK

COOK BROCCOLI ACCORDING TO PACKAGE DIRECTIONS, OR IF FRESH, UNTIL TENDER, THEN CHOP. COOK CELERY CRESCENTS IN BOILING, SALTED WATER UNTIL CRISPLY TENDER (5-6 MINS.). COMBINE THE TWO VEGETABLES IN A BUTTERED 1-1/2 QUART CASSEROLE. MELT BUTTER IN SAUCEPAN, ADD FLOUR AND BLEND. ADD MILK, STIRRING CONSTANTLY AND COOK UNTIL SMOOTH AND THICKENED. ADD SALT AND PEPPER, POUR OVER VEGETABLES. COVER WITH CHEESE AND BAKE AT 350 DEGREES FOR 15-20 MINS. 6 SERVINGS.

MAY BE MADE AHEAD OF TIME AND COOKED JUST BEFORE SERVING.

O'Brien Potatoes

1-1/2 cups milk
1/2 cup butter
6 medium potatoes, grated
1/2 green pepper, diced
1/2 sweet red pepper, diced

1/4 cup diced pimiento
5 scallions, sliced, including
  green tops
1/2 teasp. salt

Heat milk and butter together until butter melts. Place potatoes, peppers, scallions and salt in greased 2 quart casserole. Cover with warm milk mixture. Bake at 275 degrees for two hours. Leftovers may be fried. Serves 6.

Indian Cabbage

1 small cabbage, cut into
  bite-sized chunks
1 teasp. salt

3 tbsp. bacon drippings
1 small green pepper, cut in strips
1/8 teasp. pepper

Fry cabbage in bacon drippings in a large, heavy kettle over moderately high heat until cabbage begins to wilt and brown slightly, about 8-10 mins. Add green pepper and continue to fry, stirring until the raw green color goes out of pepper. Put lid on the kettle, turn heat down to low, and let cabbage "wilt" 10-15 mins. Cabbage will be lightly glazed with bacon drippings, but still somewhat crisp. Add salt and pepper, toss well to mix and serve. Serves 4-6.

Macaroni and Cheese II

1 cup macaroni, boiled
1 cup grated Cheddar cheese
2/3 cup milk

1 to 2 eggs
salt to taste
1/4 cup soft breadcrumbs

Place alternate layers of macaroni and cheese in buttered baking dish. Reserve 2 tbsp. cheese for top. Beat the eggs, add milk and salt and pour over macaroni. Sprinkle top with remaining cheese combined with breadcrumbs. Bake at 400 degrees until well-browned. Serves 4-5.

Perfection Salad

1 envelope Knox gelatin dissolved in 4 tbsp. water. Add 1 cup boiling water, 4 tbsp. vinegar, 3 tbsp. sugar, 1 tbsp. lemon juice and 1/2 teasp. salt. Cool and add chopped cabbage, celery, green pepper and grated carrots. Serves 4.

Southern Fried Apples

4 LARGE COOKING APPLES
1 TEASP. GROUND NUTMEG
1/2 TEASP. GROUND CINNAMON

1/3 CUP SUGAR
1/8 TEASP. SALT
5 TBSP. BUTTER

MIX TOGETHER SUGAR, SPICES AND SALT. WASH, CORE AND PEEL APPLES IN HALF-INCH THICK RINGS. HEAT BUTTER IN HEAVY SKILLET. ADD APPLE RINGS AND HALF OF THE SUGAR MIXTURE. COOK ABOUT 3 MINS. TURN APPLES OVER, SPRINKLE WITH REST OF SUGAR MIXTURE, AND CONTINUE COOKING UNTIL APPLES ARE ALMOST TRANSPARENT. SERVE HOT WITH HOMEMADE BISCUITS. 4-6 SERVINGS.

Baked Grits

3 CUPS COOKED GRITS
2 TBSP. BUTTER
2 EGGS, BEATEN
1 LARGE CAN EVAPORATED MILK

1-1/2 CUPS (6 OZ.) GRATED CHEDDAR
CHEESE
PAPRIKA
TABASCO SAUCE

MIX GRITS WITH MELTED BUTTER, EGGS AND MILK. STIR IN 1-1/4 CUPS OF THE CHEESE. ADD PAPRIKA AND A DROP OR TWO OF TABASCO. PLACE IN BUTTERED CASSEROLE. SPRINKLE REMAINING CHEESE ON TOP. BAKE AT 425 DEGREES UNTIL TOP IS BROWN. SERVES 6.

Creamed Spinach

4 CUPS SPINACH
1/4 CUP MARGARINE
1/2 CUP CHOPPED ONION
2 TBSP. FLOUR

1 CUP MILK
1/4 TEASP. SALT
1/4 TEASP. WHITE PEPPER
1/8 TEASP. NUTMEG

WASH SPINACH. COOK OVER LOW HEAT (WATER ON LEAVES FROM WASHING MAY BE ENOUGH TO COOK SPINACH.) SAUTÉ ONIONS IN MARGARINE. ADD FLOUR AND GRADUALLY ADD MILK. COOK, STIRRING UNTIL SMOOTH. ADD TO COOKED SPINACH. SEASON WITH PEPPER AND NUTMEG.

Green Beans

TAKE ABOUT 1-1/2 LBS. FRESH POLE OR SNAP GREEN BEANS THAT HAVE BEEN STRUNG WITH ENDS SNAPPED OFF AND BREAK INTO MEDIUM PIECES. TAKE 1/2 LB. SALT PORK, HAM HOCK, OR SEVERAL BACON STRIPS AND LET SIMMER IN SMALL AMOUNT OF WATER, ABOUT 30 MINS. THEN ADD BEANS, COVER WITH WATER, AND COOK UNTIL TENDER. ABOUT MIDWAY IN COOKING, ADD SCRUBBED, UNPEELED, SMALL NEW POTATOES AND COOK UNTIL TENDER. IF USING BACON STRIPS DO NOT COOK FIRST.

CREAMED CORN PUDDING

1 CAN CREAM CORN	1 TEASP. SALT
2 EGGS, WELL-BEATEN	1/4 TEASP. PEPPER
1/2 CUP SUGAR (SCANT)	1 CUP MILK

GREASE CASSEROLE DISH. MIX ALL INGREDIENTS WELL AND POUR INTO DISH, DOT WITH BUTTER. BAKE AT 350 DEGREES FOR 45-60 MINS., STIRRING SEVERAL TIMES UNTIL SET. SERVES 4.

MASHED TURNIPS

2-1/2 TO 3 LBS. TURNIPS, WITHOUT TOPS	SALT AND PEPPER
3 TBSP. BUTTER	

WASH TURNIPS AND PEEL WITH VERTICAL STROKES. SLICE THIN ACROSS GRAIN TO BREAK VERTICAL FIBERS. PLACE IN KETTLE WITH A LITTLE WATER (1/4 TO 1/2 CUP) AND SIMMER, COVERED, UNTIL TENDER (ABOUT 20-30 MINS.). REMOVE COVER FOR LAST FEW MINUTES TO COOK AWAY EXCESS WATER. ADD BUTTER AND SPRINKLINGS OF SALT AND PEPPER, THEN MASH. RETURN TO BURNER AND HEAT THROUGH BEFORE SERVING. SERVES 6.

NINE DAY COLESLAW

3 LBS. CABBAGE, CHOPPED	1 OR 2 CARROTS, GRATED
1 LARGE GREEN PEPPER, CHOPPED	2 MEDIUM ONIONS, CHOPPED

BRING TO BOIL:

1 CUP VINEGAR	SALT TO TASTE
1 CUP SUGAR	2 TBSP. GROUND MUSTARD OR SEEDS
2/3 CUP SALAD OIL	2 TBSP. TURMERIC

POUR OVER VEGETABLES WHILE BOILING HOT. STIR WELL. REFRIGERATE. WILL KEEP AS LONG AS IT LASTS.

MOUNTAINEER FRIED APPLES

FILL A LARGE IRON SKILLET WITH GOOD TART APPLES THAT HAVE BEEN SLICED, WITH A GOOD BIT OF PEELING LEFT ON. ADD ONE STICK OF BUTTER OR MARGARINE, A LB. OF LIGHT BROWN SUGAR AND ONE CUP WHITE CORN SYRUP. COVER WITH LID AND COOK WITHOUT STIRRING. USE A CAKE TURNER TO SLIDE UNDER APPLES TO PREVENT BURNING. WHEN APPLES ARE TENDER, IF THEY ARE VERY JUICY, REMOVE LID TO PERMIT APPLES TO BROWN AND CARMELIZE. SERVE HOT.

Easy Carrot Mold

1 SCANT CUP CRISCO	1/2 TEASP. BAKING SODA
1 TEASP. BAKING POWDER	1-1/2 CUPS GRATED CARROT
1/2 CUP DARK BROWN SUGAR	1 EGG
1/2 LEMON JUICE AND SOME RIND	1-1/4 CUPS FLOUR

SIFT DRY INGREDIENTS. COMBINE ALL INGREDIENTS AND MIX WELL. GREASE MOLD. BAKE AT 350 DEGREES FOR 45-60 MINS. SERVES 6.

Sauerkraut Salad

1 LARGE CAN (1 LB.+) SAUERKRAUT	1 CUP DICED GREEN PEPPER
1 CUP DICED CELERY	1/2 CUP DICED ONION

DRAIN (BUT DO NOT RINSE) SAUERKRAUT. MIX WITH ALL OTHER INGREDIENTS, THEN ADD:

1 CUP SUGAR	1/2 CUP SALAD OIL

MIX WELL AND CHILL OVERNIGHT, STIRRING OCCASIONALLY, IF POSSIBLE. IF CAN'T CHILL OVERNIGHT, CHILL AT LEAST 3 HOURS BEFORE SERVING. KEEPS WELL IN REFRIGERATOR FOR UP TO TWO WEEKS. WONDERFUL FOR PICNICS, COVERED-DISH AFFAIRS, OR JUST TO HAVE SOMETHING "GREEN" IN THE REFRIGERATOR TO SERVE FOR DINNER.

Triple Rice Casserole

1/2 CUP WHITE RICE	4 CUPS OR MORE CHICKEN BROTH
1/4 CUP WILD RICE	1/2 CUP BROWN RICE
1 TBSP. MINCED ONION	1 STICK BUTTER
1 CUP SLICED FRESH MUSHROOMS	1 CUP CHOPPED GREEN PEPPERS

SAUTÉ RICES AND ONIONS IN BUTTER OVER LOW HEAT FOR 10 MINS. PUT IN LARGE CASSEROLE OR SOUP POT. ADD GREEN PEPPERS, MUSHROOMS AND CHICKEN BROTH. BAKE UNCOVERED AT 325 DEGREES FOR 1-1/2 HOURS UNTIL RICE IS TENDER AND LIQUID IS ABSORBED. IF NECESSARY, ADD MORE BROTH TO KEEP RICE FROM DRYING. SERVE 8-10. *ALISON BERNARD.*

Marcy's Potato Crisps

SCRUB 2 OR MORE LARGE POTATOES. SLICE VERY THIN WITH SKINS ON. SPREAD ON BAKING SHEET COATED WITH COOKING SPRAY. SPRINKLE WITH SEASONINGS OF YOUR CHOICE (GARLIC, SALT, HERBS, ETC.). BAKE AT 375 DEGREES FOR 15-20 MINS, UNTIL TENDER AND SLIGHTLY CRISPY. *ALISON BERNARD*

BLACK-EYED PEAS WITH HAM HOCKS

3 CUPS DRIED BLACK-EYED PEAS
6 CUPS WATER
3 LBS. SMOKED HAM HOCKS
1-1/4 CUPS CHOPPED ONION
1 CUP CHOPPED GREEN PEPPER

2 BAY LEAVES
1 TEASP. SALT
1 (16 OZ.) CAN STEWED TOMATOES, CHOPPED

SORT AND WASH PEAS; PLACE IN LARGE DUTCH OVEN. COVER WITH WATER 2 INCHES ABOVE PEAS; LET SOAK 8 HOURS. DRAIN PEAS, AND RETURN TO DUTCH OVEN. ADD 6 CUPS WATER, HAM HOCKS, ONION, GREEN PEPPER, BAY LEAVES AND SALT. BRING TO A BOIL; COVER, REDUCE HEAT AND SIMMER 45 MINS., STIRRING OCCASIONALLY. ADD TOMATOES, COVER AND SIMMER AN ADDITIONAL 15 MINS. OR UNTIL PEAS ARE TENDER. REMOVE HAM HOCKS AND BAY LEAVES. CUT HAM FROM HOCKS AND CHOP, RETURN TO PEAS. 12-16 SERVINGS.

CREAMED CABBAGE

1 SMALL HEAD CABBAGE, SHREDDED
1 13-OZ. CAN EVAPORATED MILK
1 CUP DRY BREADCRUMBS

4 TBSP. BUTTER OR MARGARINE
1 TBSP. SUGAR

STEAM CABBAGE 10 MINS. PLACE IN BUTTERED CASSEROLE. POUR MILK OVER IT AND SPRINKLE WITH BREADCRUMBS AND SUGAR. DOT WITH BUTTER AND BAKE AT 350 DEGREES FOR 30 MINS. SERVES 4-6.

CORN SALAD

1 (15.25 OZ.) CAN WHOLE KERNEL CORN, DRAINED
2 TBSP. CHOPPED ONION
1 TBSP. WHITE VINEGAR
1 TEASP. SUGAR

1/8 TO 1/4 TEASP. DRIED WHOLE OREGANO
1/8 TEASP. PEPPER
1 MEDIUM CARROT, SCRAPED AND SHREDDED

COMBINE CORN, ONION, VINEGAR, SUGAR, OREGANO AND PEPPER IN SMALL SAUCEPAN; COOK OVER LOW HEAT 5 MINS. STIR IN CARROTS, AND CHILL. SERVES 4.

GAZPACHO SALAD

ARRANGE IN A GLASS BOWL ALTERNATE LAYERS OF UNPEELED AND THINLY SLICED CUCUMBERS, SKINNED AND THINLY SLICED TOMATOES, THINLY SLICED BERMUDA ONIONS AND COARSE DRY FRENCH BREADCRUMBS. POUR A TART FRENCH DRESSING OVER IT AND REFRIGERATE UNTIL ICY COLD. *MARY RANDOLPH*

CRANBERRY SALAD*

1 LB. FRESH CRANBERRIES (GROUND)
1 WHOLE APPLE, PEELED, CHOPPED
2 CUPS SUGAR
1 PACKAGE LARGE RED GELATIN, ANY KIND

1/2 CUP PECANS, FINELY CHOPPED
1 OR 2 STALKS CELERY, FINELY CHOPPED
1/2 CUP CRUSHED PINEAPPLE

DISSOLVE GELATIN IN WATER, ADD SUGAR. GRIND CRANBERRIES AND MIX WITH CHOPPED APPLE, PECANS AND CELERY. ADD PINEAPPLE. MIX TOGETHER WELL AND LET CHILL. SERVE ON LETTUCE WITH MAYONNAISE. *CARLEA DAWSON*

*CRANBERRIES GROW WILD IN SEVERAL AREAS IN WEST VIRGINIA MOST NOTABLY CRANBERRY GLADES AND ATOP SPRUCE KNOB.

HASH BROWN POTATOES I

A FAVORITE ON WEST VIRGINIA BREAKFAST MENUS. SLICE PEELED POTATOES INTO SHOESTRING STRIPS OR RUB THEM THROUGH A COARSE GRATER. HEAT 1/4 CUP BACON FAT IN AN IRON SKILLET, ADD POTATOES AND FLATTEN WITH SPATULA ON BOTTOM OF PAN. COOK VERY SLOWLY, TURNING WHEN BROWN ON BOTTOM. WHEN BROWN ON BOTH SIDES, ADD SALT AND PEPPER AND POUR ABOUT 1/2 CUP CREAM OVER POTATOES, LETTING IT BE ABSORBED WHILE COOKING A FEW MINUTES LONGER. PANFRIED POTATOES ARE DONE THE SAME WAY EXCEPT THEY'RE CUT INTO FAIRLY THICK SLICES, BROWNED IN BACON FAT AND THEN SALT AND PEPPER IS ADDED.

BEAN SALAD II

1 CAN CHICK PEAS, DRAINED
1 CAN GREAT NORTHERN BEANS, DRAINED
1/2 CUP CHOPPED CELERY
1 CUP ITALIAN DRESSING

1 CAN KIDNEY BEANS, DRAINED
1/4 CUP CHOPPED GREEN PEPPER
3 GREEN ONIONS, CHOPPED

PUT BEANS IN COLANDER, RINSE WITH COLD WATER. PLACE ALL INGREDIENTS IN A LARGE JAR AND POUR DRESSING OVER IT. PUT LID ON TIGHT AND SHAKE UNTIL ALL INGREDIENTS ARE MARINATED. REFRIGERATE AT LEAST 1 TO 2 DAYS, MIXING OCCASIONALLY, BEFORE SERVING. KEEPS WELL IN REFRIGERATOR FOR SEVERAL DAYS.

Corn Bread Salad I

2 boxes corn bread mix
1 large chopped green pepper
1 large chopped red tomato

1 large chopped purple onion
2 teasp. seasoned salt
1 cup mayonnaise

Bake corn bread mix in separate pans; cool and crumble. Add remaining ingredients. Mix well; chill at least 2 hours.

Waldorf Salad

3 large firm apples, cored, diced
2 tbsp. fresh lemon juice
3 celery stalks, diced
1 cup coarsely chopped walnuts

1 cup mayonnaise
1/2 cup dairy sour cream
Fresh lettuce leaves

In a medium-sized bowl, toss apples with lemon juice. Mix in celery and walnuts. Blend mayonnaise and sour cream. Stir into apple mixture. Serve on lettuce leaves. Serves 6-8.

Orange Beets

2-1/2 cups beets, peeled and sliced
1/2 teasp. grated orange rind
1 tbsp. sugar
2 tbsp. salt

1 cup orange juice
1 teasp. salt
2 tbsp. butter

Place uncooked beets in a greased casserole. Combine orange rind, orange juice, sugar and salt. Pour over beets. Dot with butter. Cover and bake at 425 degrees about 45 mins. or until beets are tender. 5-6 servings.

Quick Orange Beets: Use canned beets. Combine orange rind, juice, sugar and salt in a saucepan; add drained beets and heat 5-6 mins. then add butter.

Squaw Corn

5 slices diced bacon
1 teasp. sugar
1/2 teasp. salt
Dash pepper

1-1/2 to 2 cups canned whole kernel corn
1/2 cup sour cream

Cook bacon until crisp. Add remaining ingredients and heat. May garnish with broiled tomatoes and bacon curls for light main dish. Serves 5.

BROWNED RICE IN BOUILLON

1/4 CUP FAT	2 CUPS BOUILLON
1 LARGE ONION	SALT AND PEPPER
1 CLOVE GARLIC	1 CUP RAW RICE

MINCE ONION AND GARLIC. SAUTÉ ONION, RICE AND GARLIC IN FAT IN SKILLET UNTIL ALL ARE GOLDEN BROWN. PUT THE RICE MIXTURE IN A TWO-QUART CASSEROLE; ADD THE BOUILLON. COVER, BRING TO A BOIL. REDUCE HEAT TO AS LOW AS POSSIBLE AND SIMMER UNTIL RICE IS TENDER (ABOUT 20 MINS.). SERVES 6. *ALISON BERNARD*

GARDEN "CLEAN UP"

4 MEDIUM UNPEELED SUMMER SQUASH OR CUCUMBERS	2 TBSP. BUTTER
2-3 RIPE TOMATOES, PEELED AND CHOPPED	1-1/2 CUPS (8 SLICES) AMERICAN PROCESSED CHEESE, SHREDDED
6 SLICES BACON, FRIED AND CRUMBLED	1/2 CUP FINE BREADCRUMBS
1/3 CUP (1 SMALL) ONION, CHOPPED	PARMESAN CHEESE
1/2 TEASP. SALT	

PARBOIL SQUASH UNTIL SKIN IS TENDER (5-10 MINS.) COMBINE REST OF INGREDIENTS, EXCEPT CRUMBS, BUTTER AND PARMESAN. SLICE PARBOILED SQUASH THINLY. PLACE IN BAKING DISH, SPRAYED WITH COOKING SPRAY, OR LIGHTLY GREASED. ALTERNATE SQUASH WITH FILLING, SPRINKLING WITH SALT AND PEPPER AND GRATED PARMESAN. TOP WITH BREADCRUMBS AND DOT WITH BUTTER. BAKE AT 375 DEGREES FOR 30-35 MINS. 6-8 SERVINGS.

STUFFED APPLES*

8 RED COOKING APPLES (DELICIOUS, McINTOSH, WINESAP)	1/4 TEASP. THYME
4 STALKS CELERY	2 MEDIUM ONIONS
1/4 CUP BUTTER	2 TBSP. SUGAR
3 CUPS STALE BREADCRUMBS OR CUBES	1 TEASP. SALT
DASH PEPPER	1/2 TEASP. SAGE

CUT APPLES IN HALF CROSSWISE. HOLLOW OUT LOWER HALVES, LEAVING 1/2 INCH THICK SHELL. PARE, CORE AND CUT UP THE UPPER HALVES; CHOP COARSELY WITH CELERY AND ONION. HEAT BUTTER; ADD CHOPPED MIXTURE AND SPRINKLE WITH SUGAR. SIMMER UNTIL ALMOST TENDER. ADD REMAINING INGREDIENTS AND STUFF APPLE CUPS. PLACE IN SHALLOW PAN CONTAINING A SMALL AMOUNT OF WATER. BAKE IN 350 DEGREES OVEN 35-45 MINS. OR UNTIL APPLE SHELLS ARE TENDER AND STUFFING LIGHTLY BROWNED. SERVES 8.

*GOOD SERVED WITH ROAST PORK OR DUCK.

Mock Oysters

3 eggs, separated
2 cups corn, cooked and scraped
   from the cob
2 tbsp. heavy cream

1 tbsp. melted butter
2 tbsp. flour
1 teasp. salt
1/2 teasp. pepper

Beat egg yolks. Add drained corn, cream, butter, flour and seasonings. Fold in stiffly beaten egg whites. Drop by teaspoonful onto a hot greased griddle to form oyster-sized fritters. Cook until browned, turning to brown on all sides. Serves 6.

Fried Parsnips

Parsnips, now small and thin-skinned as carrots, are good raw as a snack. Need long ivory-colored plump parsnips (they taste like turnips but are more delicate and nutty). For 6 servings:

3 lbs. large parsnips, without tops
1/2 cup flour

Salt and pepper
4-6 tbsp. butter

Wash parsnips, trim off ends. Simmer in kettle covered with water for about 15 mins. or until just tender. Drain, scrape off skins and chill. Slice lengthwise in 1/8-inch strips. Season flour with salt and pepper and dredge each strip in it. Heat 2 tbsp. butter and add as many slices as will cover bottom of pan. Brown lightly a few mins., turn and cook through, about 10 mins. in all. Remove to warm platter and repeat until all slices are cooked, adding butter to skillet as needed. Best served with sprinkling of vinegar.

Southern Limas

1/4 cup butter or bacon drippings
2 tbsp. chopped green pepper
2-1/2 cups stewed or canned tomatoes
2-1/2 cups home-cooked or canned
   lima beans

2 cups ground, or finely chopped,
   cooked ham
1/2 cup buttered breadcrumbs
3 tbsp. chopped onion
2 tbsp. flour

Heat butter/drippings in skillet; add onion and green pepper. Simmer over low heat about 5 mins. or until soft but not browned. Add flour and stir until well blended. Slowly add tomatoes and cook, stirring constantly, until thickened. Season to taste. In greased casserole arrange layers of lima beans and ham; add tomato mixture. Sprinkle with buttered crumbs and a dash of paprika. Bake in 375 degree oven 25-30 mins. or until browned. Serves 6.

Corn Bread Salad II

1 (8.5 oz.) package corn bread mix
1 egg
1/3 cup milk
4 medium tomatoes, peeled and chopped
1 green pepper, chopped
1 medium onion, chopped

1/2 cup chopped sweet pickles
9 slices bacon, cooked and
    crumbled
1 cup mayonnaise
1/4 cup sweet pickle juice

Combine corn bread mix, egg and milk. Stir well. Spoon corn bread mixture into greased 8-inch-square pan. Bake at 400 degrees for 15 to 20 mins. Cool, crumble and set aside. Combine tomatoes, green pepper, onion, pickles and bacon. Toss gently. Combine mayonnaise and pickle juice, stir well. Set aside. Layer half each of corn bread, tomato mixture and mayonnaise mixture in a large glass bowl. Repeat layers. Cover and chill 2 hours. 8 servings.

Broccoli and Parmesan

2 lbs. broccoli
1 cup Parmesan
1 cup breadcrumbs
1/4 cup oil

1 clove garlic, quartered
1/2 cup hot water
1/4 teasp. salt

Boil broccoli in lightly salted water until slightly tender. Drain and arrange in a large baking dish. Combine Parmesan and breadcrumbs and sprinkle over broccoli. Heat oil in large skillet and brown garlic. Remove garlic and discard. Combine water with oil and salt. Pour oil over broccoli. Cover and bake at 350 degrees for 25-30 mins. or until hot and steaming. Serves 6-8. *Minard's Spaghetti Inn*

Stuffed Beets

6 medium beets
1/4 cup chopped onion
1 teasp. lemon juice
1/2 teasp. salt

1/4 cup diced bacon
1 tbsp. chili sauce
1/4 lb. (1/2 cup) cottage cheese
1/8 teasp. pepper

Boil whole beets about 40 mins. or until almost tender, allowing one for each serving. Rub off skin under cold water. Scoop out centers, leaving a shell about 1/2-inch thick. Sprinkle insides with a little salt. Chop the removed pulp fine and add remaining ingredients. Fill beet shells with this mixture. Place in a baking dish containing a little water. Bake in 375 degree oven about 30 mins. or until browned. Serves 6.

PICKLE SLAW

1/2 CUP SUGAR
1/2 CUP PREPARED MUSTARD
1/4 CUP WHITE VINEGAR
2 TBSP. SWEET PICKLE JUICE

1/4 TEASP. SALT
1 SMALL HEAD (6 CUPS) CABBAGE,
  GRATED
1/4 CUP CHOPPED SWEET PICKLES

COMBINE SUGAR, MUSTARD, VINEGAR, PICKLE JUICE AND SALT; WHIP WITH WIRE WHISK UNTIL SUGAR DISSOLVES. COMBINE CABBAGE AND PICKLES. ADD DRESSING AND TOSS GENTLY. CHILL 1 HOUR. SERVES 6-8.

HASH BROWN POTATOES II

4 CUPS PEELED, CUBED, RAW WHITE
  POTATOES
SALT AND PEPPER TO TASTE
6 TBSP. BACON FAT

1 MEDIUM ONION, HALVED AND
  SLICED THIN
2 TEASP. OREGANO
WORCESTERSHIRE SAUCE

SPRINKLE CUBED POTATOES WITH SALT AND PEPPER. MELT BACON FAT IN HEAVY SKILLET. ADD POTATO CUBES, TURNING UNTIL WELL-COATED. COOK FOR 10 MINS. OVER MEDIUM HEAT. ADD ONION, OREGANO, LIBERAL SQUIRTS OF WORCESTERSHIRE SAUCE AND MORE SALT AND PEPPER, IF DESIRED. COOK FOR 20-25 MINS. MORE, OR UNTIL POTATOES ARE CRUSTY BROWN AND TENDER. STIR FREQUENTLY. ADD MORE BACON FAT, IF POTATOES STICK. SERVES 4-6.

EGGPLANT PARMESAN II

1 LARGE EGGPLANT
2 TBSP. SALT
1 CUP OLIVE OIL
1 (16-OZ.) CAN TOMATOES
1 MEDIUM ONION, CHOPPED
1/2 TEASP. OREGANO
1 CUP WATER

1 STICK PEPPERONI, SLICED
1/2 LB. MOZZARELLA CHEESE
1 CUP PARMESAN CHEESE, GRATED
SALT AND PEPPER TO TASTE
BUTTERED BREADCRUMBS
3 EGGS, HARD BOILED, SLICED

PEEL AND SLICE EGGPLANT CROSSWISE AND PLACE IN BAKING DISH. POUR IN ENOUGH WATER TO COVER EGGPLANT AND ADD SALT. SOAK FOR 30 MINS. DRAIN. HEAT OLIVE OIL IN LARGE SKILLET. DRAIN TOMATOES AND SET ASIDE. SAUTÉ ONION IN HEATED OIL UNTIL TENDER. ADD SALT AND PEPPER. ADD TOMATOES, OREGANO AND WATER. SIMMER FOR 30 MINS. ROLL EGGPLANT IN FLOUR AND BROWN IN OIL. DRAIN ON PAPER TOWELS. PLACE BROWNED EGGPLANT IN BAKING DISH AND SPRINKLE WITH 1/2 OF MOZZARELLA CHEESE, 1/2 TOMATO SAUCE MIXTURE, 1/2 OF PEPPERONI, 1/2 OF EGGS AND 1/2 OF PARMESAN CHEESE. REPEAT. TOP WITH BREADCRUMBS AND BAKE AT 350 DEGREES FOR 30 MINS. SERVES 4.

Sweet Potato Casserole

3 CUPS COOKED SWEET POTATOES
1 CUP SUGAR
2 EGGS

1 STICK BUTTER
1 TBSP. VANILLA

PREHEAT OVEN TO 350 DEGREES. BEAT MASHED, COOKED SWEET POTATOES, SUGAR, SOFTENED BUTTER, VANILLA AND EGGS TOGETHER. PLACE IN GREASED CASSEROLE OR BAKING DISH. SPRINKLE WITH TOPPING AND BAKE IN 350 DEGREE OVEN FOR 1 HOUR.

Topping:

1 CUP LIGHT BROWN SUGAR
1/3 CUP BUTTER

1/3 CUP FLOUR
1 CUP NUTS, FINELY CHOPPED

MIX TOPPING TOGETHER (FINGERS WORK WELL) AND SPRINKLE OVER TOP OF CASSEROLE.

Shredded Carrot and Raisin Salad

1 (16-OZ.) PACKAGE CARROTS, PEELED
1/3 CUP MAYONNAISE OR CREAMY SALAD
   DRESSING
1/2 TEASP. SALT

1 TO 2 TBSP. GRANULATED SUGAR,
   TO TASTE
GROUND PEPPER, TO TASTE
1/2 CUP RAISINS

GRATE CARROTS IN FOOD PROCESSOR OR BY HAND TO MAKE ABOUT 2 CUPS; TOSS IN LARGE BOWL WITH RAISINS, DRESSING, SUGAR, SALT AND PEPPER. CHILL AT LEAST 1 HOUR. SERVES 4-6.

Jerusalem Artichokes Au Gratin

PREHEAT OVEN TO 375 DEGREES.

1 LB. ARTICHOKES
2 TBSP. BUTTER
2 TBSP. FLOUR
1 CUP MILK

SALT AND PEPPER
GRATED CHEESE, PARMESAN OR
   CHEDDAR
BREADCRUMBS, BUTTERED

SCRUB AND PEEL THE ARTICHOKES. CUT IN HALF AND COOK IN BOILING, SALTED WATER FOR 25 MINS. OR UNTIL TENDER. DRAIN WELL AND PUT IN SHALLOW BAKING DISH. MAKE A CREAM SAUCE WITH BUTTER, FLOUR, MILK, SALT AND PEPPER. POUR SAUCE OVER THE ARTICHOKES, SPRINKLE WITH THE CHEESE AND TOP WITH CRUMBS. BAKE IN 375 DEGREES OVEN FOR 30 MINS. OR UNTIL BROWNED. 4-6 SERVINGS.

Oven Fried Potatoes

1/4 CUP CORN OIL OR FRESH BACON FAT
3 TO 4 LARGE POTATOES, CUT INTO 1/2-INCH
   STRIPS WITH SKINS LEFT ON

1/3 CUP BUTTER
SALT AND FRESHLY GROUND PEPPER
   (WHITE PREFERRED)

PREHEAT OVEN TO 350 DEGREES. HEAT OIL IN A CAST-IRON SKILLET OVER HIGH HEAT. ADD POTATOES AND BROWN ON BOTH SIDES. SPREAD THE POTATOES IN 2 LAYERS ON A BAKING SHEET OR SHALLOW BAKING DISH. DOT WITH BUTTER. BAKE 10-15 MINS., UNTIL TENDER. DRAIN ON A PAPER TOWEL AND SEASON WITH SALT AND PEPPER. SERVES 6.

Fried Green Tomatoes

6 GREEN TOMATOES
SALT AND PEPPER

MELTED BUTTER
FLOUR

CUT THE TOPS AND BOTTOMS OFF THE TOMATOES AND SLICE IN HALF, CROSSWISE. SPRINKLE WITH SALT AND PEPPER AND DIP LIGHTLY IN FLOUR. FRY IN HOT BUTTER UNTIL BROWN ON BOTH SIDES. 6 SERVINGS.

Creamed Celery

2-1/2 CUPS CELERY CUT INTO 1-INCH PIECES
1-1/2 CUPS MILK
SALT AND PEPPER

3 TBSP. FLOUR
3 TBSP. BUTTER

WASH AND SCRAPE CELERY. COOK UNTIL TENDER IN BOILING WATER, ADDING SALT WHEN HALF DONE. DRAIN. BLEND BUTTER AND FLOUR, ADD MILK GRADUALLY. STIR CONSTANTLY UNTIL BOILING, THEN COOK 3 MINS. SEASON AND ADD CELERY UNTIL ALL IS WELL HEATED. CREAMED ONIONS, PARSNIPS OR CARROTS MAY BE PREPARED THE SAME WAY. SERVES 4.

Fresh Kale

1 LB. FRESH KALE, TRIMMED AND CUT INTO
   1-INCH SLICES, 8-10 CUPS
1/4 CUP RENDERED CHICKEN FAT OR BUTTER
1 TEASP. SALT

1/2 TEASP. PEPPER
1/2 TEASP. SUGAR
4 STRIPS BACON, COOKED
   AND CRUMBLED

BRING 2 CUPS OF WATER TO A BOIL AND ADD KALE, FAT, SALT, SUGAR AND PEPPER; REDUCE HEAT TO LOW AND SIMMER, COVERED, ABOUT 30-40 MINS., UNTIL KALE IS TENDER. STIR OCCASIONALLY. WHEN DONE, MIX IN CRUMBLED BACON AND SERVE. SERVES 6-8.

Carrot Salad

3 CARROTS, FINELY DICED
2 STALKS CELERY, FINELY DICED
SALT AND PEPPER TO TASTE

3 HARD BOILED EGGS, FINELY DICED
MAYONNAISE

MIX FINELY CHOPPED CARROTS, CELERY AND EGG. MIX WITH MAYONNAISE UNTIL WELL-MOISTENED AND SALT AND PEPPER TO TASTE. CHILL. SERVES 4. TO INCREASE NUMBER OF SERVINGS ALWAYS USE SAME NUMBER OF CARROTS AND EGGS AND ONE LESS CELERY STALK. *ROSEMOND S. BEURY*

Cheese Parsnips

4 PARSNIPS, HALVED AND COOKED
2 TBSP. BUTTER
3 TBSP. FLOUR
1/4 TEASP. WORCESTERSHIRE SAUCE
1/4 TEASP. PREPARED MUSTARD

1/2 CUP GRATED CHEDDAR CHEESE
1 CUP PARSNIP COOKING LIQUID
FEW DROPS ONION JUICE OR DASH OF
    ONION POWDER

MELT BUTTER IN ONE QUART SAUCEPAN; ADD FLOUR, STIRRING CONSTANTLY. ADD LIQUID FROM PARSNIPS, STIRRING UNTIL THICKENED. ADD SEASONINGS. ARRANGE PARSNIPS IN 8-INCH BAKING DISH. COVER WITH SAUCE, TOP WITH GRATED CHEESE AND BAKE AT 350 DEGREES FOR 20-30 MINS. SERVES 4.

Baked Winter Squash

1 LB. WINTER SQUASH
1/4 LB. BUTTER
1/2 TEASP. SALT

1/2 CUP FIRMLY PACKED LIGHT
    BROWN SUGAR
FRESHLY GROUND PEPPER TO TASTE

PREHEAT OVEN TO 375 DEGREES. WASH SQUASH AND SPLIT OPEN. REMOVE SEEDS AND PEEL. CUT INTO CUBES ABOUT 1-INCH SQUARE. PLACE IN A BAKING DISH IN LAYERS, DOTTING EACH LAYER WITH BUTTER AND BROWN SUGAR. SPRINKLE SALT AND PEPPER ON TOP. POUR 1/4 CUP COLD WATER OVER SQUASH. BAKE 1 HOUR, OR UNTIL SQUASH IS TENDER, STIRRING GENTLY ONCE OR TWICE DURING COOKING PERIOD. SERVES 4.

Pea Salad I

1 SMALL CAN PEAS, DRAINED
2 GREEN ONIONS
1 OR 2 STALKS CELERY

SALT AND PEPPER TO TASTE
1 TBSP. MAYONNAISE (OR ENOUGH
    TO HOLD SALAD TOGETHER)

DRAIN PEAS, FINELY CHOP GREEN ONIONS AND CELERY. CHILL WELL. SERVES 2.

SCALLOPED POTATOES

PREHEAT OVEN TO 325 DEGREES. SLICE PARED POTATOES AS THIN AS POSSIBLE. PLACE LAYER OF POTATOES IN A CASSEROLE. DUST WITH A LITTLE FLOUR, SEASON WITH SALT, PEPPER, CHOPPED ONION (ABOUT 1 SLICE) AND DOT WITH BUTTER. REPEAT LAYERS UNTIL CASSEROLE IS FULL. ADD ENOUGH MILK TO REACH TOP LAYER. BAKE IN 325 DEGREE OVEN FOR 1-1/2 HOURS. NUMBER SERVED DEPENDS ON SIZE OF CASSEROLE.

MAPLE BAKED CARROTS

4 LARGE CARROTS, PEELED AND DICED
2 MEDIUM APPLES
2 TBSP. MAPLE SYRUP

2 TBSP. BROWN SUGAR
2 TBSP. BUTTER

PREHEAT OVEN TO 375 DEGREES. COOK CARROTS IN A SMALL AMOUNT OF BOILING SALTED WATER 20 MINS., OR UNTIL JUST TENDER. GREASE A 1-1/2 QUART BAKING DISH. DRAIN CARROTS. PEEL, CORE AND THINLY SLICE APPLES. PLACE CARROTS AND APPLES IN BAKING DISH. MIX MAPLE SYRUP AND BROWN SUGAR AND POUR OVER TOP. DOT WITH BUTTER. BAKE 30-40 MINS. OR UNTIL APPLES ARE TENDER, STIRRING ONCE OR TWICE DURING COOKING. SERVES 4-6.

GREEN TOMATO CASSEROLE

IN A LARGE HEAVY SKILLET, COOK 8 MEDIUM GREEN TOMATOES AND 3 LARGE ONIONS, ALL SLICED, UNTIL THEY ARE MUSHY. STIR IN CURRY POWDER, SALT AND PAPRIKA TO TASTE. LET MIXTURE COOL AND STIR IN ABOUT 1-1/2 CUPS SOUR CREAM. POUR MIXTURE INTO A CASSEROLE AND SPRINKLE COARSE BREADCRUMBS OVER TOP (OLD BISCUITS ARE GOOD), BUTTERED BEFORE CRUMBLING AND GRATED PARMESAN CHEESE. BAKE IN 350 DEGREE OVEN UNTIL THE VEGETABLE MIXTURE BUBBLES AND CRUMBS ARE WELL BROWNED. *MRS. DELCIE COLLINS*

BAKED TURNIPS WITH MAPLE SUGAR

5-6 CUPS GRATED YELLOW TURNIPS
1 MEDIUM APPLE, PEELED, CORED, DICED
2 TBSP. MAPLE SUGAR

1 TEASP. SALT
1/4 TEASP. PEPPER
3 TBSP. BUTTER, MELTED

PREHEAT OVEN TO 350 DEGREES. GREASE 1-1/2 QUART BAKING DISH. COMBINE TURNIPS AND DICED APPLES. STIR IN MAPLE SUGAR, SALT, PEPPER AND BUTTER. MIX THOROUGHLY. TURN INTO BAKING DISH AND BAKE 1-1/2 HOURS. SERVES 6.

Baked Macaroni and Cheese

1 TBSP. SALT
2 CUPS UNCOOKED ELBOW MACARONI
1/2 STICK BUTTER OF MARGARINE, MELTED
2 EGGS, LIGHTLY BEATEN

12 OZ. SHARP CHEDDAR CHEESE, GRATED
1-1/2 CUPS EVAPORATED MILK
PAPRIKA

PREHEAT OVEN TO 375 DEGREES. FILL A 3-QUART SAUCEPAN WITH WATER AND PLACE OVER A HIGH FLAME. WHEN WATER IS BOILING RAPIDLY, ADD SALT AND ELBOW MACARONI. ADD GRADUALLY SO WATER DOES NOT STOP BOILING. COOK, UNCOVERED FOR 8-9 MINS. REMOVE AND DRAIN IN COLANDER, THEN RINSE WITH COLD WATER FOR A FEW SECONDS. PUT MACARONI IN A 2-QUART CASSEROLE AND ADD MELTED BUTTER, 8 OZ. OF GRATED CHEESE, EGGS AND MILK. MIX LIGHTLY. SPRINKLE REMAINING CHEESE OVER THE TOP AND DUST WITH PAPRIKA. BAKE IN 375 DEGREE OVEN FOR 30 MINS. SERVES 8.

Noodle Pudding

1/2 LB. MEDIUM NOODLES
6 TBSP. BUTTER
2 CUPS CREAM-STYLE COTTAGE CHEESE

SALT AND PEPPER
2 CUPS SOUR CREAM

COOK NOODLES IN RAPIDLY BOILING, SALTED WATER UNTIL NOT QUITE TENDER, AL DENTE. DRAIN. TURN NOODLES INTO A GENEROUSLY BUTTERED 1-1/2 QUART BAKING DISH. MIX IN REST OF INGREDIENTS, USING ONLY 4 TBSP. BUTTER. DOT WITH REMAINING 2 TBSP. AND BAKE IN 350 DEGREE OVEN FOR ABOUT 30 MINS. OR UNTIL GOLDEN BROWN AND BUBBLY. SERVES 4-6.

Young Greens with Bacon Dressing

4 SLICES BACON, DICED
1/2 CUP SUGAR
1/2 TEASP. SALT
1 TBSP. CORN STARCH
1 EGG, LIGHTLY BEATEN
1/4 CUP CIDER VINEGAR

1 CUP LIGHT CREAM
4 CUPS YOUNG TENDER, DANDELION, CREASY OR NEW GARDEN LETTUCE, CLEANED AND DRIED
1 HARD-COOKED EGG, CHOPPED

COOK BACON UNTIL CRISP. COMBINE SUGAR, SALT AND CORNSTARCH. COMBINE EGG, VINEGAR AND CREAM, BLEND WELL. STIR INTO SUGAR MIXTURE. POUR INTO COOKED BACON WITH DRIPPINGS. COOK OVER MEDIUM HEAT, STIRRING CONSTANTLY, UNTIL MIXTURE THICKENS. POUR OVER GREENS, TOSSING LIGHTLY. GARNISH WITH HARD-COOKED EGG AND SERVE WHILE DRESSING IS STILL WARM. SERVES 6.

Candied Sweet Potatoes

6 SWEET POTATOES	1/2 CUP WATER
1/2 TEASP. SALT	4 TBSP. BUTTER
1 CUP DARK BROWN SUGAR	1 TBSP. LEMON JUICE

PREHEAT OVEN TO 375 DEGREES. COOK SWEET POTATOES IN JACKETS IN BOILING, SALTED WATER UNTIL NEARLY TENDER. DRAIN, PEEL AND CUT IN SLICES ABOUT 1/2-INCH THICK. PLACE IN GREASED, SHALLOW BAKING DISH AND SPRINKLE WITH SALT. COOK BROWN SUGAR, WATER AND BUTTER TOGETHER IN SEPARATE PAN FOR SEVERAL MINUTES. STIR IN LEMON JUICE AND POUR OVER POTATOES. BAKE IN 375 DEGREE OVEN FOR 20-25 MINS., BASTING OCCASIONALLY WITH SYRUP. SERVES 4-6.

Baked Onion Rings

6 MEDIUM OR LARGE ONIONS	1 CUP MILK
1 TBSP. ALL-PURPOSE FLOUR	1 TEASP. SALT
FRESHLY GROUND PEPPER, TO TASTE	CHOPPED PARSLEY
3 TBSP. BUTTER	

PREHEAT OVEN TO 450 DEGREES. PEEL AND SLICE ONIONS VERY THIN. SEPARATE INTO RINGS. TOSS WITH FLOUR. PLACE IN A DEEP BAKING DISH. SPRINKLE LIGHTLY WITH PEPPER. DOT WITH BUTTER AND POUR MILK OVER TOP. BAKE ABOUT 45 MINS., OR UNTIL ONIONS ARE TENDER. SPRINKLE WITH SALT AND PARSLEY AND SERVE. SERVES. 4.

Squash Casserole

1/8 CUP VEGETABLE OIL	SALT AND PEPPER
1/3 CUP DICED SUMMER SQUASH	8 EGGS
2/3 CUP (EACH) DICED ZUCCHINI, RED	1/2 CUP MILK
BELL PEPPER, ONION	1-1/2 TEASP. DRIED SWEET BASIL
1/4 LB. MUSHROOMS, SLICED	3/4 CUP GRATED PARMESAN CHEESE

PREHEAT OVEN TO 350 DEGREES. HEAT VEGETABLE OIL IN LARGE SKILLET. ADD SQUASH, ZUCCHINI, RED PEPPER AND ONION AND SAUTÉ UNTIL ALMOST TENDER. ADD MUSHROOMS AND SAUTÉ ANOTHER MINUTE OR TWO. SALT AND PEPPER TO TASTE. TRANSFER VEGETABLES TO WELL-BUTTERED 8x8 BAKING DISH. WHISK EGGS AND MILK TOGETHER AND ADD BASIL. POUR EGG MIXTURE OVER VEGETABLES. BAKE 30 MINS. REMOVE FROM OVEN AND TOP WITH PARMESAN CHEESE. RETURN TO OVEN FOR 5-6 MINS. TO MELT CHEESE. SERVE WITH ITALIAN BREAD. 4 SERVINGS.

Baked Garlic Grits

1 cup grits
4 cups boiling water
1/2 teasp. salt
2 eggs, slightly beaten
1 tbsp. parsley flakes

6 oz. pasteurized cheese
  (Velveeta is good)
1 clove garlic, finely chopped
  or 1/2 teasp. garlic powder
1/2 cup margarine

Cook grits in boiling water about 5 mins. Stir a small amount of the cooked grits into the beaten eggs. Add to remainder of grits and stir well. Stir in margarine, cheese and garlic. Bake in 2-quart casserole for 1 hour.

Lima Bean Salad

2 packages frozen lima beans
2 packages frozen green beans
2 packages frozen green peas
6 hard-cooked eggs, chopped
1 small onion, grated
1 cup mayonnaise

2 teasp. mustard
1 dash Tabasco
4 teasp. salad oil
4 tbsp. olive oil
1 dash Worcestershire sauce

Cook and drain the beans and peas. Fold in the eggs, onion, mayonnaise, mustard, Tabasco, salad oil, olive oil and Worcestershire sauce. Mix and let stand overnight.

Broccoli Casserole

2 (10 oz.) packages, frozen,
  chopped broccoli
1 tbsp. butter
1 tbsp. minced onion
1 (10-1/2 oz.) can cream of mushroom soup

1/3 cup milk
1/3 cup grated cheese
1 egg
1/2 cup buttered breadcrumbs

Cook broccoli according to directions on package. Drain. Preheat oven to 350 degrees. In a 3-quart saucepan, melt butter and cook onion until it is translucent. Pour in mushroom soup and milk. Add cheese. Heat until cheese is melted, then whisk in the egg. Combine the broccoli and sauce and transfer to a 9x13 baking dish. Sprinkle with the buttered breadcrumbs and bake 30 mins. or until the sauce bubbles and the crumbs are brown. Serves 6. From *General Lewis Inn, Lewisburg, W.Va.*

Sautéed or Fried Cucumbers

Pare 2 medium cucumbers, then slice about 1/4-inch thick. Pat with paper towels to remove all moisture.

Sauté: Sprinkle with salt and pepper and coat lightly with flour. Cook in 1/4 cup melted butter until golden brown on both sides.

Fry: Dip each slice in fine dry breadcrumbs, then in slightly beaten egg, then again in the crumbs. Fry several minutes in fat heated to 385 degrees or until 1-inch cube of bread browns in 60 secs. When slices are golden, drain on paper towels and season with salt and pepper. 4 servings.

Sweet and Sour Bean Salad

1 can each (16 oz.) green, wax, baby lima and red kidney beans
1 cup celery cut into thin 1-inch strips
2 medium onions sliced and separated into rings

1-1/2 cups sugar
1/2 cup salad oil
1 small jar pimiento strips
salt and pepper
1 cup vinegar

Drain canned beans (wash kidney beans) and place in large bowl. Add celery, pepper, pimiento and onion. Mix well. Combine oil, vinegar and sugar in pan and bring to boil. Pour over bean mixture and refrigerate overnight. Stores well in refrigerator.

12-Hour Slaw

1 large cabbage, shredded
1 Bermuda onion (thinly sliced)

1 green pepper (chopped)

Pack in bowl, cabbage, onion and green pepper in layers until bowl is filled. Pour 1 cup sugar over top. **Do not stir.**

Mix:

1 cup cider vinegar
3/4 cup salad oil
1 tbsp. celery seed

1 tbsp. sugar
1 tbsp salt
1 teasp. dried mustard

Heat this combination in saucepan and let come to a hard boil. Pour over the cabbage combination. Seal tight with lid and let stand overnight. Toss next day. Will keep in refrigerator for two weeks.

Turnip Greens and Dumplings

2 QUARTS TURNIP GREENS	2 QUARTS BOILING WATER
1 LB. TURNIPS	1 HAM HOCK OR PIECE OF SALT PORK
1 TEASP. SALT	

WASH GREENS THOROUGHLY. PARE AND DICE TURNIPS. BRING 2 QUARTS OF WATER TO BOIL IN LARGE KETTLE. ADD HAM HOCK, GREENS, TURNIPS AND 1 TEASP. SALT. COVER, SIMMER FOR 2 HOURS. REMOVE 1 CUP OF "POT LIKKER."

Dumplings

1-1/2 CUPS WHITE CORNMEAL	1/2 TEASP. SALT
1/2 CUP FLOUR	3 TBSP. BUTTER, MELTED
1 TEASP. BAKING POWDER	1 EGG, BEATEN
1 TEASP. SUGAR	

STIR TOGETHER CORNMEAL, FLOUR, BAKING POWDER, SUGAR AND SALT. STIR IN BUTTER AND "POT LIKKER." STIR IN EGG. DROP 1 TBSP. AT A TIME INTO SIMMERING GREENS. COVER AND SIMMER FOR 30 MINS. SERVES 6-8.

Potato Cakes

4 TBSP. (1/2 STICK) UNSALTED BUTTER, SOFTENED	1/4 CUP MILK
	1-1/2 CUPS COLD MASHED POTATOES
2 CUPS SELF-RISING FLOUR	1 TEASP. SALT

PREHEAT OVEN TO 450 DEGREES. MIX BUTTER INTO FLOUR WITH HANDS. THEN BLEND IN POTATOES, MILK AND SALT WITH WOODEN SPOON. AFTER ALL IS WELL MIXED, ROLL OUT ON FLOURED BOARD TO THICKNESS OF ABOUT 1-1/4 INCHES. CUT WITH 3-INCH BISCUIT CUTTER AND PLACE ON GREASED COOKIE SHEET. BAKE 25-30 MINS. UNTIL GOLDEN BROWN. SERVE HOT, SPLIT, WITH BUTTER.

Creamed Tomatoes

2 CUPS TOMATOES OR TOMATO JUICE	1 TBSP. MARGARINE
2 TBSP. ALL-PURPOSE FLOUR	1/4 CUP WATER
2 TBSP. EVAPORATED MILK	SALT AND PEPPER TO TASTE

MIX FLOUR, MILK AND WATER TOGETHER IN A SMALL BOWL, SET ASIDE. BRING TOMATOES TO A BOIL, ADD SALT AND PEPPER. WHILE BOILING, ADD FLOUR MIXTURE, STIRRING CONSTANTLY. REMOVE FROM HEAT. POUR INTO SERVING BOWL, TOP WITH MARGARINE PAT.

POTATO AND BEET SALAD

4-6 MEDIUM POTATOES, SLICED   1 (16 OZ.) CAN BEETS, WHOLE

DRESSING:

1/2 CUP OLIVE OIL   1 CLOVE GARLIC, CRUSHED
1/4 CUP WINE VINEGAR   SALT AND PEPPER TO TASTE

BOIL, COOL AND PEEL POTATOES. SLICE POTATOES AND DRAINED BEETS INTO ROUND SLICES, ABOUT 1/4-INCH THICK AND PLACE IN LARGE BOWL. COMBINE DRESSING INGREDIENTS AND POUR OVER POTATOES AND BEETS. TOSS GENTLY. LET STAND SEVERAL HOURS. TOSS BEFORE SERVING. SERVE AT ROOM TEMPERATURE. 4-6 SERVINGS.

COLESLAW I

1 CUP CORN OIL   1 LARGE CABBAGE, COARSELY
1 CUP SUGAR   SHREDDED
1 CUP APPLE CIDER VINEGAR   1 LARGE ONION, SLICED INTO RINGS
2 TEASP. CELERY SEED   2 GREEN PEPPERS, COARSELY CHOPPED
SALT AND PEPPER TO TASTE   2 TEASP. POWDERED MUSTARD

COMBINE CORN OIL, SUGAR AND VINEGAR, AND BOIL SLOWLY FOR 5 MINS. IN ENAMEL OR STAINLESS SAUCEPAN. ADD CELERY SEED, MUSTARD, SALT AND PEPPER. COOL SLIGHTLY. COMBINE CABBAGE, ONION AND GREEN PEPPERS WITH MARINADE AND MIX WELL. REFRIGERATE FOR AT LEAST 24 HOURS. SERVES 20 OR MORE.

CORN CUSTARD PUDDING

2 CUPS FROZEN LOOSE-PACK WHOLE   1 TBSP. SUGAR
   KERNEL CORN   1 TEASP. SALT
2 CUPS MILK OR DAIRY HALF-AND-HALF   1/8 TEASP. WHITE PEPPER
2 TBSP. MELTED BUTTER OR MARGARINE   3 EGGS

ADD CORN, MILK, BUTTER, SUGAR, SALT AND PEPPER TO EGGS; STIR TO COMBINE WELL. TURN INTO WELL-GREASED 1-1/2 QUART CASSEROLE. PLACE IN PAN OF HOT WATER. BAKE IN MODERATE OVEN (350 DEGREES) 45 MINS., OR UNTIL PUDDING IS SET. SERVES 4.

N.B. MAY SUBSTITUTE 1 (1 LB.) CAN CREAM-STYLE CORN FOR FROZEN WHOLE CORN, BUT USE 1 CUP OF MILK OR DAIRY HALF-AND-HALF INSTEAD OF 2.

Succotash

2 CUPS FRESH LIMA BEANS OR	1/2 CUP WATER
2 PACKAGES FROZEN LIMAS	1 TEASP. SALT
2 CUPS WHOLE KERNEL CORN (FRESH,	DASH OF PEPPER
FROZEN OR CANNED)	1 TEASP. SUGAR
2 TBSP. BUTTER	1/4 CUP HEAVY CREAM

COOK LIMA BEANS IN BOILING, SALTED WATER UNTIL TENDER (IF FROZEN, ACCORDING TO PACKAGE DIRECTIONS). MIX COOKED BEANS WITH CORN (IF FRESH OR CANNED, DRAIN, IF FROZEN USE STRAIGHT FROM THE PACKAGE), BUTTER, SALT, PEPPER, SUGAR AND WATER. COOK OVER LOW HEAT FOR 10-15 MINS. DRAIN, THEN ADD CREAM. HEAT THROUGH BUT DO NOT BOIL.

Pea Salad II

3/4 CUP SPANISH PEANUTS	1 CHOPPED TOMATO
3/4 CUP SOUR CREAM	1/4 CUP MINCED GREEN ONION
1 TEASP. SEASONED SALT	1 CUP DICED CUCUMBER
1/4 TEASP. GARLIC POWDER	3 SMALL SWEET PICKLES, CHOPPED
1/4 TEASP. PEPPER	1/2 CUP CELERY HEARTS, CHOPPED
2 (10 OZ.) PACKAGES FROZEN ENGLISH	2 TBSP. MAYONNAISE
PEAS, THAWED	6 SLICES CRISP BACON, CRUMBLED

MIX WELL. SPOON MIXTURE INTO BOWL LINED WITH LETTUCE LEAVES. ARRANGE TOMATO WEDGES OVER TOP. SPRINKLE WITH 6 SLICES CRISP BACON, CRUMBLED.

Sweet-Sour Baked Beans

8 SLICES BACON, PAN-FRIED UNTIL CRISP,	1 (1 LB.-11 OZ.) CAN BAKED BEANS,
DRAINED AND CRUMBLED	UNDRAINED
4 LARGE ONION, CUT INTO RINGS	1 TEASP. DRY MUSTARD
1/2 TO 1 CUP BROWN SUGAR*	1 TEASP. SALT
1/2 TEASP. GARLIC POWDER (OPTIONAL)	2 (15 OZ.) CANS DRIED LIMA BEANS,
1/2 CUP CIDER VINEGAR	DRAINED, OR 1 BOX, FROZEN, COOKED
1 (1 LB.) CAN DARK RED KIDNEY BEANS, DRAINED	

PLACE ONIONS IN SKILLET, ADD SUGAR, MUSTARD, GARLIC POWDER, SALT AND VINEGAR. COOK 20 MINS., COVERED. ADD ONION MIXTURE TO BEANS. ADD CRUMBLED BACON. POUR INTO 3 QUART CASSEROLE AND BAKE AT 350 DEGREES FOR 1 HOUR.

*USE FULL AMOUNT OF SUGAR IF YOU LIKE BEANS ON THE SWEET SIDE.

Caillette (Cabbage Roll-Ups)

Large head of cabbage
1 cup milk
3 cups dry breadcrumbs
2 eggs, slightly beaten
salt and pepper

Dash nutmeg
Chicken or beef broth
1 cup grated Cheddar or Swiss
cheese

Remove 12-14 large outer leaves from cabbage and cut off some of the thick rib. Cover with boiling water to soften. Heat milk and pour over crumbs. Thoroughly mix in eggs, cheese, salt, pepper and nutmeg. Put a heaping tablespoon of the mixture on each drained cabbage leaf, folding sides and ends to make neat package. Fasten with toothpicks or tie with string and drop into gently boiling broth. Cook for 30 mins. or until cabbage is tender. Lift from broth and serve immediately. Serves 4-6.

===============

Creamy Cheese Potatoes

1-1/4 cups milk
4 cups cooked potatoes, cubed
(about 4 medium)
1 (8 oz.) package cream cheese

1/2 teasp. salt
1 tbsp. snipped fresh chives
1 teasp. minced dry onion

Over low heat blend milk into cream cheese. If necessary, beat with rotary beater. Stir in chives, onion and salt. Add potatoes and stir carefully to coat. Turn mixture into 1-1/2 quart casserole; sprinkle with paprika. Bake at 350 degrees for 40 mins. Serves 8.

===============

Homestead Salad

1 (10 oz.) package frozen mixed
vegetables
1 (17 oz.) can red kidney beans,
drained
1/2 cup chopped green pepper
1 tbsp. all-purpose flour

1/2 cup vinegar
1 cup diced celery
1/2 cup diced onion
3/4 cup sugar
1 tbsp. prepared mustard

Cook mixed vegetables according to package directions, drain. Set aside to cool. Rinse kidney beans and drain well. Combine celery, onion, pepper, mixed vegetables and kidney beans. Combine sugar, flour, mustard and vinegar. Cook over medium heat, stirring constantly, until clear and thick. Let cool; then stir into vegetable mixture. Refrigerate for 24 hours, stirring occasionally.

MASHED PARSNIPS AND CARROTS

4 LARGE CARROTS
6 LARGE PARSNIPS
1 TEASP. SUGAR

2 TBSP. BUTTER
1/2 TEASP. SALT

PEEL CARROTS AND SLICE IN ROUNDS. WASH AND PEEL PARSNIPS, SPLIT IN TWO LENGTH-WISE. SPLIT IN QUARTERS AND CUT OUT THE PITHY CORE. CUT INTO SLICES. PLACE CARROTS AND PARSNIPS IN A SAUCEPAN WITH SALT, SUGAR AND WATER TO COVER. BRING TO A BOIL AND REDUCE HEAT. COOK ABOUT 30 MINS. OR UNTIL TENDER. DRAIN WELL. MASH WITH POTATO MASHER; ADD BUTTER AND BEAT UNTIL WELL BLENDED. REHEAT OVER BOILING WATER, IF NECESSARY, TO SERVE HOT. SERVES 4.

FRESH CORN CASSEROLE

6 SLICES BACON
3/4 CUP CHOPPED GREEN PEPPER
1/2 CUP CHOPPED ONION
2 FIRM, RIPE TOMATOES, PEELED AND SLICED

8 EARS OF FRESH CORN, CUT FROM
  COB, WITH ALL POSSIBLE JUICES
1/2 TEASP. PEPPER
1 TEASP. SALT

FRY BACON UNTIL BROWN, DRAIN AND CRUMBLE. REMOVE ALL BUT 2 TBSP. OF BACON GREASE FROM SKILLET. ADD CORN, GREEN PEPPER AND ONION. COOK OVER HIGH HEAT FOR 5 MINS. ADD CRUMBLED BACON, SALT AND PEPPER. IN 2-QUART CASSEROLE, ALTERNATE LAYERS OF CORN MIXTURE AND TOMATO SLICES. BAKE UNCOVERED FOR 30-40 MINS. SERVES 6.

COLESLAW II

1 QUART CABBAGE, CHOPPED
1/2 CUP CHOPPED ONION
1/2 CUP CHOPPED CELERY

1/2 CUP CHOPPED CARROT
1/2 CUP CHOPPED GREEN PEPPER
1 TBSP. SALT

SOAK THE VEGETABLES IN COLD WATER WITH THE SALT FOR 30 MINS. DRAIN AND RINSE WELL, DRAIN AGAIN.

DRESSING:

1/2 CUP OIL
1/2 CUP VINEGAR

1 CUP SUGAR

BRING TO BOIL IN SMALL SAUCEPAN. COOL. THEN TOSS WITH VEGETABLES. CHILL WELL BEFORE SERVING.

SWEET POTATO PUFFS

SWEET POTATOES
BROWN SUGAR TO TASTE
BUTTER TO TASTE

PECANS, WALNUTS, GROUND
(A LITTLE LESS THAN 1/2 CUP
PER POTATO)

USE AS MANY SWEET POTATOES AS YOU WISH. BOIL UNTIL TENDER. PEEL AND MASH. ADD BROWN SUGAR AND BUTTER. FORM INTO BALLS (MAY ROLL AROUND MARSHMALLOWS TO HELP FORM). ROLL EACH BALL INTO GROUND NUTS UNTIL ENTIRE SURFACE IS COVERED. PLACE IN A WARM OVEN UNTIL READY TO SERVE.

PINTO-BEAN SALAD

1-1/2 TBSP. FRESH LEMON JUICE
1 TBSP. VEGETABLE OIL
2 TEASP. SOY SAUCE
1 CAN (15-1/2 OZ.) PINTO BEANS, DRAINED
1/2 CUP THINLY SLICED RADISHES

2 TBSP. SLICED GREEN ONION
2 TBSP. CHOPPED FRESH PARSLEY
1/2 TEASP. MINCED GARLIC
2 CUPS LOOSELY PACKED TORN
ROMAINE OR ESCAROLE

IN A MEDIUM-SIZED BOWL, WHISK LEMON JUICE, OIL AND SOY SAUCE. ADD REMAINING INGREDIENTS EXCEPT LETTUCE. TOSS TO COAT. COVER AND CHILL 30 MINS. FOR FLAVORS TO BLEND. ARRANGE ON LETTUCE-LINED SERVING PLATTER OR PLATES. MAKES 4 SIDE-DISH SERVINGS.

TURNIP GREENS II

3 CUPS WATER
1 SMALL HAM HOCK

2 LBS. TURNIP GREENS
6 SMALL TURNIPS, DICED

SIMMER WATER, GREENS AND HAM HOCK FOR 30 MINS. ADD DICED TURNIPS AND SIMMER ABOUT ANOTHER 30 MINS. SERVE WITH CORN BREAD TO DIP INTO "POT LIKKER." 6 SERVINGS.

CRUNCHY ZUCCHINI STICKS

3 MEDIUM ZUCCHINI
1/2 CUP WHEAT GERM
1/4 CUP MELTED BUTTER OR MARGARINE

1/4 CUP GRATED PARMESAN CHEESE
1/2 TEASP. SALT
1/2 CUP FINELY CHOPPED ALMONDS

CUT ZUCCHINI IN HALF AND THEN LENGTHWISE TO FORM ABOUT 16 STICKS EACH. MIX OTHER INGREDIENTS, EXCEPT BUTTER, IN PLASTIC BAG. DIP STICKS IN BUTTER, THEN SHAKE IN BAG UNTIL EVENLY COATED. PLACE IN SINGLE LAYER ON UNGREASED COOKIE SHEET AND BAKE AT 350 DEGREES ABOUT 15 MINS., OR UNTIL CRISP AND TENDER.

BREADS

Since corn was a new product, introduced to the first settlers by the Indians, it's amazing what these early housewives learned to do with it. Particularly in the bread department: spoon bread, corn bread, pone muffins, griddle cakes, etc., all came from their ingenuity.

Baking bread was no easy feat with only the trial and error method to develop a "feel" for when the coals were right. Yet every pioneer wife developed her own many, and varied recipes, which were a mainstay of the family's diet.

POTATO ROLLS

3 CUPS WATER
1 MEDIUM POTATO
1 TBSP. SALT
1 TBSP. SUGAR

1/2 CUP SHORTENING
1 PACKAGE DRY YEAST
1/2 CUP LUKEWARM WATER
4-5 CUPS FLOUR

COOK POTATO IN 3 CUPS WATER UNTIL DONE; REMOVE AND MASH ADDING WATER IT WAS COOKED IN. MIX UNTIL SMOOTH; ADD SALT, SUGAR AND SHORTENING. MIX YEAST IN 1/2 CUP LUKEWARM WATER UNTIL DISSOLVED. ADD POTATO MIXTURE AND YEAST TO FLOUR. MIX, WORKING WELL. LEAVE IN MIXING BOWL, COVER AND LET RISE UNTIL DOUBLE IN BULK. WORK DOWN AND LET RISE AGAIN. MAKE ROLLS, LET RISE UNTIL DOUBLE IN BULK. BAKE IN 400 DEGREE OVEN UNTIL GOLDEN BROWN AND DONE. GREASE TOP WITH BUTTER OR MARGARINE.

MAYO BISCUITS

1 CUP SELF-RISING FLOUR (SIFTED)
2 TBSP. MAYONNAISE

1/2 CUP MILK

BLEND ALL INGREDIENTS, JUST UNTIL FLOUR IS MOISTENED. GREASE MUFFIN TINS AND FILL HALF FULL WITH BATTER. BAKE AT 350 DEGREES FOR 20-25 MINS.

BROCCOLI BREAD

1 (10-OZ.) PACKAGE BROKEN BROCCOLI,
   THAWED, DRAINED
1 LARGE ONION, CHOPPED
1/2 CUP MARGARINE, MELTED

4 EGGS, BEATEN
1 TEASP. SALT
1 SMALL BOX CORN BREAD MIX

MIX BROCCOLI, ONION, MARGARINE, EGGS AND SALT IN A BOWL. STIR IN CORN BREAD MIX. POUR INTO GREASED 9x13 PAN AND BAKE AT 400 DEGREES FOR 25 MINS. SERVES 9.

POTATO SCONES

1 LB. POTATOES, COOKED AND MASHED
2 TBSP. BUTTER, MELTED

1 CUP SIFTED ALL-PURPOSE FLOUR
1/2 TEASP. SALT

MIX ALL INGREDIENTS TO MAKE A SOFT DOUGH. PAT OUT INTO A 1/2-INCH THICK CIRCLE. CUT IN 8 PIE-SHAPED WEDGES. HEAT A GRIDDLE OVER MEDIUM HEAT. BUTTER HOT GRIDDLE LIGHTLY AND COOK SCONES ABOUT 4 MINS. ON EACH SIDE, OR UNTIL LIGHTLY BROWNED AND CRISP. SPLIT AND SERVE HOT WITH BUTTER. 4 SERVINGS.

CORNMEAL BISCUITS

3/4 CUP MILK	3/4 TEASP. SALT
1 CUP CORNMEAL	3/4 CUP SIFTED ALL-PURPOSE FLOUR
2 TBSP. SHORTENING	4 TEASP. BAKING POWDER

PREHEAT OVEN TO 425 DEGREES. SCALD MILK. COMBINE CORNMEAL, SHORTENING AND SALT IN MIXING BOWL. STIR IN HOT MILK UNTIL MIXTURE IS SMOOTH AND SHORTENING HAS MELTED. COOL. SIFT FLOUR AND BAKING POWDER TOGETHER AND STIR INTO COLD CORNMEAL MIXTURE. DUMP ONTO A LIGHTLY FLOURED BOARD AND ROLL ABOUT 3/4-INCH THICK. CUT WITH SMALL BISCUIT CUTTER, PLACE ON UNGREASED COOKIE SHEET AND BAKE IN 425 DEGREE OVEN FOR 15-20 MINS. BISCUITS HAVE CRUNCHY TEXTURE. SERVE WITH BUTTER, HONEY OR MAPLE SYRUP, IF DESIRED.

WATERCRESS BISCUITS

2 CUPS SIFTED ALL-PURPOSE FLOUR	3 TEASP. BAKING POWDER
1 TEASP. SALT	4 TBSP. SHORTENING
1 BUNCH OF WATERCRESS	ABOUT 3/4 CUP MILK

SIFT DRY INGREDIENTS TOGETHER. CUT SHORTENING INTO THIS USING TWO KNIVES OR A PASTRY BLENDER, UNTIL MIXTURE IS CONSISTENCY OF COARSE CORN MEAL. DISCARD STEMS OF WATERCRESS. COARSELY CUT LEAVES AND ADD TO MIXTURE. ADD ENOUGH MILK, WHILE STIRRING WITH FORK, TO MAKE A SOFT DOUGH THAT CAN BE EASILY HANDLED. TURN ONTO A LIGHTLY FLOURED BOARD AND KNEAD LIGHTLY ABOUT 20 SECS. ROLL 1/2-INCH THICK. CUT INTO BISCUITS OF DESIRED SIZE. MAKES ABOUT 30 1-1/2-INCH BISCUITS OR 18 2-INCH.

HOMEMADE NOODLES*

2 CUPS FLOUR	1/2 TEASP. SALT
2 EGGS, WELL-BEATEN	2 TBSP. WARM WATER

SIFT FLOUR AND SALT ONTO PASTRY BOARD. MAKE A WELL IN THE CENTER AND ADD EGGS AND WATER. WORK THE FLOUR INTO THE EGG MIXTURE, ADDING MORE WATER, IF NECESSARY TO MAKE A STIFF, BUT MALLEABLE DOUGH. KNEAD ON THE BOARD UNTIL SMOOTH. DIVIDE DOUGH IN HALF AND LET IT REST FOR 30 MINS., COVERED. ROLL OUT AS THIN AS POSSIBLE AND CUT INTO ANY DESIRED SHAPES. SPREAD NOODLES ON THE BOARD AND LET THEM DRY WELL BEFORE USING.

*OLD-FASHIONED WAY SANS A PASTA MACHINE.

BOILED NOODLES: DROP DRIED NOODLES IN BOILING, SALTED WATER. BOIL ABOUT 10 MINS., OR UNTIL JUST TENDER. DRAIN AND BUTTER WELL BEFORE SERVING.

CHEDDAR BISCUITS

1 CUP SIFTED ALL-PURPOSE FLOUR
1/4 TEASP. SALT

1/3 CUP BUTTER
1 CUP GRATED CHEDDAR CHEESE

PREHEAT OVEN TO 350 DEGREES. SIFT FLOUR AND SALT TOGETHER IN BOWL. CUT IN BUTTER WITH PASTRY BLENDER OR KNIVES, THEN MIX IN CHEESE. MIX LIGHTLY WITH YOUR HANDS UNTIL DOUGH HOLDS TOGETHER. ROLL ABOUT 1/2-INCH THICK ON LIGHTLY FLOURED BOARD. CUT WITH SMALL BISCUIT CUTTER AND PRICK TOPS WITH FORK. PLACE ON UNGREASED COOKIE SHEET AND BAKE FOR 12-15 MINS. SHOULD BE RICH CHEDDAR COLOR NOT BROWN. GOOD COLD. KEEP WELL. YIELD: 22-24 BISCUITS.

SOUR-MILK GRAHAM BREAD*

1 EGG
2 TBSP. MELTED BUTTER
2 CUPS SOUR MILK
1-1/2 CUPS WHITE FLOUR

2 TBSP. SUGAR
1 TEASP. BAKING SODA
1-1/2 CUPS GRAHAM FLOUR

BEAT THE EGG WITH THE SUGAR, POUR IN MELTED BUTTER. DISSOLVE SODA IN 2 SPOONS-FUL OF HOT WATER AND ADD SOUR MILK. STIR INTO THE FLOUR. POUR INTO LOAF PAN AND BAKE ON LOW HEAT (250 DEGREES) FOR 1 HOUR OR UNTIL DONE.

*ONE WAY TO USE UP MILK THAT HAS SOURED (BUT NOT SEPARATED NOR BECOME BITTER.)

BEER BREAD I

3 CUPS SELF-RISING FLOUR
1 (12-OZ.) CAN BEER

3 TBSP. SUGAR

MIX INGREDIENTS. BAKE AT 350 DEGREES IN GREASED BREAD PAN FOR 45 MINS. TO AN HOUR. MAKES 1 LOAF.

BEER BREAD II

3 CUPS SELF-RISING FLOUR
1/4 CUP SUGAR

1 (12-OZ.) CAN BEER
MELTED BUTTER

PREHEAT OVEN TO 350 DEGREES. GREASE AND FLOUR LOAF PAN. MIX FLOUR, SUGAR AND BEER AND POUR INTO PAN. POUR MELTED BUTTER OVER TOP AND BAKE FOR ABOUT 45 MINS. MAKES ONE LOAF.

Basic Dumplings

1-1/2 CUPS FLOUR
3 TEASP. BAKING POWDER
3/4 TEASP. SALT

1-1/2 TBSP. SHORTENING
3/4 CUP MILK
2 OR 3 PINTS OF BOILING BROTH

SIFT TOGETHER THE DRY INGREDIENTS AND CUT INTO SHORTENING. STIR IN MILK SLOWLY, MIXING ONLY TO MOISTEN DOUGH THOROUGHLY. FIRST DIP A TEASPOON IN THE HOT BROTH AND THEN IN THE DOUGH AND DROP DUMPLING MIX, ONE SPOONFUL AT A TIME, INTO BOILING BROTH. COVER KETTLE AND COOK 15 MINS. MAKES 6 SERVINGS. (BROTH CAN BE CHICKEN, PINTO BEANS, TOMATO, POTATO, ETC.)

Firm, Chewy Dumplings

2 EGGS

1 CUP FLOUR

MIX TO MAKE A STIFF DOUGH, ADDING A LITTLE WATER, IF NECESSARY. THE DOUGH SHOULD BE STIFF ENOUGH SO THAT IT WILL NOT SEPARATE WHEN ADDED TO BOILING WATER. DROP BY TEASPOONSFUL INTO WATER WITH SALT ADDED TO TASTE; COOK UNTIL ALMOST DONE, THEN ADD TO CHICKEN, STEW OR SOUP.

Drop Dumplings

2 CUPS FLOUR
3 TEASP. BAKING POWDER
3/4 CUP MILK

1/2 TEASP. SALT
1 TBSP. SHORTENING

SIFT FLOUR, MEASURE AND ADD BAKING POWDER AND SALT. CUT IN SHORTENING. ADD MILK TO MAKE A DROP BATTER. DROP BY SPOONFULS INTO BOILING BROTH OR LIQUID. COVER AND COOK 10 MINS. SERVE AT ONCE. SERVES 8. (LIQUID MUST REMAIN BOILING DURING THE 10 MINS.)

Sesame Crackers

6 TBSP. OIL
1/4 CUP UNHULLED SESAME SEEDS
1 CUP FINELY GROUND OATMEAL

1/2 CUP WATER
1 CUP WHOLE WHEAT FLOUR
1/2 CUP BRAN

COMBINE WET INGREDIENTS. ADD DRY INGREDIENTS. GREASE COOKIE SHEET. ROLL DOUGH AS THIN AS POSSIBLE ONTO SHEET. BAKE 10 MINS. AT 350 DEGREES. LOOSEN AND COOL.

Quick Sally Lunn

2 CUPS FLOUR
1/2 TEASP. SALT
2 EGGS, SEPARATED
3/4 CUP MILK

1 TBSP. BAKING POWDER
3 TBSP. BUTTER
1/2 CUP SUGAR

PREHEAT OVEN TO 350 DEGREES. IN A BOWL, SIFT FLOUR, BAKING POWDER AND SALT. CUT IN THE BUTTER UNTIL MIXTURE IS LIKE COARSE CORNMEAL. IN ANOTHER BOWL, BEAT TOGETHER EGG YOLKS AND SUGAR UNTIL THICK AND PALE. ADD FLOUR AND MILK ALTERNATELY TO EGG MIXTURE, BEATING WELL AFTER EACH ADDITION. BEAT EGG WHITES UNTIL STIFF AND FOLD GENTLY INTO BATTER. TURN BATTER INTO WELL-GREASED 8x8 BAKING PAN. SPREAD OUT WITH SPATULA. BAKE 40-45 MINS. OR UNTIL TESTS DONE. SERVES 6.

Cheddar Cheese Muffins

2 CUPS ALL-PURPOSE FLOUR
3 TEASP. BAKING POWDER
1/2 TEASP. SALT
1 CUP MILK
1 TBSP. SUGAR

1-1/2 CUPS GRATED SHARP CHEDDAR
  CHEESE
1 EGG
3 TBSP. BUTTER, SOFTENED

PREHEAT OVEN TO 400 DEGREES. MIX FLOUR, BAKING POWDER, SUGAR AND SALT IN MEDIUM BOWL. SET ASIDE. PUT EGG, MILK AND BUTTER INTO BLENDER AND WHIRL UNTIL SMOOTH. STIR IN GRATED CHEESE. POUR WET INGREDIENTS INTO DRY AND MIX UNTIL JUST MOISTENED. SPOON INTO GREASED AND FLOURED MUFFIN TINS (3/4 FULL) AND BAKE FOR 20-25 MINS. YIELDS ABOUT 15 MUFFINS.

Apple Corn Bread

2 CUPS WHITE CORN MEAL
1/4 CUP SUGAR, DIVIDED
1/2 TEASP. SALT
1 TEASP. CREAM OF TARTAR
1 TEASP. BAKING SODA

1-1/2 CUPS MILK
3 TO 4 TART APPLES, PEELED, CORED
  AND THINLY SLICED
1 TEASP. GROUND CINNAMON

PREHEAT OVEN TO 375 DEGREES. GREASE AN 8x11 BAKING PAN. MIX CORN MEAL, 2 TBSP. SUGAR, SALT, CREAM OF TARTAR AND BAKING SODA. ADD MILK AND BEAT UNTIL SMOOTH. TURN INTO BAKING PAN. COVER WITH OVERLAPPING LAYERS OF APPLE. COMBINE REMAINING SUGAR AND CINNAMON AND SPRINKLE OVER TOP OF APPLES. BAKE 30-35 MINS. OR UNTIL TOOTHPICK INSERTED INTO CENTER COMES OUT CLEAN. SERVES 8.

SOUTHERN CORN BREAD

1 TBSP. MELTED SHORTENING
1 CUP CORN MEAL
1/2 CUP FLOUR
1/2 TEASP. SALT

1/2 TEASP. SODA
1 EGG, BEATEN
1 CUP BUTTERMILK

PREHEAT OVEN TO 450 DEGREES. HEAT SHORTENING IN BREAD PAN OR SKILLET. SIFT DRY INGREDIENTS AND ADD EGG AND BUTTERMILK. MIX WELL, THEN ADD HOT SHORTENING. STIR AND POUR INTO HOT PAN OR SKILLET. BAKE 25 MINS. OR UNTIL GOLDEN BROWN.

GREENBRIER BISCUITS

1 PACKAGE YEAST
1 CUP WARM WATER
1/4 CUP COOKING OIL
1/2 CUP DRY MILK

2 TEASP. SUGAR
2 TEASP. BAKING POWDER
1 TEASP. SALT
ENOUGH FLOUR TO MAKE STIFF DOUGH

DISSOLVE YEAST IN WARM WATER; ADD OTHER INGREDIENTS AND MIX WELL. KNEAD AND ROLL OUT (ABOUT 1/2-INCH THICK) ON A FLOURED BOARD. CUT INTO BISCUITS. BUTTER TOPS AND PLACE ONE ON TOP OF ANOTHER. LET RISE 30 MINS. AND BAKE AT 450 DEGREES FOR ABOUT 12 MINS.

MARIA FLOR'S RYE BREAD

1 PACKAGE ACTIVE DRY YEAST
3 CUPS SIFTED RYE FLOUR
1/3 CUP SHORTENING
2 CUPS BOILING WATER

1/2 CUP WARM WATER
3/4 CUP DARK MOLASSES
2 TEASP. SALT
5 TO 5-1/2 CUPS WHITE FLOUR*

SOFTEN ACTIVE DRY YEAST IN WARM WATER. COMBINE RYE FLOUR, MOLASSES, SHORTENING AND SALT. ADD BOILING WATER AND BLEND WELL. COOL TO LUKEWARM. ADD SOFTENED YEAST. GRADUALLY STIR IN WHITE FLOUR TO MAKE SOFT DOUGH. MIX WELL. TURN OUT ON FLOURED BOARD. COVER AND LET RISE 10 MINS. KNEAD UNTIL DOUGH IS SMOOTH AND SATINY, ABOUT 10 MINS. PLACE IN LIGHTLY GREASED BOWL, TURNING ONCE TO GREASE SURFACE. COVER AND LET RISE IN WARM PLACE (80-85 DEGREES) UNTIL ABOUT DOUBLE, APPROXIMATELY 30 MINS. TURN OUT ON LIGHTLY FLOURED SURFACE AND DIVIDE INTO THREE EQUAL PARTS. FORM ROUND LOAVES AND PLACE ON GREASED BAKING SHEET. COVER AND LET RISE UNTIL ALMOST DOUBLE AGAIN, ABOUT 1 HOUR. BRUSH LOAVES WITH SLIGHTLY BEATEN EGG. BAKE IN 350 DEGREE OVEN FOR 35-40 MINS. MAKES 3 LOAVES.

*IF DARKER BREAD IS DESIRED, SUBSTITUTE WHOLE WHEAT FLOUR FOR WHITE.

Yeast Biscuits

1 PACKAGE YEAST
1 CUP WARM BUTTERMILK
2-1/2 CUPS ALL-PURPOSE FLOUR
1/2 TEASP. SODA

4 TBSP. SUGAR
1/2 TEASP. SALT
6 TBSP. OIL

DISSOLVE YEAST IN WARM BUTTERMILK. ADD OTHER INGREDIENTS QUICKLY AND KNEAD ON BOARD. ROLL OUT 1/4-INCH THICK AND CUT. BRUSH WITH OIL OR BUTTER AND PLACE SECOND HALF ON TOP. LET RISE 1-1/2 TO 2 HOURS. BAKE 20 MINS. AT 350 TO 400 DEGREES.

Tomato Bread

1 CAKE COMPRESSED YEAST
2 CUPS LUKEWARM TOMATO JUICE
APPROX. 6 CUPS ALL-PURPOSE FLOUR,
    SIFTED

2 TEASP. SALT
1/4 CUP LUKEWARM WATER
1/4 CUP SUGAR
2 TBSP. MELTED SHORTENING

SOFTEN YEAST IN LUKEWARM WATER; ADD TOMATO JUICE, SUGAR, SALT AND SHORTENING. ADD ENOUGH FLOUR TO MAKE A STIFF DOUGH AND MIX THOROUGHLY. TURN OUT ON LIGHTLY FLOURED BOARD AND KNEAD ABOUT 10 MINS. OR UNTIL SMOOTH AND SATINY. PLACE DOUGH IN A WARM GREASED BOWL; BRUSH SURFACE VERY LIGHTLY WITH MELTED SHORTENING. COVER AND LET RISE IN A WARM PLACE (80 TO 85 DEGREES) ABOUT 2 HOURS OR UNTIL DOUBLED IN BULK. PUNCH DOWN THOROUGHLY. TURN OUT ONTO BOARD AND DIVIDE INTO TWO EQUAL PORTIONS, MOLDED INTO BALLS. LET REST, CLOSELY COVERED, FOR 10 MINS. SHAPE INTO 2 LOAVES. PLACE IN GREASED LOAF PANS (9-1/2x5-1/2). BRUSH TOPS WITH MELTED SHORTENING; COVER AND LET RISE ABOUT 1 HOUR OR UNTIL DOUBLED AGAIN. BAKE IN 375 DEGREE OVEN FOR ABOUT 45 MINS. MAKES 2 1-LB. LOAVES.

Corn Bread

1 CUP YELLOW CORN MEAL
3/4 CUP ALL-PURPOSE FLOUR
3/4 CUP INSTANT NONFAT DRY MILK
2 TEASP. BAKING POWDER
1/2 TEASP. BAKING SODA
1/8 TEASP. SALT

1 CUP WATER
1 LARGE EGG
2 TBSP. HONEY (OPTIONAL)
2 TBSP. LIGHT MOLASSES
3 TBSP. VEGETABLE OIL
1 TEASP. VANILLA

HEAT OVEN TO 400 DEGREES. SPRAY AN 8-INCH SQUARE PAN WITH NONSTICK VEGETABLE SPRAY. IN A MEDIUM-SIZED BOWL, MIX CORN MEAL, FLOUR, DRY MILK, BAKING POWDER, SODA AND SALT. IN A SMALL BOWL, BEAT REMAINING INGREDIENTS. ADD TO FLOUR MIXTURE AND STIR JUST UNTIL BLENDED. POUR INTO PAN. BAKE 20 TO 25 MINS. UNTIL GOLDEN AND TOOTHPICK INSERTED IN CENTER COMES OUT CLEAN. COOL IN PAN ON RACK 10 MINS. CUT INTO SQUARES. MAKES 8 SERVINGS.

CHEDDAR SPOON BREAD

1 CUP YELLOW CORN MEAL	DASH CAYENNE PEPPER
2 CUPS WATER	1 TEASP. SALT
12 OZ. SHARP CHEDDAR CHEESE, SHREDDED	2 TBSP. BUTTER
3 EGGS, SEPARATED (WHITES IN MEDIUM	1 CUP MILK
BOWL, YOLKS IN SMALL)	1 TEASP. BAKING POWDER

PREHEAT OVEN TO 375 DEGREES. COMBINE CORN MEAL AND SALT IN MEDIUM BOWL. MIX WELL. BRING WATER AND BUTTER TO A BOIL IN MEDIUM SAUCEPAN. ADD TO CORN MEAL MIXTURE, STIRRING WITH A WIRE WHISK. ADD CHEESE AND STIR UNTIL MELTED. ADD MILK AND BEAT UNTIL SMOOTH. REMOVE FROM HEAT AND LET COOL. GREASE A 2 QUART CASSEROLE DISH LIGHTLY. BEAT EGG WHITES UNTIL STIFF PEAKS FORM. WHIP EGG YOLKS UNTIL THICK AND LIGHT. FOLD EGG WHITES, YOLKS, CAYENNE PEPPER AND BAKING POWDER INTO CORN MEAL MIXTURE UNTIL COMBINED. DO NOT MIX TOO THOROUGHLY. TURN INTO CASSEROLE DISH. BAKE 55-60 MINS., UNTIL BREAD IS PUFFED AND GOLDEN BROWN. SERVES 8.

INDIAN BEAN BREAD

2 CUPS CORN MEAL	1-1/2 TEASP. SALT
1 TEASP. BAKING POWDER	2 EGGS, SLIGHTLY BEATEN
1-1/2 CUPS MILK	1 TBSP. MELTED BACON DRIPPINGS OR
2 CUPS COOKED, WELL-DRAINED	VEGETABLE SHORTENING
PINTO BEANS	

STIR CORN MEAL, SALT AND BAKING POWDER TOGETHER IN MEDIUM BOWL. COMBINE EGGS, MILK, MELTED DRIPPINGS/SHORTENING. POUR INTO DRY INGREDIENTS AND STIR UNTIL JUST MIXED. FOLD IN PINTO BEANS. SPOON INTO WELL-GREASED 9x9x2 BAKING PAN AND BAKE IN VERY HOT (450 DEGREE) OVEN ABOUT 20 MINS. OR UNTIL BREAD BEGINS TO PULL FROM SIDES OF PAN AND IS LIGHTLY BROWNED ON TOP. COOL BREAD IN PAN FOR 10 MINS., THEN CUT INTO SQUARES AND SERVE. A HEAVY BREAD, HIGH IN PROTEIN. YIELDS 1 LOAF.

BAB'S QUICKIE BISCUITS

2 CUPS BUTTERMILK	2 TBSP. MELTED SHORTENING
ENOUGH SELF-RISING FLOUR TO MAKE STIFF DOUGH	

MIX INGREDIENTS AND TURN DOUGH OUT ON FLOURED BOARD AND ROLL ABOUT ONE-INCH THICK. CUT WITH BISCUIT CUTTER INTO ROUNDS. BAKE AT 450 DEGREES ABOUT 10 MINS. YIELDS ABOUT 12 BISCUITS.

Mexican Corn Bread I

1 CUP SELF-RISING CORN MEAL
1 CUP ALL-PURPOSE FLOUR
1/2 CUP CREAM-STYLE CANNED CORN
1/4 CUP SUGAR
1/4 CUP ONION, CHOPPED

1 CUP LONGHORN CHEESE, GRATED
1/2 CUP VEGETABLE OIL
1 GREEN PEPPER, DICED
1/2 TEASP. RED CAYENNE PEPPER
1 CUP SWEET MILK

COMBINE INGREDIENTS. BAKE IN GREASED IRON SKILLET AT 425 DEGREES FOR 25-30 MINS. OR UNTIL DONE.

Ham Muffins

1-1/2 CUPS FLOUR
1/2 TEASP. SALT
1/2 CUP BRAN
2 EGGS, SLIGHTLY BEATEN
3 TBSP. MELTED SHORTENING

2-1/2 TEASP. BAKING POWDER
1 TBSP. SUGAR
3/4 CUP GROUND COOKED HAM
1 CUP MILK

SIFT FLOUR; MEASURE; ADD BAKING POWDER, SALT AND SUGAR; SIFT AGAIN. ADD BRAN AND HAM, MIX WELL. COMBINE EGGS, MILK AND MELTED SHORTENING (SLIGHTLY COOLED); POUR INTO FLOUR MIXTURE AND STIR JUST TO MOISTEN DRY INGREDIENTS. DO NOT BEAT. FILL GREASED MUFFIN TINS 2/3 FULL AND BAKE IN 400 DEGREE OVEN FOR 20-25 MINS. YIELD: 12-15 MEDIUM-SIZED MUFFINS.

Chewy Flat Bread

3 EGGS, BEATEN UNTIL FLUFFY
ADD:
1 TEASP. SALT
1 TEASP. SUGAR
4 TBSP. OIL
4-1/2 CUPS FLOUR

1 PACKAGE YEAST DISSOLVED IN
  2 TBSP. WARM WATER
3/4 CUP MILK

KNEAD AND LET STAND 20 MINS. PUNCH DOWN AND LET STAND ANOTHER 20 MINS. ROLL OUT AND SPREAD WITH BUTTER. FOLD AND ROLL 1/2-INCH THICK. PRICK WITH FORK. BAKE AT 350 DEGREES FOR 25-30 MINS.

Pan-Fried Bread

MIX UP DESIRED BISCUIT OR CORN BREAD RECIPE. USING A LARGE SPOON, DROP BATTER IN PATTIES INTO A HEATED FRYING PAN WITH 1/4-INCH GREASE OR OIL. LET COOK AND BROWN SLOWLY ON ONE SIDE, THEN TURN AND BROWN.

Oatcakes

8 OZ. OATMEAL

1 TEASP. SALT

2 TEASP. SUGAR

4 TBSP. COLD WATER

4 OZ. FLOUR

2 TEASP. BAKING POWDER

3 OZ. MARGARINE

SIEVE FLOUR, SALT AND BAKING POWDER INTO A BOWL THEN ADD OATMEAL AND SUGAR. MIX IN MARGARINE. MIX WITH WATER TO A FIRM CONSISTENCY. KNEAD LIGHTLY ON A SURFACE SPRINKLED WITH OATMEAL. ROLL OUT 1/4-INCH THICK AND CUT INTO ROUNDS. BAKE 15 MINS. AT 350 DEGREES. COOL ON WIRE RACK. SERVE WITH BUTTER AND CHEESE OR SYRUP.

Mexican Corn Bread II

1 CUP CORN MEAL

1/2 TEASP. SALT

1 CUP CREAM-STYLE CORN

2 EGGS

1 SMALL CAN GREEN CHILI PEPPERS

2/3 CUP BUTTERMILK

1/2 TEASP. SODA

1/3 CUP SHORTENING

1 CUP GRATED SHARP CHEESE

SIFT DRY INGREDIENTS. ADD REMAINING INGREDIENTS AND MIX WELL. POUR INTO HEATED AND OILED PAN. BAKE 20-25 MINS. AT 450 DEGREES.

Delicious with a big pot of beans!

Salt-rising Bread

STARTER:

3 MEDIUM POTATOES

1 TEASP. SUGAR

4 CUPS BOILING WATER

3 TBSP. CORN MEAL

1 TEASP. SALT

DOUGH:

2 CUPS LUKEWARM MILK

1/8 TEASP. SODA

1 CUP WATER

2 TBSP. MELTED SHORTENING

1/8 TEASP. SALT

FLOUR

PARE AND SLICE POTATOES. ADD CORN MEAL, SUGAR, 1 TEASP. SALT AND BOILING WATER. WRAP BOWL IN A HEAVY CLOTH. COVER AND ALLOW TO STAND IN A WARM PLACE OVERNIGHT. IN THE MORNING REMOVE POTATOES. ADD MILK, SODA, SALT AND SHORTENING. ADD SUFFICIENT FLOUR TO MAKE A DOUGH JUST STIFF ENOUGH TO KNEAD. KNEAD UNTIL SMOOTH AND ELASTIC. FORM INTO LOAVES. PLACE IN WELL-OILED PANS. COVER AND LET RISE UNTIL DOUBLE IN BULK. BAKE IN MODERATE OVEN (400 DEGREES) ABOUT 45 MINS. MAKES 3 LOAVES.

CHEESE SCONES

8 OZ. FLOUR
1/2 TEASP. SALT
1 TEASP. SODA
1 TEASP. CREAM OF TARTAR

1-1/2 OZ. MARGARINE
3 OZ. GRATED CHEESE
LARGE PINCH CAYENNE PEPPER
1/4 PINT MILK

SIEVE DRY INGREDIENTS, CUT IN MARGARINE AND ADD CHEESE. MIX WITH MILK UNTIL SOFT, ELASTIC DOUGH FORMS. KNEAD LIGHTLY AND ROLL OUT 1/2-INCH THICK. CUT WITH BISCUIT CUTTER, LAY ON BAKING SHEET AND BRUSH TOP WITH MILK. BAKE 10-12 MINS. IN HOT (425 DEGREE) OVEN. COOL ON WIRE RACK.

SOUTHERN EGG BREAD

2 CUPS WHITE CORN MEAL
1 TEASP. SALT
3 TEASP. BAKING POWDER
1 CUP COLD BOILED RICE

3 EGGS, WELL-BEATEN
1 TBSP. MELTED SHORTENING
1-1/2 CUPS MILK

COMBINE CORN MEAL, SALT AND BAKING POWDER; ADD EGGS, MELTED SHORTENING, MILK AND RICE. BEAT THOROUGHLY, POUR INTO A SHALLOW, WELL-GREASED PAN AND BAKE IN MODERATE OVEN (400 DEGREES) ABOUT 30 MINS. SERVES 6.

ZUCCHINI BREAD*

3 EGGS, BEATEN UNTIL FOAMY
2 CUPS SUGAR
1 TBSP. VANILLA
1/4 TEASP. (GENEROUS) BAKING POWDER
1 TEASP. SALT (OPTIONAL)
1/2 TO 1 CUP RAISINS (OPTIONAL)

1 CUP VEGETABLE OIL
2 CUPS PEELED, GRATED ZUCCHINI
1 TEASP. BAKING SODA
1 TBSP. CINNAMON
1/2 TO 1 CUP CHOPPED NUTS (OPTIONAL)
3 CUPS FLOUR

MIX TOGETHER EGGS AND DRY INGREDIENTS. ADD REMAINING INGREDIENTS, MIXING WELL, BUT DO NOT BEAT. DIVIDE BATTER INTO 2 LARGE, GREASED LOAF PANS. BAKE AT 350 DEGREES APPROXIMATELY 1 HOUR, OR UNTIL CAKE TESTER COMES OUT CLEAN. MAKES 2 LOAVES.

*ZUCCHINI IS THE ONE VEGETABLE EVERYONE CAN RELY ON TO REALLY GROW IN THE GARDEN, AND EVERYONE ALWAYS HAS MORE PRODUCE THAN THEY KNOW WHAT TO DO WITH. THIS BREAD FREEZES WELL AND WHILE YOU ARE SICK OF ZUCCHINI AT HARVEST TIME, IT IS A DELIGHT TO SERVE IN THE MIDDLE OF WINTER.

No-Knead Herb Bread

2 PACKAGES DRY YEAST
2 CUPS WARM WATER (105-115 DEGREES)
1/2 CUP SUGAR
2 TEASP. SALT
2 CUPS WHOLE-WHEAT FLOUR, DIVIDED

4-5 CUPS ALL-PURPOSE FLOUR, DIVIDED
1 EGG
1/4 CUP VEGETABLE OIL
3/4 TEASP. DRIED WHOLE SAGE
3/4 TEASP. DRIED WHOLE BASIL

DISSOLVE YEAST IN WATER. COMBINE YEAST MIXTURE, SUGAR, SALT, 1 CUP WHOLE-WHEAT FLOUR AND 2 CUPS ALL-PURPOSE FLOUR IN A LARGE MIXING BOWL. BEAT WITH ELECTRIC MIXER 2 MINS. ADD EGG, OIL, HERBS AND 1/2 CUP ALL-PURPOSE FLOUR; BEAT ANOTHER 2 MINS. COMBINE REMAINING FLOUR, STIRRING WELL; GRADUALLY STIR INTO BATTER; USING ENOUGH TO FORM A MODERATELY STIFF DOUGH. DIVIDE DOUGH IN HALF; PLACING EACH PORTION IN A GREASED BOWL. TURN ONCE TO GREASE BOTH SIDES. COVER AND LET RISE IN A WARM PLACE (85 DEGREES), FREE FROM DRAFTS, UNTIL DOUBLED IN BULK. PUNCH DOUGH DOWN, AND SHAPE INTO 2 LOAVES. PLACE IN GREASED 9x5x3 LOAF PANS. COVER AND LET RISE UNTIL DOUBLED IN BULK. BAKE AT 375 DEGREES FOR 25-35 MINS. OR UNTIL LOAVES SOUND HOLLOW WHEN TAPPED. YIELD: 2 LOAVES.

Cranberry Bread

1 CUP CRANBERRIES, COARSELY CHOPPED
1 TBSP. GRATED ORANGE RIND
2 TBSP. OIL
HOT WATER
2 CUPS WHOLE WHEAT FLOUR
1/2 TEASP. BAKING SODA

1/2 CUP ORANGE JUICE
1-1/2 TEASP. BAKING POWDER
1/2 TEASP. SALT
1/2 CUP HONEY
1 EGG
1/2 CUP CHOPPED NUTS

TO 1/2 CUP ORANGE JUICE AND 1 TBSP. GRATED ORANGE RIND ADD OIL AND ENOUGH HOT WATER TO MAKE 3/4 CUP LIQUID. ADD SIFTED DRY INGREDIENTS. BLEND IN HONEY AND EGG; FOLD IN CRANBERRIES AND NUTS. BAKE AT 325 DEGREES IN GREASED 9x5x3 LOAF PAN FOR 1 HOUR. COOL IN PAN 15 MINS. AND INVERT ONTO WIRE RACK TO FINISH COOLING. MAKES 1 LOAF. FREEZES WELL.

Lacy Corn Cakes

1-1/3 CUPS YELLOW CORN MEAL
2 EGGS, WELL-BEATEN
4 TBSP. MELTED SHORTENING

1 TEASP. SALT
2 CUPS MILK

COMBINE CORN MEAL AND SALT. COMBINE EGGS, MILK AND MELTED SHORTENING; POUR INTO CORN MEAL AND STIR UNTIL WELL MIXED. BAKE ON A HOT GRIDDLE, STIRRING BATTER EACH TIME BEFORE REMOVING A SPOONFUL. SERVE HOT WITH BUTTER AND SYRUP OR HONEY. MAKES ABOUT 8 SERVINGS (ABOUT 40 THIN CAKES).

BUTTERSCOTCH BREAD

2 CUPS FLOUR
3/4 TEASP. BAKING SODA
1/2 CUP CHOPPED WALNUTS
1 CUP BROWN SUGAR
1 TBSP. MELTED SHORTENING

1-1/4 TEASP. BAKING POWDER
1/4 TEASP. SALT
1 EGG, SLIGHTLY BEATEN
1 CUP SOUR MILK OR BUTTERMILK

SIFT FLOUR; MEASURE; ADD BAKING POWDER, SODA AND SALT. SIFT AGAIN, THEN ADD CHOPPED WALNUTS AND MIX WELL. COMBINE EGG, BROWN SUGAR, SOUR MILK/BUTTERMILK AND MELTED SHORTENING (SLIGHTLY COOLED). POUR INTO FLOUR MIXTURE AND STIR JUST TO MOISTEN DRY INGREDIENTS. **DO NOT BEAT.** TURN INTO GREASED LOAF PAN (9-1/2x5-1/2) AND BAKE IN 350 DEGREE OVEN FOR 45-50 MINS. MAKES 1 LOAF.

SESAME BANANA BREAD

1/4 LB. BUTTER, SOFTENED
1/2 CUP SUGAR
2 EGGS
1/4 CUP MILK
2 CUPS ALL-PURPOSE FLOUR

1/2 TEASP. SALT
3 RIPE BANANAS, MASHED
1 TEASP. VANILLA EXTRACT
1 TEASP. BAKING SODA
1 CUP SESAME SEEDS

PREHEAT OVEN TO 350 DEGREES. CREAM BUTTER AND SUGAR TOGETHER UNTIL FLUFFY. ADD EGGS, ONE AT A TIME. STIR IN BANANAS, MILK AND VANILLA. ADD REMAINING INGREDIENTS AND MIX WELL. POUR INTO OILED 9x5 LOAF PAN. BAKE 50-60 MINS. REMOVE FROM PAN, SLICE AND SERVE HOT OR COOL ON RACK, WRAP AND FREEZE FOR FUTURE USE. MAKES 1 LOAF.

APPLESAUCE MUFFINS

2 STICKS BUTTER, ROOM TEMPERATURE
2 CUPS SUGAR
3 TEASP. VANILLA
2 TEASP. BAKING SODA
2 TEASP. GROUND ALLSPICE

2 CUPS APPLESAUCE
2 EGGS
4 CUPS ALL-PURPOSE FLOUR
1 TBSP. GROUND CINNAMON
1 TEASP. GROUND CLOVES

PREHEAT OVEN TO 350 DEGREES. BUTTER A 12-CUP MUFFIN TIN, OR USE PAPER LINERS. IN A LARGE BOWL, COMBINE BUTTER, SUGAR, EGGS AND VANILLA. IN ANOTHER BOWL, COMBINE FLOUR, BAKING SODA AND SPICES. ADD TO BUTTER MIXTURE AND STIR WELL. ADD APPLESAUCE AND MIX WELL AGAIN. SPOON BATTER INTO MUFFIN TINS. BAKE FOR 20-25 MINS. OR UNTIL CAKE TESTER INSERTED IN MIDDLE COMES OUT CLEAN. REPEAT WITH REMAINING BATTER, AFTER LETTING FIRST BATCH COOL IN MUFFIN TIN PLACED ON CAKE RACK. MAKES 2 DOZEN.

LEMON YOGURT BREAD

3 CUPS ALL-PURPOSE FLOUR
1 TEASP. BAKING SODA
1 CUP FINELY CHOPPED BLANCHED ALMONDS
1-3/4 CUPS SUGAR
1 TBSP. LEMON EXTRACT

1 TEASP. SALT
1/2 TEASP. BAKING POWDER
3 EGGS
1 CUP VEGETABLE OIL
1 PINT LEMON YOGURT

PREHEAT OVEN TO 325 DEGREES. SIFT TOGETHER FLOUR, SALT, BAKING SODA AND BAKING POWDER. STIR IN NUTS AND SET ASIDE. BEAT EGGS IN LARGE MIXING BOWL. ADD OIL AND SUGAR; CREAM WELL. ADD LEMON YOGURT AND EXTRACT. COMBINE WET AND DRY INGREDIENTS; BEAT THOROUGHLY. SPOON BATTER INTO 2 WELL-GREASED 9x5 LOAF PANS OR 1 LARGE BUNDT PAN. BAKE 1 HOUR OR UNTIL TOOTHPICK INSERTED IN CENTER COMES OUT CLEAN. COOL IN PAN 10 MINS. TURN OUT ONTO WIRE RACK AND CONTINUE COOLING. MAKES 2 LOAVES.

SESAME ZUCCHINI BREAD

3 EGGS
1 CUP VEGETABLE OIL
3 TEASP. VANILLA
1 TEASP. SALT
1-1/2 TEASP. BAKING POWDER
1-1/2 CUPS SESAME SEEDS

1 CUP SUGAR
2 CUPS GRATED ZUCCHINI
3 CUPS ALL-PURPOSE FLOUR
1 TEASP. BAKING SODA
3 TEASP. GROUND CINNAMON

PREHEAT OVEN TO 350 DEGREES. BEAT EGGS UNTIL LIGHT AND FOAMY. ADD SUGAR, OIL, ZUCCHINI AND VANILLA. MIX LIGHTLY, THEN BEAT WELL. ADD REMAINING INGREDIENTS AND MIX WELL. DIVIDE BATTER INTO 2 OILED 9x5 LOAF PANS. BAKE 1 HOUR. REMOVE FROM PAN, SLICE AND SERVE HOT OR COOL ON RACK, WRAP AND STORE FOR FUTURE USE. MAKES 2 LOAVES.

BLACK WALNUT BREAD

3 CUPS SIFTED ALL-PURPOSE FLOUR
4-1/2 TEASP. BAKING POWDER
1/2 CUP SUGAR
1 TEASP. SALT

1 CUP CHOPPED BLACK WALNUTS
2 EGGS
1 CUP MILK
1/4 CUP BUTTER, MELTED

PREHEAT OVEN TO 350 DEGREES. SIFT FLOUR, BAKING POWDER, SUGAR AND SALT TOGETHER, THEN STIR IN NUTS. BEAT EGGS, MILK AND MELTED BUTTER. ADD TO FLOUR MIXTURE AND STIR UNTIL THOROUGHLY BLENDED. DON'T WORRY ABOUT LUMPS. SPOON INTO GREASED LOAF PAN AND BAKE IN 350 DEGREE OVEN FOR 1 HOUR. TURN OUT OF PAN AND COOL BEFORE SERVING. MAKES 1 LOAF.

Molasses Sweet Bread

2 CUPS FLOUR
1/2 TEASP. SALT
1-2 TEASP. GROUND GINGER
2 TEASP. BAKING POWDER
1/4 TEASP. SODA
1/2 CUP MELTED BUTTER

1 CUP MOLASSES OR 1/2 CUP MOLASSES
  AND 1/2 CUP SUGAR
3/4 CUP BUTTERMILK
1 EGG
1 TEASP. CINNAMON

SIFT TOGETHER DRY INGREDIENTS AND ADD MELTED BUTTER AND MOLASSES. MIX WELL. ADD BUTTERMILK AND EGG. POUR INTO LOAF PAN AND BAKE AT 350 DEGREES FOR 45-50 MINS.

Oatmeal-Carrot Muffins

1 CUP FLOUR
1/2 TEASP. SALT
2 TEASP. BAKING POWDER
1/2 TEASP. BAKING SODA
1/2 TEASP. CINNAMON
1/2 CUP PACKED BROWN SUGAR

1 CUP MILK
1 EGG, BEATEN
1/4 CUP MELTED BUTTER
1/2 CUP GRATED CARROTS
1-1/2 CUPS QUICK COOKING OATS

MIX FLOUR, BAKING POWDER, SODA, SALT AND CINNAMON. ADD BROWN SUGAR, MILK, EGG AND BUTTER. MIX WITH WIRE WHIP. ADD CARROTS AND OATS; MIX WELL. SPOON INTO GREASED MUFFIN CUPS (ABOUT 2/3 FULL). BAKE AT 375 DEGREES FOR 25 MINS.

**FOR MORE CARROT TASTE, PUT IN 1 CUP GRATED CARROTS AND ONLY 1 CUP OATS.

Mountain Applesauce Bread

1 CUP UNSWEETENED APPLESAUCE
1/2 CUP MELTED BUTTER
1/2 CUP HONEY
2 EGGS
1-1/2 CUPS WHOLE WHEAT FLOUR
1/2 CUP WHEAT GERM OR 1-1/2 CUPS
  ROLLED OATS
1 TEASP. VANILLA

1 TEASP. BAKING SODA
1 TEASP. BAKING POWDER
1/2 TO 1 TEASP. CINNAMON
1/4 TO 1/2 TEASP. NUTMEG
1/2 TO 1 CUP RAISINS
1/2 CUP NUTS
1/2 TEASP. SALT

BEAT TOGETHER BUTTER AND HONEY. ADD EGGS AND MIX WELL. ADD VANILLA AND APPLESAUCE. COMBINE DRY INGREDIENTS, RAISINS AND NUTS. ADD TO LIQUID. BAKE AT 350 DEGREES IN GREASED 9x5x3 LOAF PAN FOR 55-60 MINS. ALLOW TO COOL IN PAN 30-45 MINS. WRAP AND STORE OVERNIGHT BEFORE SLICING. FREEZES WELL.

BLUEBERRY MUFFINS

1-1/2 CUPS SIFTED ALL-PURPOSE FLOUR
1-1/2 TEASP. BAKING POWDER
1/4 TEASP. SALT
5 TBSP. SOFTENED BUTTER

1/2 CUP SUGAR
1 EGG
1/2 CUP MILK
1 CUP FRESH BLUEBERRIES

PREHEAT OVEN TO 400 DEGREES. SIFT TOGETHER FLOUR, BAKING POWDER AND SALT. SET ASIDE. CREAM BUTTER, ADD SUGAR A LITTLE AT A TIME UNTIL MIXTURE IS SMOOTH AND FLUFFY. BEAT EGG VIGOROUSLY. THEN STIR IN FLOUR COMBINATION AND MILK, ALTERNATING THEM AND BEGINNING AND ENDING WITH FLOUR. FOLD IN BLUEBERRIES AND SPOON INTO WELL-GREASED MUFFIN TIN. BAKE FOR 25-30 MINS. YIELD: 12 MUFFINS.

ZUCCHINI-PINEAPPLE BREAD

3 EGGS
2 CUPS SUGAR
1 CUP OIL
2 CUPS GRATED ZUCCHINI
3 CUPS FLOUR
1 TEASP. EACH OF BAKING POWDER,
    SODA AND SALT

3 TEASP. CINNAMON
1 8-OZ. CAN CRUSHED PINEAPPLE,
    DRAINED
1 CUP CHOPPED WALNUTS OR PECANS
3 TEASP. VANILLA
1/2 CUP RAISINS

BEAT EGGS UNTIL FLUFFY. ADD SUGAR, OIL, VANILLA AND ZUCCHINI AND MIX WELL. BLEND IN PINEAPPLE, WALNUTS AND RAISINS. POUR INTO 2 GREASED AND FLOURED LOAF PANS. BAKE AT 325 DEGREES ABOUT 55 MINS.

PUMPKIN CORN BREAD

2 TEASP. OIL/MELTED BUTTER
2 EGGS
1 CUP COOKED, MASHED PUMPKIN
2 TEASP. BAKING POWDER
2/3 CUP DRY MILK

1/3 CUP HONEY
2 TEASP. VANILLA
1/4 CUP CORN MEAL
1/2 TEASP. SALT

MIX OIL, HONEY, EGGS AND VANILLA. STIR IN PUMPKIN. COMBINE CORN MEAL, BAKING POWDER, SALT AND DRY MILK. MIX INTO LIQUIDS. BAKE AT 350 DEGREES IN GREASED 9x5x3 LOAF PAN FOR 40 MINS. COOL IN PAN 15 MINS. INVERT ONTO WIRE RACK TO FINISH COOLING. YIELD: 1 LOAF.

Boston Brown Loaf

2-1/2 cups whole wheat flour
1 teasp. salt
1/2 cup dark molasses
1/2 cup chopped nuts

2 teasp. baking soda
2 cups buttermilk
1 cup raisins

Mix dry ingredients, add raisins and nuts. Combine buttermilk and molasses and stir into mixture until just moist. Spoon into a 9x5x3 loaf pan or 4 (1-1/2) cup loaf pans. Bake at 350 degrees for 40-50 mins., or until knife comes out clean. Remove from pan and cool on wire rack. Makes 1 large loaf or 4 small loaves.

Oatmeal and Black Walnut Pancakes

1-1/2 cups uncooked rolled oats
2 tbsp. brown sugar
3 teasp. baking powder
1-1/2 cups milk
2 tbsp. butter, melted

1 cup all-purpose flour
1/4 teasp. salt
1/2 cup chopped black walnuts or
    pecans
2 eggs

Combine oats, flour, brown sugar, salt, baking powder and black walnuts (pecans). Set aside. Whish together milk, eggs and melted butter. Pour over dry ingredients and mix until just combined. Spoon by quarter cupfuls onto heated, lightly oiled griddle. Cook until bubbles form on the surface and edges become dry. Flip over and cook until golden brown. Serve with orange sauce. Makes 16 (4-inch) pancakes.

Orange Sauce

3/4 cup brown sugar
1/2 cup fresh orange juice

4 tbsp. butter
1 tbsp. grated orange rind

Combine ingredients in saucepan and simmer 5 mins., stirring constantly. Cool slightly and serve over cakes.

Muffins

1 English muffin
8 eggs
2 tbsp. milk

1 cup grated Cheddar cheese
1-1/4 cups diced ham

Preheat oven to 350 degrees. Render English muffin into very fine crumbs. Beat eggs with fork. Add milk, breadcrumbs, cheese and ham. Mix thoroughly. Spoon mixture into greased muffin tins (3/4 full) and bake until plump and firm, about 20-25 mins. Makes 10-12.

THE FOLLOWING TWO RECIPES ARE FROM A LADY NAMED ELIZABETH CADE, WHO WAS ONCE THE COOK AT WEST VIRGINIA'S 'FIRST' COUNTRY INN, "FARAWAY HILLS" AT BEVERLY, W.VA. THE INN IS NO LONGER IN OPERATION, BUT ANYONE WHO EVER STAYED THERE WILL REMEMBER THE WONDERFUL FOOD.

ORANGE BREAD

2 CUPS FLOUR	1 TEASP. BAKING SODA
1 TEASP. BAKING POWDER	2 TBSP. BUTTER
1/2 TEASP. SALT	2 TBSP. ORANGE RIND
2 TEASP. VANILLA	1 EGG
1/2 CUP ORANGE JUICE	1 CUP SUGAR
1/2 CUP BOILING WATER	

MEASURE DRY INGREDIENTS. MELT BUTTER IN BOILING WATER, BLEND IN ORANGE RIND, ORANGE JUICE, SUGAR, VANILLA AND EGG. MIX WITH DRY INGREDIENTS. POUR INTO LARGE LOAF PAN AND BAKE AT 325-350 DEGREES FOR ABOUT AN HOUR. SLICE THIN AND SERVE WITH CREAM CHEESE THAT HAS BEEN SOFTENED WITH ORANGE JUICE. ONE LOAF.

CARROT CAKE

4 EGGS	2 CUPS SUGAR
2 CUPS SELF-RISING FLOUR	1 TEASP. CINNAMON
1 CUP VEGETABLE OIL	1 BUNCH CARROTS (4-5) GRATED OR
1 CUP NUTS (BLACK WALNUTS ARE GOOD)	GROUND CARROTS
OR 1/2 CUP NUTS AND 1/2 CUP RAISINS	1 TEASP. VANILLA

BEAT EGGS, ADD SUGAR AND BEAT WELL. SIFT FLOUR AND CINNAMON AND ADD ALTERNATELY WITH OIL TO EGG MIXTURE. ADD VANILLA, CARROTS AND NUTS. POUR INTO GREASED AND FLOURED ANGEL FOOD CAKE PAN, AND BAKE 350 DEGREES FOR 1 HOUR 15 MINS.

GLAZE

MIX 1 CUP SUGAR AND 1/2 CUP BUTTERMILK. BRING TO A BOIL. BOIL FOR 1 MIN., REMOVE FROM HEAT. ADD 1 TEASP. VANILLA AND 1/2 TEASP. BAKING SODA, MIX WELL. POUR ON CAKE WHILE STILL WARM.

PUMPKIN BREAD

2-1/2 CUPS PLUS 4 TBSP. FLOUR
3 CUPS SUGAR
2 TEASP. SODA
2 TEASP. CINNAMON
1-1/2 TEASP. NUTMEG
1-1/2 TEASP. SALT

2 CUPS CANNED PUMPKIN
4 EGGS
1 CUP WESSON OIL
1/2 CUP WATER PLUS 3 TBSP.
1/2 CUP BROKEN PECANS (OPTIONAL)

MIX FIRST 6 INGREDIENTS. MAKE A WELL AND ADD PUMPKIN, EGGS, OIL, WATER AND NUTS. MIX AND BAKE 1 HOUR AT 350 DEGREES OR UNTIL DONE. ONE LOAF.

BISHOP BREAD

3 EGGS, WELL-BEATEN
1 CUP SUGAR
1 CUP WALNUT HALVES
1 CUP WHOLE BRAZIL NUTS
1-1/2 CUPS SIFTED FLOUR

1-1/2 TEASP. BAKING POWDER
1 CUP WHOLE DATES
1 CUP WHOLE MARASCHINO CHERRIES
2/3 TO 1 CUP CHOCOLATE CHIPS OR
    HERSHEY'S KISSES

BEAT EGGS AND SUGAR TOGETHER. ADD FLOUR AND BAKING POWDER. FOLD IN REMAINING INGREDIENTS. GREASE AND FLOUR LOAF PAN. BAKE AT 325 DEGREES FOR 1 HOUR 15 MINS. TO 1 HOUR 25 MINS. ONE LOAF.

BUCKWHEAT CAKES

3/4 CUP BUCKWHEAT FLOUR
3/4 CUP SIFTED UNBLEACHED WHITE FLOUR
2-1/4 TEASP. BAKING POWDER
3 TBSP. GRANULATED SUGAR
3/4 TEASP. SALT

1 CUP MILK OR 1/2 CUP EVAPORATED
    MILK AND 1/2 CUP WATER
1 EGG, BEATEN
3 TBSP. MELTED SHORTENING

COMBINE ALL DRY INGREDIENTS. ADD THE MILK, EGGS AND MELTED SHORTENING, AND STIR UNTIL SMOOTH. DROP ON A HOT GRIDDLE AND BROWN ON BOTH SIDES. MAKES ABOUT 1 DOZEN CAKES.

OATMEAL PANCAKES

1/2 CUP WHOLE WHEAT FLOUR
1-1/2 CUPS ROLLED OATS
1 TBSP. BAKING POWDER
1 TEASP. SALT

1 EGG, BEATEN
1 TBSP. OIL
1 TBSP. HONEY
1-1/2 CUPS MILK

POUR ALL INGREDIENTS INTO A BLENDER AND MIX WELL. POUR ONTO HOT GRIDDLE FOR PANCAKES OR ONTO AN IRON FOR WAFFLES. SERVES 4.

Rhubarb Bread

2 CUPS FINELY DICED RHUBARB
2/3 CUP OIL
1-1/2 CUPS BROWN SUGAR, PACKED
1 EGG
1 TEASP. VANILLA

2-1/2 CUPS WHOLE WHEAT FLOUR
1 TEASP. BAKING SODA
1 TEASP. SALT
1/2 CUP CHOPPED NUTS
1 CUP BUTTERMILK

MIX TOGETHER OIL, BROWN SUGAR, EGG, VANILLA AND BUTTERMILK. ADD SIFTED DRY INGREDIENTS. FOLD IN RHUBARB AND NUTS. POUR INTO TWO GREASED 9x5x3 LOAF PANS. BAKE AT 350 DEGREES FOR 60 MINS. STORE IN REFRIGERATOR. TWO LOAVES.

Blueberry-Rice Pancakes

2 CUPS FRESH BLUEBERRIES
1/4 CUP SUGAR
2 CUPS DAIRY SOUR CREAM
2 TBSP. BAKING SODA
2 EGGS, WELL-BEATEN

1 CUP SIFTED ALL-PURPOSE FLOUR
1 CUP COOKED RICE
1 TEASP. SALT
2 TBSP. MELTED BUTTER

RINSE BLUEBERRIES IN A COLANDER AND SPREAD ON ABSORBENT PAPER TO DRY. PLACE IN A BOWL WITH SUGAR AND SET ASIDE. COMBINE SOUR CREAM AND BAKING SODA; STIR INTO EGGS. ADD FLOUR, RICE, SALT AND MELTED BUTTER. FOLD IN BLUEBERRIES. BAKE ON BOTH SIDES ON A HOT GRIDDLE. MAKES THICK GRIDDLE CAKES. 1 DOZEN CAKES.

Vegetable Pizza

2 PACKAGES CRESCENT ROLLS
2 PACKAGES CREAM CHEESE
1 CUP MAYONNAISE
1 TEASP. SEASONING SALT
1/2 TEASP. GARLIC SALT

1/4 TEASP. CURRY POWDER
1/4 CUP RED SWEET PEPPERS
1/4 CUP BROCCOLI
1/4 CUP CAULIFLOWER
1/2 CUP SLICED GREEN OLIVES

ROLL CRESCENT ROLL DOUGH OUT ONTO PIZZA PAN. BAKE AS DIRECTED. COOL. MIX CREAM CHEESE, MAYONNAISE, SEASONING SALT, GARLIC SALT AND CURRY POWDER UNTIL CREAMY. SPREAD OVER COOLED PASTRY. DICE PEPPERS, BROCCOLI, CAULIFLOWER AND SLICED OLIVES AND SPRINKLE OVER TOP. CUT INTO DESIRED PIECES (SMALL IS BEST). MAKES DELICIOUS SNACKS OR PARTY HORS D'OEUVRES.

Cornmeal Batter Cakes

1 cup white cornmeal, sifted
1/2 teasp. sugar
1/4 teasp. salt
2 teasp. baking powder

1 egg, beaten
1 cup milk
2 tbsp. salad oil
1-2 teasp. white flour

Sift together cornmeal, sugar, salt and baking powder. Beat egg until light and combine with milk and salad oil. Mix all together and sift in a very small amount of white flour (1-2 teasp.). Fry on lightly greased hot griddle.

Oyster Stuffing

6 cups soft breadcrumbs
2/3 cup butter
2 medium onions, chopped
2 teasp. salt
2 cups drained, chopped oysters

1/2 teasp. pepper
2 teasp. poultry seasoning
grated rind of one lemon
2 tbsp. chopped parsley
1 cup chopped celery

Melt butter, add onions and cook gently until soft. Add to rest of ingredients and mix well. Use as stuffing for turkey. For chicken stuffing, reduce all ingredients by half.

Johnny Cakes

2 cups sour milk (or sour cream)
2 eggs, well-beaten
1 teasp. sugar (optional)
1 teasp. salt

1 tbsp. melted butter
1 rounded teasp. soda
1-2 cups cornmeal

Sift soda with one cup cornmeal; mix with salt and sugar. Mix eggs with sour milk (cream); then mix in dry ingredients, adding more cornmeal to make a batter as for a layer cake. Stir in melted butter. Fry on hot greased griddle or turn into greased drippings pan and bake 25-30 mins. at 425 degrees.

120

$\mathcal{D}ESSERTS$

Almost every settler crossing the mountains into West Virginia brought at least one cow, and a few chickens, so milk, butter and eggs were usually plentiful. Add some stone ground flour, rendered lard, honey, molasses or maple syrup, potash or soda and voilà: a cake.

But for family eating - puddings were a favorite. Pioneers had plenty of milk products, eggs, berries and fruit and this type of dessert was nutritious and filling. Or these same fruits and berries were baked into delicious pies which were not as time-consuming as cake baking...remember, the first egg beater wasn't patented until 1870.

Cakes

Cookies

Custards

Doughnuts

Frostings

Pies

Puddings

Butterscotch Pie

1 (9-inch) unbaked pie shell
2 tbsp. butter
1 cup packed brown sugar
4 eggs, separated
1/2 teasp. vanilla extract

1 tbsp. all-purpose flour
1-1/2 cups milk
1/4 cup plus 2 tbsp. granulated
  sugar

Preheat oven to 375 degrees. In a saucepan, cook the butter until browned. Add the flour, brown sugar, milk and beaten egg yolks. Mix well. Cook until thick over low heat. Pour into pie shell. Bake until crust is browned and filling is set, 20-25 mins.

Meringue Topping: Beat egg whites until stiff. Gradually fold in granulated sugar and vanilla. Smooth meringue over top of pie, slightly overlapping edges of pie crust. Bake about 5 mins. to brown.

Cottage Cheese Pie

1-1/2 cups cottage cheese
1/2 cup sugar
2 eggs, separated
1/4 teasp. cinnamon
1 (9-inch) pie shell

1/2 tbsp. flour
1/4 teasp. salt
2 cups milk
1/2 teasp. lemon rind, grated
  (optional)

Combine cottage cheese, sugar, flour, salt, lemon rind and cinnamon. Add beaten egg yolks and mix thoroughly. Add milk gradually and stir until smooth. Fold in beaten egg whites and pour into pie shell. Bake at 350 degrees, about 1 hour.

Oatmeal Pie

1/4 cup butter
1/2 cup sugar
1 cup oatmeal
3 eggs
1/2 teasp. cinnamon

1/4 cup chopped walnuts
1/4 teasp. salt
1 cup dark corn syrup
1/2 teasp. vanilla
1 unbaked (9-inch) pie shell

Cream together butter and sugar. Add cinnamon and salt. Stir in syrup and vanilla. Add eggs, one at a time, stirring after each addition, until blended. Stir in oatmeal and walnuts. Pour into unbaked pie shell and bake in 350 degree oven for about an hour or until knife inserted in center comes out clean. Oatmeal forms nutty, chewy crust on top of pie.

CUSTARD PIE

4 EGGS	2-1/2 CUPS WHOLE MILK
1/2 CUP SUGAR	1 TEASP. VANILLA
1/2 TEASP. SALT	1 UNBAKED (9-INCH) PIE SHELL

MIX ALL INGREDIENTS AND POUR INTO PIE SHELL. SPRINKLE NUTMEG OVER TOP. BAKE ABOUT 10 MINS. AT 450 DEGREES, REDUCE HEAT TO 325 DEGREES FOR ABOUT 30 MINS. OR UNTIL SET. DRAINED FRUIT MAY BE ADDED OR COCONUT SPRINKLED OVER TOP.

VIRGINIA HAM AND APPLE PIE

3 TBSP. ALL-PURPOSE FLOUR	3/4 CUP FIRMLY PACKED BROWN SUGAR
1/2 TEASP. GROUND CINNAMON	1/2 TEASP. MACE
FEW GRINDS FRESH BLACK PEPPER	5 MEDIUM APPLES, PEELED, CORED
1-1/2 CUPS DICED COOKED HAM	AND SLICED

PIE CRUST: (FAVORITE RECIPE OR)	
1 CUP ALL-PURPOSE FLOUR	1/4 TEASP. SALT
4 TBSP. BUTTER, CUT INTO SMALL CHUNKS	3 TBSP. COLD WATER

6 SLICES EDAM CHEESE

PREHEAT OVEN TO 350 DEGREES. COMBINE FLOUR, BROWN SUGAR, CINNAMON, MACE AND BLACK PEPPER. SET ASIDE. GREASE 7x10 BAKING DISH. LAYER A THIRD OF APPLES WITH HALF OF THE HAM IN BOTTOM OF DISH. SPRINKLE WITH HALF THE SEASONINGS. LAYER ANOTHER THIRD OF APPLES AND REMAINING HAM AND SEASONINGS. TOP WITH REMAINING APPLES. SET ASIDE.

TO MAKE PIE CRUST: COMBINE FLOUR AND SALT. CUT IN BUTTER WITH PASTRY BLENDER. ADD WATER, A LITTLE AT A TIME, TO FORM DOUGH INTO A BALL. ROLL OUT ON FLOURED BOARD TO 7-1/2x10-1/2 RECTANGLE.

COVER APPLES WITH PIE CRUST DOUGH, SEALING EDGES. BAKE FOR 1 HOUR. REMOVE FROM OVEN AND CUT INTO SIX SQUARES. TOP EACH WITH THIN SLICE OF EDAM CHEESE. RETURN TO OVEN UNTIL CHEESE IS MELTED AND SERVE IMMEDIATELY. SERVES 6.

LEMON CHESS PIE

1 STICK BUTTER, SOFTENED	1 TBSP. LEMON EXTRACT
2-1/2 CUPS SUGAR	2 CUPS MILK
8 TEASP. FLOUR	2 TBSP. VINEGAR
4 EGGS	1 UNBAKED (9-INCH) PIE SHELL

CREAM BUTTER AND SUGAR IN BOWL. MIX IN FLOUR, EGGS, FLAVORING, MILK AND VINEGAR. POUR INTO PIE SHELL AND BAKE AT 350 DEGREES FOR 1 HOUR. SERVES 6.

Old-Fashioned Chess, Custard, Vinegar Pie
(Favorite of Confederate President Jefferson Davis)

1/4 lb. (1 stick) butter, room temp.
1-1/2 cups sugar
3 eggs

2 tbsp. cider vinegar
1 (8-inch) unbaked pie crust

Preheat oven to 375 degrees. Cream butter and sugar together until light and fluffy. Add eggs one at a time, beating well after each addition. Turn into pie shell. Bake for about one hour, or until set. Let cool before serving.

For crisper crust: brush about 1 teasp. of unbeaten egg white over bottom and sides of shell before adding filling. Since this is a very thin filling, you may want to place pie shell in oven and then fill.

Peanut Butter Pie

1 cup sugar
3 eggs, slightly beaten
1/3 cup salted, blanched peanuts, chopped (optional)

1/2 teasp. vanilla
1 cup dark corn syrup
1/2 cup crunchy peanut butter

Combine sugar, corn syrup and eggs; mix well. Add peanut butter, peanuts and vanilla; mixing until well blended. Pour filling into pastry-lined pie pan. Bake at 400 degrees for 15 mins., reduce heat to 350 degrees and bake 45 mins. longer or until set. Top with chopped peanuts, if desired.

Fried Fruit Pies

1 (8-oz.) package dried fruit (apples, peaches, apricots or mixed)
2 cups water
1/2 cup sugar or to taste

Pie crust, enough for two 9-inch pies
Shortening or oil for deep frying

In heavy saucepan, combine fruit and water. Simmer, covered over low heat for 20 mins. Add sugar and continue cooking for 10-15 mins. Mash fruit to thick consistency. If fruit is still too moist, cook a bit longer. Cool. Roll out pastry to 1/8-inch thickness. Cut into 4 to 4-1/2 inch rounds. Place about 1 tbsp. fruit into center. Wet edges with water and fold over to completely enclose filling, making half-moon shapes. Seal edges by pressing with fork. Heat shortening in deep fryer to 375 degrees and fry a few pies at a time for about 3-4 mins. on each side, until golden. Drain on paper towels and serve hot or cold. Makes about 1 dozen 4-1/2 inch pies.

BLACK WALNUT PIE

1 9-INCH PIE SHELL
2/3 CUP SUGAR
1/3 CUP BUTTER, MELTED
1/2 TEASP. SALT

1 CUP DARK CORN SYRUP
3 EGGS
1 CUP BLACK WALNUTS

BEAT TOGETHER SUGAR, BUTTER, SALT, CORN SYRUP AND EGGS. MIX IN BLACK WALNUTS.
POUR INTO 9-INCH UNBAKED PIE SHELL. SET OVEN BETWEEN 350-375 DEGREES. BAKE UNTIL
SET AND PASTRY IS NICELY BROWNED, ABOUT 50 MINS. COOL. SERVE COLD OR SLIGHTLY
WARM.

CARROT PIE

2 CUPS CHOPPED, COOKED CARROTS
2 EGGS
1 CUP EVAPORATED MILK
3/4 CUP SUGAR
2/3 TEASP. LEMON JUICE

1/2 TEASP. SALT
1/2 TEASP. NUTMEG
1 TEASP. **EACH** CINNAMON AND GINGER
1/8 TEASP. GROUND CLOVES
1 UNBAKED (9-INCH) PIE SHELL

COMBINE FIRST 6 INGREDIENTS IN BLENDER CONTAINER, ADD SPICES AND PROCESS UNTIL
SMOOTH. POUR INTO PIE SHELL AND BAKE AT 400 DEGREES FOR 40-45 MINS. OR UNTIL SET.
SERVES 6. *MARY HUDKINS, HARRISON COUNTY, WV.*

STRAWBERRY CRUMB PIE

3 PINTS FRESH STRAWBERRIES,
  CLEANED AND HALVED
3/4 CUP SUGAR
1/4 CUP CORNSTARCH
1-1/3 CUPS SIFTED ALL-PURPOSE FLOUR
1/2 TEASP. GROUND CINNAMON

1/2 TEASP. SALT
1/2 CUP SHORTENING
1/4 CUP FIRMLY PACKED LIGHT BROWN
  SUGAR
CREAM (OPTIONAL)

PREHEAT OVEN TO 400 DEGREES. COMBINE STRAWBERRIES WITH SUGAR AND CORN-
STARCH. SET ASIDE. COMBINE FLOUR AND SALT IN A BOWL. CUT IN SHORTENING UNTIL
COARSE. SET ASIDE 2/3 CUP OF MIXTURE. SPRINKLE 2-3 TBSP. WATER OVER REMAINDER AND
TOSS WITH A FORK UNTIL MIXED AND STICKING TOGETHER. PRESS WITH HANDS INTO A BALL.
ROLL OUT ON LIGHTLY FLOURED BOARD INTO A CIRCLE 1/2-INCH LARGER THAN INVERTED
9-INCH PIE PLATE. FIT DOUGH CAREFULLY INTO PLATE. TURN UNDER EDGES TO MAKE
DOUBLE THICKNESS AROUND EDGE AND FLUTE SO EDGE IS HIGH. FILL WITH BERRY
MIXTURE. COMBINE RESERVED FLOUR MIXTURE, BROWN SUGAR AND CINNAMON; BLEND
WELL. SPRINKLE OVER STRAWBERRIES. PLACE IN OVEN ON A SHEET OF ALUMINUM FOIL.
BAKE 45 MINS. OR UNTIL CRUST IS BROWNED. SERVE WARM OR COLD WITH CREAM, IF
DESIRED. ONE 9-INCH PIE.

Rhubarb Pie

1 CUP SUGAR
1/2 TEASP. CINNAMON
1/4 TEASP. NUTMEG
SMALL HUNK BUTTER

4 CUPS RHUBARB, CUT INTO SMALL
PIECES
1 TBSP. FLOUR

MIX ALL INGREDIENTS. BAKE IN A DOUBLE PIE SHELL IN MODERATE OVEN (350-375 DEGREES) ABOUT 1 HOUR.

Brown Sugar Pie

PREHEAT OVEN TO ABOUT 375 DEGREES. CREAM 1/2 CUP BUTTER AND 1-1/2 CUPS BROWN SUGAR. ADD YOLKS OF 2 EGGS AND BEAT UNTIL FLUFFY. ADD 5 TBSP. COGNAC. BEAT 3 EGG WHITES UNTIL STIFF, BUT NOT DRY. FOLD INTO SUGAR MIXTURE AND TURN AT ONCE INTO UNBAKED PIE SHELL. BAKE ON LOWER SHELF OF OVEN FOR ABOUT 45 MINS. COOL. SERVES 6 OR 8.

Blender Pumpkin Pie

4 EGGS
3/4 CUP SUGAR
1/2 CUP FLOUR
1 STICK MARGARINE, SOFTENED

1 CUP EVAPORATED MILK
1 CUP MILK
1 CUP COOKED PUMPKIN
1 TEASP. NUTMEG

MIX ALL INGREDIENTS TOGETHER IN BLENDER. POUR INTO 2 GREASED PIE PANS AND BAKE ABOUT 1 HOUR AT 350 DEGREES. MAKES ITS OWN CRUST AS IT BAKES!

Old-Fashioned Vinegar Pie

1 BAKED PIE SHELL
1 CUP ALL-PURPOSE FLOUR
1/4 CUP COLD WATER

1 CUP SUGAR
3/4 CUP CIDER VINEGAR

MIX SUGAR AND FLOUR TOGETHER TO PREVENT LUMPING, THEN ADD VINEGAR AND WATER TO MAKE BATTER. BRING 3 CUPS OF WATER TO A GOOD BOIL AND STIR IN YOUR BATTER. STIR CONSTANTLY TO PREVENT STICKING AND BURNING. COOK UNTIL THOROUGHLY DONE. COOL SLIGHTLY AND PUT IN BAKED PIE SHELL. EAT WITH CREAM OR PLAIN.

SHOO FLY PIE

3 UNBAKED 9-INCH PIE SHELLS
1 CUP MOLASSES
1 CUP BOILING WATER
1 TEASP. SODA

4 CUPS UNSIFTED FLOUR
1 CUP BROWN SUGAR
3/4 CUP LARD OR VEGETABLE
   SHORTENING

MIX 1 CUP MOLASSES AND 1 CUP BOILING WATER, SLIGHTLY COOLED, TO WHICH 1 TEASP. SODA HAS BEEN ADDED. MIX 4 CUPS UNSIFTED FLOUR, 1 CUP BROWN SUGAR AND 3/4 CUP SHORTENING UNTIL NICE AND CRUMBLY. POUR MOLASSES MIXTURE INTO UNBAKED CRUSTS AND PUT CRUMBLY MIXTURE ON TOP. BAKE ABOUT 25 MINS. AT 350 DEGREES. THIS MAKES 3 PIES.

SPICY OATMEAL COOKIES

1 CUP BUTTER, SOFTENED
1 CUP PACKED BROWN SUGAR
1/2 CUP GRANULATED SUGAR
2 EGGS
1 TEASP. BAKING SODA
1/2 TEASP. SALT

1-1/2 CUPS ALL-PURPOSE FLOUR
1 TEASP. GROUND CINNAMON
3/4 TEASP. EACH, GROUND CLOVES AND
   GROUND GINGER
3 CUPS ROLLED OATS, QUICK OR
   OLD-FASHIONED

PREHEAT OVEN TO 350 DEGREES. IN LARGE BOWL BEAT BUTTER, BROWN SUGAR, GRANULATED SUGAR AND EGGS UNTIL LIGHT AND FLUFFY. MIX IN REMAINING INGREDIENTS. SHAPE DOUGH INTO BALLS THE SIZE OF WALNUTS; PLACE 2-INCHES APART ON UNGREASED BAKING SHEETS. WITH A GLASS DIPPED IN WATER, PRESS COOKIES TO 1/4-INCH THICK. BAKE 8-10 MINS. OR UNTIL GOLDEN AND CRISP. COOL ON RACK. MAKES ABOUT 60 COOKIES.

MOLASSES APPLESAUCE COOKIES

2 CUPS SIFTED ALL-PURPOSE FLOUR
1 TEASP. BAKING SODA
1 TEASP. SALT
2 TEASP. CINNAMON
1/2 TEASP. GROUND CLOVES
1/2 CUP SHORTENING

1/2 CUP SUGAR
1/2 CUP MOLASSES
1 EGG
1 CUP APPLESAUCE
1/2 CUP CHOPPED RAISINS
1/2 CUP CHOPPED NUTS

PREHEAT OVEN TO 350 DEGREES. SIFT TOGETHER FLOUR, BAKING SODA, SALT, CINNAMON AND CLOVES. CREAM TOGETHER SHORTENING, SUGAR AND MOLASSES. BEAT IN EGG. BLEND IN DRY INGREDIENTS AND APPLESAUCE. STIR IN RAISINS AND NUTS. DROP BY TEASPOONSFUL ONTO LIGHTLY GREASED BAKING SHEET. BAKE 10-12 MINS., OR UNTIL LIGHTLY BROWN. REMOVE AND COOL ON WIRE RACKS. APPROX. 7-1/2 DOZEN.

LEMON CHEESE BARS

1 YELLOW CAKE MIX
1 (8 OZ.) PACKAGE CREAM CHEESE, SOFTENED
1/3 CUP SUGAR
1/3 CUP OIL

1 TEASP. LEMON JUICE OR 1/2 TEASP.
   LEMON FLAVORING
2 EGGS

MIX DRY CAKE MIX, EGGS AND OIL UNTIL CRUMBLY. RESERVE 1 CUP OF MIXTURE. PAT REMAINING MIXTURE LIGHTLY IN UNGREASED 13x9 PAN. BAKE 15 MINS. AT 350 DEGREES. BEAT CREAM CHEESE, SUGAR AND LEMON JUICE UNTIL LIGHT AND FLUFFY. SPREAD OVER BAKED LAYER, SPRINKLING RESERVED CRUMB MIXTURE OVER TOP. RETURN TO OVEN AND BAKE 15 MINS. COOL AND CUT INTO BARS.

GINGER COOKIES

2/3 CUP BUTTER
1/2 CUP SUGAR
1 EGG
1 CUP LIGHT MOLASSES

1 TBSP. CIDER VINEGAR
4-1/2 CUPS SIFTED ALL-PURPOSE FLOUR
1 TBSP. GROUND GINGER
1 TBSP. BAKING SODA

PREHEAT OVEN TO 350 DEGREES. CREAM TOGETHER BUTTER AND SUGAR UNTIL LIGHT AND FLUFFY. BEAT THE EGG INTO MIXTURE AND BLEND WELL. STIR IN MOLASSES, VINEGAR AND 2 TBSP. COLD WATER. SIFT TOGETHER FLOUR, GINGER AND BAKING SODA. ADD GRADU-ALLY TO BUTTER MIXTURE, STIRRING TO MAKE STIFF DOUGH. CHILL THOROUGHLY, ABOUT 1 HOUR. ROLL DOUGH OUT, A LITTLE AT A TIME, ON A LIGHTLY FLOURED BOARD; THICK OR THIN, AS DESIRED. CUT INTO DESIRED SHAPES AND PLACE ON LIGHTLY GREASED BAKING SHEETS. BAKE 12-14 MINS. OR UNTIL LIGHTLY BROWNED AND SET. LOOSEN IMMEDIATELY AND COOL ON RACKS. THICK COOKIES MAY BE SPRINKLED WITH CONFECTIONERS SUGAR. APPROX. 6 DOZEN.

SOFT MOLASSES COOKIES

1/4 CUP SHORTENING
1 EGG, BEATEN
1-1/2 CUPS ALL-PURPOSE FLOUR
1/4 TEASP. SODA
1/2 TEASP. GROUND CINNAMON
1/4 CUP BUTTERMILK

1/4 CUP GRANULATED SUGAR
1/2 CUP MOLASSES
1-1/2 TEASP. BAKING POWDER
1/4 TEASP. SALT
1/4 TEASP. GROUND CLOVES
1/2 CUP RAISINS

CREAM SHORTENING AND SUGAR UNTIL LIGHT AND FLUFFY; ADD EGG AND MIX WELL. STIR IN MOLASSES. COMBINE DRY INGREDIENTS. ADD TO CREAMED MIXTURE ALTERNATELY WITH BUTTERMILK, MIXING WELL AFTER EACH ADDITION. STIR IN RAISINS. DROP DOUGH BY TEASPOONSFUL ONTO LIGHTLY GREASED COOKIE SHEETS, ABOUT 2 INCHES APART. BAKE AT 375 DEGREES FOR 10 MINS. OR UNTIL DONE. ABOUT 3-1/2 DOZEN.

LEMON SQUARES

1 CUP SIFTED FLOUR   1/4 CUP POWDERED SUGAR
1/2 CUP MELTED BUTTER

MIX ALL THE ABOVE AND PRESS INTO AN 8-INCH SQUARE PAN. BAKE AT 350 DEGREES FOR
20 MINS.
THEN MIX TOGETHER:

2 BEATEN EGGS   1 CUP GRANULATED SUGAR
3 GENEROUS TBSP. LEMON JUICE   1/2 TEASP. BAKING POWDER
2 TBSP. FLOUR

POUR ON TOP OF FIRST MIXTURE AND BAKE FOR 25 MINS. CUT INTO SMALL SQUARES AND
SPRINKLE WITH POWDERED SUGAR WHILE STILL HOT.

PAWPAW COOKIES

PAWPAWS ARE BETTER KNOWN IN THE MOUNTAINS AS "APPALACHIAN BANANAS" AND
HAVE A TASTE YOU EITHER LOVE OR HATE. THE SKIN ON RIPE PAWPAWS TURNS BLACK AND
THE PULP GETS MUSHY LIKE OVER-RIPE BANANAS.

1-1/2 CUPS MASHED RIPE PAWPAWS   2 CUPS FLOUR
1 TEASP. SODA   1 TEASP. SALT
1/2 CUP SHORTENING   1 CUP SUGAR
2 EGGS   1 TEASP. GRATED LEMON RIND
1 CUP CHOPPED BLACK WALNUTS

PREHEAT OVEN TO 350 DEGREES. SIFT TOGETHER FLOUR, SODA AND SALT. CREAM
SHORTENING AND SUGAR; BEAT IN EGGS. ADD LEMON RIND, FLOUR MIXTURE AND PAWPAW
PULP. FOLD IN BLACK WALNUTS. DROP ON GREASED COOKIE SHEET AND BAKE FOR 15 MINS.

GINGERBREAD

2 CUPS MOLASSES   1 TEASP. BAKING POWDER
1 CUP (2 STICKS) UNSALTED BUTTER   4 TBSP. GINGER
1 CUP SUGAR   1 TBSP. ALLSPICE
4 CUPS UNBLEACHED WHITE FLOUR   4 EGGS

PREHEAT OVEN TO 375 DEGREES. IN DOUBLE BOILER MELT BUTTER AND MOLASSES. STIR
IN SUGAR UNTIL DISSOLVED. ALLOW TO COOL. IN BOWL MIX FLOUR, BAKING POWDER,
GINGER, ALLSPICE AND EGGS WITH WOODEN SPOON. ADD THIS MIXTURE TO COOLED
MOLASSES MIXTURE, BEATING WELL. POUR INTO GREASED 8x8 PAN. BAKE 50-60 MINS.
UNTIL RICH BROWN AND TOOTHPICK IN CENTER COMES OUT CLEAN. YIELDS ONE CAKE —
12-16 SERVINGS.

OLD-FASHIONED AMMONIA COOKIES

A REAL BIT OF NOSTALGIA. REMEMBER AMMONIA COKES?

1 OZ. AMMONIUM CARBONATE (BAKER'S
   AMMONIUM, AVAILABLE AT DRUGSTORES)
1/4 CUP WATER
2 CUPS GRANULATED SUGAR
1 TEASP. SALT

1-1/4 CUPS MILK
1 CUP SHORTENING
3 EGGS, WELL-BEATEN
2 TEASP. LEMON OIL
6-7 CUPS ALL-PURPOSE FLOUR

STIR AMMONIA IN WATER AND SET ASIDE. CREAM SHORTENING AND SUGAR UNTIL LIGHT AND FLUFFY. ADD EGGS AND BLEND WELL; THEN ADD SALT AND LEMON OIL. COMBINE AMMONIA WATER WITH MILK AND MIX ALTERNATELY WITH FLOUR TO SHORTENING MIXTURE UNTIL BATTER CAN BE EASILY HANDLED. PRESS BATTER ONTO FLOURED BOARD WITH HANDS, THEN CUT INTO SQUARES OR CIRCLES. BAKE AT 400 DEGREES UNTIL LIGHT BROWN. MAKES 5 DOZEN.

APPLE COOKIES

2 CUPS PEELED, CHOPPED APPLES
1 CUP GRANULATED SUGAR
1/2 CUP BUTTER, SOFTENED
3/4 TEASP. GROUND CLOVES
2 CUPS ALL-PURPOSE FLOUR
1 TEASP. SODA
1 CUP CHOPPED NUTS

1 CUP STRONG COFFEE
1 CUP RAISINS
1 TEASP. GROUND CINNAMON
3/4 TEASP. GROUND NUTMEG
1/4 TEASP. SALT
1 TEASP. VANILLA EXTRACT

COMBINE APPLES, COFFEE, SUGAR, RAISINS, BUTTER, CINNAMON, NUTMEG AND CLOVES IN SAUCEPAN; COOK OVER LOW HEAT UNTIL APPLES ARE TENDER. REMOVE FROM HEAT AND COOL. COMBINE FLOUR, SALT AND SODA. STIR INTO APPLE MIXTURE. ADD VANILLA AND NUTS, STIRRING WELL. DROP BY TEASPOOONSFUL ONTO UNGREASED COOKIE SHEETS. BAKE AT 375 DEGREES FOR 15 MINS. 4-1/2 DOZEN COOKIES.

BLACK WALNUT BARS

1/2 CUP BUTTER
1/2 TEASP. SALT
1 CUP PLUS 2 TBSP. FLOUR

1/2 CUP BROWN SUGAR, FIRMLY PACKED
1/2 CUP CHOPPED BLACK WALNUTS

COMBINE BUTTER AND SALT. ADD BROWN SUGAR. CREAM WELL. ADD FLOUR AND WALNUTS; BLEND. SPREAD EVENLY IN A GREASED 8x12 PAN. BAKE IN SLOW OVEN, ABOUT 325 DEGREES, ABOUT 20 MINS. OR UNTIL EVENLY BROWNED. COOL AND CUT INTO SQUARE BARS.

Easy Oatmeal Cookies

1 CUP SHORTENING
1 CUP GRANULATED SUGAR
2 EGGS
1 TEASP. SODA
1/2 TEASP. CINNAMON
1/2 CUP BLACK WALNUTS

1 CUP BROWN SUGAR
1/2 TEASP. VANILLA EXTRACT
1-1/4 CUPS ALL-PURPOSE FLOUR
1/2 TEASP. SALT
3 CUPS QUICK OATS

MIX SHORTENING, SUGARS, VANILLA AND EGGS TOGETHER WITH BEATER. SET ASIDE. COMBINE FLOUR, SODA, SALT AND CINNAMON. COMBINE WITH FIRST MIXTURE. FOLD IN OATS AND WALNUTS. DROP BY TABLESPOONSFUL ONTO UNGREASED COOKIE SHEETS. BAKE AT 350 DEGREES FOR 12-15 MINS. ABOUT 3 DOZEN COOKIES.

Sour-Milk Doughnuts

1 CUP RICH SOUR MILK
1/2 TEASP. SODA
1 EGG, WELL BEATEN
1 CUP SUGAR

1/2 TEASP. SALT
1/2 TEASP. NUTMEG
FLOUR

SIFT FLOUR, MEASURE AND SIFT 1 CUP WITH SODA, SALT AND NUTMEG. COMBINE EGG, SUGAR, SHORTENING, SOUR MILK AND DRY INGREDIENTS. ADD SUFFICIENT FLOUR TO MAKE A SOFT ROLL DOUGH. CHILL. TURN ONTO LIGHTLY FLOURED BOARD. ROLL IN SHEET 1/3-·INCH THICK. CUT WITH FLOURED CUTTER (OR INTO STRIPS). FRY IN OIL, 365 DEGREES, UNTIL BROWN. DRAIN ON PAPER TOWELS. SPRINKLE WITH SUGAR IF DESIRED.

Old-Fashioned Apple Butter Cake

2-1/4 CUPS FLOUR
1 TEASP. SODA
1/2 TEASP. SALT
1/2 CUP BUTTER
1 CUP SOUR CREAM

1 TEASP. BAKING POWDER
1 CUP SUGAR
2 EGGS
3/4 CUP APPLE BUTTER
1 TEASP. VANILLA EXTRACT

SIFT TOGETHER FLOUR, BAKING POWDER, SODA AND SALT. CREAM SUGAR AND BUTTER UNTIL FLUFFY AND LIGHT. ADD EGGS AND BEAT UNTIL BLENDED. ADD APPLE BUTTER AND VANILLA. ADD SIFTED DRY INGREDIENTS SLOWLY, ALTERNATELY WITH SOUR CREAM. MIX UNTIL WELL BLENDED. POUR 1/2 CAKE BATTER INTO A GREASED, FLOURED LOAF PAN. MIX TOGETHER: 1/2 CUP SUGAR, 1/2 TEASP. NUTMEG, 1 TEASP. CINNAMON AND 1/2 CUP CHOPPED WALNUTS. SPRINKLE HALF THIS TOPPING OVER MIXTURE, THEN POUR REMAINING BATTER OVER TOP AND SPRINKLE REST OF TOPPING ON TOP LAYER. BAKE AT 350 DEGREES ABOUT 40-50 MINS. SERVE WARM OR COLD WITH WHIPPED CREAM OR TOPPING.

HICKORY NUT DROPS

2 CUPS SUGAR
2 CUPS HICKORY NUTS, CHOPPED FINE

6 EGG WHITES
3 TBSP. FLOUR

BEAT EGG WHITES UNTIL LIGHT, ADD SUGAR GRADUALLY, THEN ADD NUTS. LAST ADD FLOUR AND FOLD IN LIGHTLY UNTIL ALL IS WELL MIXED. DROP ONTO GREASED COOKIE SHEET AND BAKE AT 350 DEGREES ABOUT 10 MINS.

ALMOND CHEESECAKES

1/4 LB. SHELLED ALMONDS
3 EGGS
1/4 CUP SOFT BUTTER

6 UNBAKED 4-INCH TART SHELLS
6 TBSP. SUGAR
1 TEASP. ROSE WATER*

PREHEAT OVEN TO 375 DEGREES. PUT ALMONDS IN BLENDER AND PROCESS AT LOW SPEED UNTIL CHOPPED VERY FINE. ADD EGGS AND BEAT UNTIL WELL MIXED. ADD BUTTER, SUGAR AND ROSE WATER AND BLEND THOROUGHLY. DIVIDE AMONG TART SHELLS. BAKE 20-25 MINS., OR UNTIL TARTS ARE PUFFY AND SET. 6 SERVINGS.

*IF ROSE WATER IS UNAVAILABLE, USE EQUAL AMOUNT OF LEMON JUICE OR 1/4 TEASP. VANILLA EXTRACT.

APPLESAUCE SQUARES

1/2 CUP BUTTER
1-1/2 CUPS BROWN SUGAR, FIRMLY PACKED
2 EGGS, WELL BEATEN
2 CUPS SIFTED FLOUR
1-1/2 TEASP. SODA

1/2 TEASP. SALT
1 TEASP. CINNAMON
1/2 TEASP. ALLSPICE
1/2 TEASP. CLOVES
1-1/2 CUPS APPLESAUCE

CREAM BUTTER AND BROWN SUGAR; ADD EGGS AND BEAT WELL. SIFT FLOUR; ADD SODA, SALT AND SPICES, THEN SIFT AGAIN. ADD ALTERNATELY WITH APPLESAUCE TO CREAMED MIXTURE; BEATING WELL AFTER EACH ADDITION. SPREAD ON GREASED AND FLOURED 11x16x1 COOKIE SHEET. BAKE AT 350 DEGREES ABOUT 30 MINS. WHEN COOL, FROST WITH CARAMEL ICING AND CUT INTO SQUARES.

CARAMEL ICING

1/2 CUP (1 STICK) BUTTER, MELTED
1 CUP BROWN SUGAR

1/2 CUP EVAPORATED MILK
1 LB. POWDERED SUGAR, SIFTED

COMBINE MELTED BUTTER, BROWN SUGAR AND MILK. BOIL FOR ONE MINUTE STIRRING CONSTANTLY. REMOVE FROM HEAT AND ADD SIFTED POWDERED SUGAR. BEAT UNTIL CREAMY. *MRS. WILLIAM WALLACE BARRON*

POUND CAKE

1 CUP PURE WHITE VEGETABLE SHORTENING	2 CUPS SUGAR
3 CUPS FLOUR	4 EGGS
1 CUP BUTTERMILK	1/2 TEASP. BAKING POWDER AND
1 TEASP. VANILLA OR ALMOND FLAVORING	BAKING SODA

CREAM SUGAR AND SHORTENING. SIFT DRY INGREDIENTS TOGETHER AND ADD EGGS, FLAVORING AND HALF THE MILK. BEAT TWO MINS. AND ADD REMAINING MILK. BEAT TWO MORE MINS. BAKE IN TWO GREASED, WAX PAPER-LINED 8x3 LOAF PANS IN 325 DEGREES OVEN FOR 45-50 MINS.

POPPY SEED THUMBPRINTS

1 CUP BUTTER OR MARGARINE, SOFTENED	2-1/2 CUPS UNSIFTED ALL-PURPOSE
1/2 CUP PACKED BROWN SUGAR	FLOUR
2 LARGE EGGS	2 TBSP. POPPY SEEDS
1 TEASP. VANILLA	FAVORITE JAM OR JELLY

IN LARGE BOWL, BEAT AT MEDIUM SPEED, BUTTER, SUGAR, EGGS AND VANILLA UNTIL BLENDED. STIR IN FLOUR AND POPPY SEEDS, MIXING JUST UNTIL DOUGH HOLDS TOGETHER. COVER WITH PLASTIC WRAP; REFRIGERATE UNTIL FIRM, ABOUT 30 MINS. PREHEAT OVEN TO 350 DEGREES. ROLL 1 TABLESPOON DOUGH INTO A BALL FOR EACH COOKIE. PLACE 1-INCH APART ON UNGREASED COOKIE SHEET. WITH FLOURED THUMB, PRESS TOP CENTER OF EACH BALL TO MAKE A DEEP THUMBPRINT. BAKE 15 MINS. OR UNTIL GOLDEN. COOL ON WIRE RACKS. FILL EACH THUMBPRINT WITH 1 TEASPOON JELLY.

POOR MAN'S CAKE

2 CUPS DARK RAISINS	1/2 TEASP. FRESHLY GRATED NUTMEG
2 CUPS SUGAR	1/2 TEASP. GROUND ALLSPICE
3/4 CUP LARD OR VEGETABLE SHORTENING	3-1/2 CUPS ALL-PURPOSE FLOUR
2 CUPS WATER	1 TEASP. BAKING SODA
2 TEASP. GROUND CINNAMON	1 TEASP. BAKING POWDER

PREHEAT OVEN TO 350 DEGREES. GREASE AND FLOUR TWO 9x5 LOAF PANS. IN MEDIUM SAUCEPAN, COMBINE RAISINS, SUGAR, LARD OR SHORTENING, WATER AND SPICES. BRING TO BOIL, STIRRING. BOIL 5 MINS. REMOVE FROM HEAT, COOL TO ROOM TEMPERATURE. STIR IN FLOUR, BAKING SODA AND POWDER. DIVIDE BATTER BETWEEN PANS AND BAKE 30-35 MINS. OR UNTIL TOOTHPICK INSERTED IN CENTER COMES OUT CLEAN. COOL ON RACK.

LOAVES MAY BE ICED OR JUST SERVED SPREAD WITH BUTTER.

Oatmeal Lace Cookies

2-1/4 cups regular oatmeal
2-1/4 cups light brown sugar
3 tbsp. flour
1 teasp. salt

1 cup butter, melted
1 egg
1 teasp. vanilla

Preheat oven to 350 degrees. Lightly mix oatmeal, sugar, flour and salt in a bowl by hand. Add melted butter and stir. Add slightly beaten egg and vanilla. Mix well. Grease cookie sheet and drop small quarter-sized circles of dough onto sheet. Bake 8-10 mins.

Date Cake

1 cup chopped dates
2-1/2 tbsp. shortening
1 teasp. baking soda
1 cup boiling water
1 egg, lightly beaten

1-3/4 cups all-purpose flour
1 teasp. vanilla extract
3/4 cups sugar
1 teasp. salt
1/2 cup chopped walnuts

Preheat oven to 350 degrees. To dates add shortening and baking soda. Pour boiling water over mixture. Add egg and sugar, mix well. Stir in flour and salt. Add vanilla and nut meats. Mix all ingredients thoroughly. Pour batter into greased 9x5 loaf pan and bake 55-60 mins.

Mock Chocolate Eclair Cake

2 boxes instant French vanilla pudding
1 (9 oz.) carton Cool Whip

3 cups milk
box of graham crackers

Mix pudding with milk. Fold in Cool Whip. Line 13x9 pan with graham crackers. Spread 1/2 of pudding mixture over top and layer again with graham crackers and pudding, ending with graham crackers.

Frosting

2 squares unsweetened chocolate
6 tbsp. margarine
1 teasp. vanilla

1-1/2 cups powdered sugar
2 tbsp. milk
2 tbsp. corn syrup

Melt chocolate with margarine, corn syrup, milk and vanilla. Add powdered sugar. Pour over graham crackers; refrigerate overnight.

West Virginia Blackberry Jam Cake

1 CUP SHORTENING
2 CUPS SUGAR
3 EGGS YOLKS, WELL BEATEN
1 CUP BLACKBERRY JAM
3 CUPS FLOUR

1/2 TEASP. SALT
1 TEASP. SODA
1 TEASP. CINNAMON
1 CUP BUTTERMILK
1/2 CUP CHOPPED NUTS (OPTIONAL)

CREAM SHORTENING AND SUGAR; ADD EGG YOLKS AND JAM. MIX WELL. SIFT DRY INGREDIENTS TOGETHER; ADD ALTERNATELY WITH BUTTERMILK, BEATING SMOOTH AFTER EACH ADDITION. ADD CHOPPED NUTS IF DESIRED. BAKE IN GREASED SHEET PAN FOR 30 MINS. AT 350 DEGREES. COOL AND FROST WITH CARAMEL ICING.

Caramel Icing

2 CUPS LIGHT BROWN SUGAR
1/4 LB. (1 STICK) BUTTER

1/2 CUP EVAPORATED MILK

COMBINE ALL INGREDIENTS; BRING TO A BOIL AND COOK 1 MIN. REMOVE FROM HEAT. START BEATING IMMEDIATELY AND CONTINUE UNTIL MIXTURE REACHES SPREADING CONSISTENCY. ICING WILL BE ALMOST COLD BEFORE READY TO SPREAD ON CAKE. LEAVE IN PAN FOR EASY HANDLING.

Old-Fashioned Parsnip Cake

2-3/4 CUPS WHOLE WHEAT FLOUR
1-1/2 TEASP. BAKING SODA
1 TEASP. SALT
1/4 LB. BUTTER, MELTED
1 TEASP. EACH GROUND CINNAMON, GROUND
    NUTMEG, GROUND CLOVES, GROUND ALLSPICE
1-3/4 CUPS APPLESAUCE

2/3 CUP CHOPPED WALNUTS
1 CUP DICED RAW PARSNIPS
1 TEASP. BAKING POWDER
2 EGGS
2 CUPS SUGAR
1/2 CUP WATER
1 CUP RAISINS

PREHEAT OVEN TO 350 DEGREES. COMBINE FLOUR, SODA, BAKING POWDER AND SALT. WHISK TOGETHER EGGS, BUTTER AND SUGAR; ADD TO DRY INGREDIENTS. STIR IN REMAINING INGREDIENTS UNTIL THOROUGHLY BLENDED. POUR BATTER INTO LIGHTLY OILED 9-INCH BUNDT PAN AND BAKE 40 MINS. TURN OUT ONTO WIRE RACK AND COOL COMPLETELY. COMBINE ICING INGREDIENTS, STIRRING UNTIL SMOOTH. SPREAD ON CAKE.

Icing

1/2 CUP FIRMLY PACKED DARK BROWN SUGAR
1/2 CUP POWDERED SUGAR

1/4 LB. BUTTER, MELTED

BUTTERMILK PIE

3 EGGS	1/2 TEASP. VANILLA
2 TBSP. CREAM	2 CUPS BUTTERMILK
1/2 CUP SUGAR	DASH OF NUTMEG
1/8 TEASP. SALT	1 9-INCH UNBAKED PIE SHELL

BEAT EGGS; ADD CREAM, SUGAR, SALT AND VANILLA. STIR IN BUTTERMILK. POUR INTO UNBAKED PIE CRUST. SPRINKLE LIGHTLY WITH NUTMEG. BAKE IN HOT (450 DEGREE) OVEN FOR 10 MINS. OR JUST ENOUGH TO SET CRUST. REDUCE HEAT TO 325 DEGREES AND BAKE 30 TO 40 MINS. LONGER, OR UNTIL KNIFE INSERTED IN CENTER COMES OUT CLEAN.

MOLASSES CAKES

1 TEASP. SODA	1 TEASP. SALT
1/4 CUP WARM WATER	DASH OF PEPPER
1 CUP MOLASSES	2-1/2 TEASP. GINGER
3/4 CUP SUGAR	4 CUPS FLOUR

PREHEAT OVEN TO 350 DEGREES. DISSOLVE SODA IN WATER, THEN ADD INGREDIENTS IN ORDER GIVEN. ADD A LITTLE MORE FLOUR, IF NEEDED. ROLL ALL, OR PART ON A FLOURED BOARD AND CUT WITH A BISCUIT CUTTER OR JELLY GLASS. PUT ON A GREASED COOKIE SHEET AND BAKE 10 MINS. OR UNTIL LIGHTLY BROWNED. MAKES 4 TO 6 DOZEN.

FRIED APPLE PIES

2/3 CUP SHORTENING	2 CUPS FLOUR
1/2 TEASP. SALT	

WORK SHORTENING INTO FLOUR AND SALT. ADD ENOUGH COLD WATER TO FORM DOUGH. ROLL SMALL PORTIONS OF DOUGH OUT INTO SMALL ROUNDS.

APPLESAUCE FILLING

2 CUPS SWEETENED APPLESAUCE	2 TBSP. TAPIOCA
1 TEASP. ALLSPICE	

BRING APPLESAUCE, TAPIOCA AND ALLSPICE TO A BOIL; PLACE A HEAPING TABLESPOON OF MIXTURE ONTO EACH ROUND. FOLD DOUGH OVER, SHAPE INTO CRESCENTS AND CRIMP EDGES. FRY IN DEEP FAT AT 360 DEGREES UNTIL GOLDEN BROWN.

OLD-FASHIONED BREAD PUDDING

4 CUPS MILK, SCALDED
4 CUPS COARSE DRY BREADCRUMBS
1/4 CUP BUTTER, MELTED
4 EGGS, SLIGHTLY BEATEN
1/2 CUP SEEDLESS RAISINS

1/3 CUP SUGAR
1/4 TEASP. SALT
1/2 TEASP. FRESHLY GRATED NUTMEG
1/2 TEASP. GROUND CINNAMON
1 PINT VANILLA ICE CREAM (OPTIONAL)

PREHEAT OVEN TO 350 DEGREES. GREASE AN 8x12 CAKE PAN. IN LARGE MIXING BOWL, POUR MILK OVER BREADCRUMBS. IN A SMALL MIXING BOWL COMBINE ALL REMAINING INGREDIENTS AND ADD TO BREAD AND MILK MIXTURE. MIX THOROUGHLY AND POUR INTO CAKE PAN. BAKE 40 MINS. OR UNTIL KNIFE INSERTED INTO CENTER OF PUDDING COMES OUT CLEAN. CUT INTO SQUARES AND SERVE HOT WITH A SMALL SCOOP OF VANILLA ICE CREAM, IF DESIRED. SERVES 12.

INDIAN PUDDING

4 CUPS MILK
1/3 CUP YELLOW CORNMEAL
2 TBSP. BUTTER
1/2 CUP MOLASSES
1/2 CUP BROWN SUGAR
1/2 TEASP. SALT

1 TEASP. CINNAMON
1/4 TEASP. GINGER
2 EGGS
1 CUP COLD MILK
LIGHT CREAM

PREHEAT OVEN TO 350 DEGREES. IN THE TOP OF A DOUBLE BOILER, SCALD THE MILK. ADD CORNMEAL AND COOK FOR 15 MINS., STIRRING FREQUENTLY. THEN ADD BUTTER, MOLASSES, SUGAR, SALT, SPICES AND EGGS. WHEN WELL-BLENDED POUR INTO A BUTTERED MEDIUM-SIZED CASSEROLE DISH. POUR COLD MILK ON TOP WITHOUT STIRRING IT IN AND BAKE FOR 1 HOUR. SERVE HOT, TOPPED WITH CREAM. SERVES 6.

OZARK PUDDING

1 EGG, WELL BEATEN
3/4 CUP FIRMLY PACKED LIGHT BROWN SUGAR
3/4 CUP UNSIFTED ALL-PURPOSE FLOUR
1-1/2 TEASP. BAKING POWDER
1/2 TEASP. CINNAMON

1 TEASP. VANILLA
3/4 CUP FINELY CHOPPED, PEELED
   APPLES
1/2 CUP FINELY CHOPPED, PECANS OR
   BLACK WALNUTS

BEAT EGG AND SUGAR WELL IN SMALL MIXING BOWL; SIFT FLOUR WITH BAKING POWDER AND CINNAMON AND MIX IN. STIR IN VANILLA, APPLES AND NUTS. SPOON BATTER INTO WELL-GREASED AND FLOURED 8x8x2 PAN AND BAKE AT 350 DEGREES FOR 30 MINS. OR UNTIL CRUSTY-BROWN ON TOP. LET COOL ABOUT HALF AN HOUR BEFORE SERVING. TOP WITH WHIPPED TOPPING OR CREAM.

APPLE PUDDING I

1 EGG	1/2 CUP CHOPPED APPLES
2 TBSP. FLOUR	PINCH OF SALT
1 TEASP. VANILLA	3/4 CUP SUGAR
1 CUP CHOPPED WALNUTS/HICKORY NUTS	1-1/2 TEASP. BAKING POWDER

BEAT EGG AND SUGAR UNTIL SMOOTH; ADD VANILLA. STIR IN FLOUR, BAKING POWDER AND SALT. ADD APPLES AND NUTS. BAKE IN A GREASED PAN AT 325 DEGREES FOR 30 MINS. SERVE WITH WHIPPED TOPPING OR ICE CREAM.

APPLE PUDDING II

MIX AND SET ASIDE:

1 EGG	2 CUPS CHOPPED APPLES (FRESH OR
1/3 CUP OIL OR SHORTENING	FROZEN)

THEN MIX TOGETHER:

1 CUP FLOUR	1 CUP SUGAR
1 TEASP. SODA	1/2 TEASP. SALT
1 TEASP. CINNAMON	1/4 TEASP. CLOVES

ADD DRY INGREDIENTS TO APPLE MIXTURE. DOUGH WILL SEEM STIFF BUT KEEP MIXING, DO NOT ADD ADDITIONAL OIL OR OTHER LIQUID. BAKE FOR 45 MINS. AT 325 DEGREES. SERVE WARM OR COLD WITH CREAM. BEST IF BAKED IN GLASS DISH. RECIPE MAY BE DOUBLED.

BAKED PEACH PUDDING

6-7 LARGE RIPE, BUT FIRM PEACHES, STONED AND SLICED (ENOUGH TO FILL A 1-1/2 QUART BAKING DISH)	1 CUP FLOUR
	3 TBSP. BUTTER
	1 CUP GRANULATED SUGAR
3 TBSP. BROWN SUGAR	1 TEASP. BAKING POWDER
1 EGG	

PREHEAT OVEN TO 350 DEGREES. TURN PEACHES INTO BUTTERED 1-1/2 QUART BAKING DISH. SPRINKLE WITH BROWN SUGAR AND DOT WITH THE BUTTER. BEAT THE EGG AND SIFT THE GRANULATED SUGAR, FLOUR AND BAKING POWDER INTO IT. STIR UNTIL MIXTURE IS WELL-BLENDED AND CRUMBLY. SPREAD ACROSS TOP OF PEACHES AND BAKE FOR ABOUT 35 MINS. SERVE WITH HEAVY CREAM OR ICE CREAM. MAY BE MADE WITH TART APPLES. SERVES 4-6.

APPLE CRISP

6 CUPS SLICED APPLES (6-8 MED.)
1 CUP SUGAR
2 TBSP. FLOUR

1/2 TEASP. GROUND CINNAMON
2 TBSP. BUTTER/MARGARINE

TOPPING

1 CUP SUGAR
1 CUP SIFTED ALL-PURPOSE FLOUR
1 TEASP. BAKING POWDER

1 TEASP. GROUND CINNAMON
1/2 TEASP. SALT
1 LARGE EGG, SLIGHTLY BEATEN

MIX APPLES WITH SUGAR, FLOUR AND CINNAMON; PLACE IN WELL-BUTTERED 8x8x2 BAKING DISH AND DOT WELL WITH BUTTER. MIX TOPPING, EXCEPT FOR EGG, MAKE WELL IN CENTER OF TOPPING AND PUT IN EGG, FORK TOGETHER UNTIL CRUMBLY. SCATTER OVER APPLES AND BAKE IN 325 DEGREES OVEN FOR ABOUT 1 HOUR OR UNTIL BUBBLY AND LIGHTLY BROWNED. SERVE WITH WHIPPED TOPPING OR ICE CREAM.

PERSIMMON PUDDING I

1-1/2 CUPS SIFTED FLOUR
1/2 TEASP. SALT
1-1/2 TEASP. BAKING SODA
1/2 CUP CHOPPED DATES
1/2 CUP RAISINS
1 CUP SOFT BREADCRUMBS

1 CUP CHOPPED PECANS
1-1/2 TEASP. BUTTER
1/2 CUP MILK
1 CUP SUGAR
1-1/2 TEASP. BAKING POWDER
1 CUP PERSIMMON PULP

RESIFT FLOUR WITH SUGAR, SALT, BAKING POWDER AND SODA. ADD OTHER INGREDIENTS AND MIX THOROUGHLY. GREASE 9x5x3 LOAF PAN AND LINE WITH WAX PAPER. ADD MIXTURE TO PAN AND BAKE AT 350 DEGREES FOR ABOUT 1-1/2 HOURS OR UNTIL CENTER IS FIRM. SERVE WITH WHIPPED CREAM, IF DESIRED.

QUICK RICE PUDDING

1 CUP MINUTE RICE
3 TBSP. RAISINS
1/8 TEASP. CINNAMON

1/4 TEASP. SALT
1 (3 OZ.) PACKAGE VANILLA PUDDING

BRING RICE, 1 CUP WATER, RAISINS AND SALT TO BOIL IN SAUCE PAN. COOL. PREPARE PUDDING MIX ACCORDING TO DIRECTIONS, ADDING CINNAMON. FOLD INTO RICE MIXTURE IN A BOWL. CHILL UNTIL SERVING TIME. SERVES 4.

Pear and Cranberry Crunch

4 RIPE PEARS, PEELED, CORED AND SLICED
1 (12-OZ.) BAG FRESH CRANBERRIES
1/3 CUP SUGAR
1 TEASP. GROUND CINNAMON

3/4 CUP ROLLED OATS
1/2 CUP ALL-PURPOSE FLOUR
3 TBSP. FIRMLY PACKED BROWN SUGAR
1/4 LB. BUTTER

PREHEAT OVEN TO 375 DEGREES. COMBINE PEAR SLICES, CRANBERRIES, SUGAR, CINNAMON AND 3 TBSP. FLOUR. PLACE IN BUTTERED 9x13 DISH. MIX BROWN SUGAR, OATS AND 1/2 CUP FLOUR. CUT BUTTER INTO SMALL PIECES AND CUT INTO OATS MIXTURE WITH KNIFE/ FORK OR PASTRY CUTTER. SPRINKLE OVER PEAR/CRANBERRY MIXTURE. BAKE 45 MINS. CUT INTO SQUARES TO SERVE. 8-10 SERVINGS.

Rhubarb Pudding

1-1/2 CUPS MILK
3 EGGS, SEPARATED
8 SLICES WHITE BREAD, CUT INTO CUBES
1 LB. FRESH RHUBARB CUT INTO 1/2-INCH
    CUBES (ABOUT 4 CUPS)

1-1/2 CUPS LIGHT BROWN SUGAR,
    FIRMLY PACKED
1 TEASP. VANILLA
WHIPPED TOPPING

PREHEAT OVEN TO 350 DEGREES. BLEND TOGETHER MILK, BROWN SUGAR, EGG YOLKS AND VANILLA. MIX IN BREAD CUBES UNTIL MOISTENED THOROUGHLY. STIR IN RHUBARB. BEAT EGG WHITES UNTIL STIFF, BUT NOT DRY. FOLD INTO BREAD MIXTURE. POUR INTO GREASED 1-1/2 QUART BAKING DISH. BAKE ABOUT 50 MINS. OR UNTIL RHUBARB IS COOKED. SERVED WITH WHIPPED TOPPING OR WHIPPED CREAM.

Persimmon Pudding II

2 OR 3 VERY RIPE PERSIMMONS
3/4 CUP BROWN SUGAR, FIRMLY PACKED
1 CUP MILK
1/4 CUP BUTTER, MELTED
1 CUP SIFTED ALL-PURPOSE FLOUR

2 TEASP. BAKING POWDER
1/4 TEASP. SALT
1/4 TEASP. CINNAMON
HEAVY CREAM

PREHEAT OVEN TO 325 DEGREES. PEEL PERSIMMONS AND BLEND IN ELECTRIC BLENDER. MEASURE 1 CUP PERSIMMON PULP AND COMBINE WITH BROWN SUGAR, MILK AND BUTTER. SIFT TOGETHER FLOUR, BAKING POWDER, SALT AND CINAMMON AND STIR INTO PULP UNTIL SMOOTH. POUR INTO BUTTERED 1-1/2 QUART BAKING DISH AND BAKE FOR 1 HOUR OR UNTIL PUDDING PULLS AWAY FROM SIDES OF DISH (SURFACE SHOULD BE SOFT). SERVE WARM OR COOL WITH WHIPPED CREAM OR TOPPING. SERVES 4-6.

Bread Pudding

2 CUPS BREADCRUMBS	2 EGGS, BEATEN
1/4 TEASP. SALT	1 TEASP. VANILLA
3 CUPS HOT MILK	1/2 CUP CHOPPED NUTS OR RAISINS
1 TBSP. FAT	2/3 CUP SUGAR

COMBINE CRUMBS, MILK, EGGS, SUGAR, SALT AND FAT. MIX. ADD VANILLA AND NUTS OR RAISINS. TURN INTO GREASED PAN. BAKE AT 350 DEGREES FOR 35-40 MINS. OR UNTIL FIRM. SPRINKLE NUTMEG ON TOP BEFORE BAKING. SERVE WITH WHIPPED TOPPING. MAKES 6 SERVINGS.

Sweet Potato Pie

3/4 CUP BROWN SUGAR	1/2 TEASP. SALT
1-1/2 CUPS EVAPORATED MILK	2 EGGS, WELL BEATEN
1 TEASP. CINNAMON	1/2 TEASP. GINGER
2 TBSP. ALL-PURPOSE FLOUR	1-1/2 CUPS COOKED SWEET POTATOES
2 TBSP. MELTED BUTTER	(CANNED OR FRESH), MASHED
1/2 TEASP. NUTMEG	10-INCH UNBAKED PIE SHELL

LIGHTLY BLEND SUGAR, FLOUR AND SALT. ADD ALL REMAINING INGREDIENTS AND MIX WELL. POUR INTO UNBAKED PIE SHELL AND BAKE IN 450 DEGREE OVEN FOR 10 MINS., REDUCE HEAT TO 350 DEGREES AND BAKE AN ADDITIONAL 35-40 MINS. OR UNTIL FILLING TESTS DONE (KNIFE IN CENTER COMES OUT CLEAN).

Molasses Taffy

COOK ONE CAN OF EAGLE BRAND MILK, 1/2 CUP MOLASSES AND 1 PINCH SALT UNTIL HARD BALL FORMS IN COLD WATER. COOL ON BUTTERED PLATE AND PULL UNTIL FIRM.

Baked Custard

3 EGGS	1/3 CUP SUGAR
3 CUPS WATER	1/4 TEASP. SALT
1 CUP DRY MILK POWDER	1 TEASP. VANILLA

BREAK EGGS IN SAUCEPAN. ADD LIQUID, THEN REMAINING INGREDIENTS. BEAT UNTIL SMOOTH. HEAT TO LUKEWARM, POUR INTO BAKING DISH AND SET IN PAN OF HOT WATER. BAKE AT 325 DEGREES UNTIL SET. FOR PIE FILLING, REDUCE WATER TO 2 CUPS; BAKE AT 450 DEGREES, THEN REDUCE TO 325 DEGREES AND CONTINUE BAKING UNTIL SET.

BLUEBERRY BREAD PUDDING

3 BLUEBERRY MUFFINS
1-1/2 CUPS MILK
3 EGGS, BEATEN
1 CUP FRESH OR FROZEN BLUEBERRIES

2 TBSP. HONEY
2 TBSP. BUTTER
2 TBSP. GRATED LEMON RIND

PREHEAT OVEN TO 350 DEGREES. CRUMBLE MUFFINS INTO A GREASED 1-QUART CASSE-
ROLE. MIX MILK AND HONEY WITH BEATEN EGGS; POUR OVER MUFFINS. DOT WITH BUTTER
AND TOP WITH BLUEBERRIES. SPRINKLE WITH GRATED LEMON RIND. BAKE 40 MINS. UNTIL
SET. MAKES 4-6 SERVINGS.

MAPLE CUP CUSTARD

4 EGGS, LIGHTLY BEATEN
3 CUPS MILK
3/4 CUP MAPLE SYRUP

PINCH OF SALT
1/4 TEASP. VANILLA EXTRACT

PREHEAT OVEN TO 350 DEGREES. BEAT TOGETHER EGGS, MILK, MAPLE SYRUP, SALT AND
VANILLA. POUR INTO 6-8 CUSTARD CUPS. SET CUPS IN A PAN OF HOT WATER. BAKE ABOUT
45 MINS. OR UNTIL KNIFE INSERTED IN CENTER OF CUSTARD COMES OUT CLEAN. REMOVE
CUPS FROM OVEN AND COOL BEFORE SERVING. MAKES 6-8 SERVINGS.

SWEET POTATO PUDDING

2 CUPS COOKED, MASHED SWEET
  POTATOES
2 EGGS, BEATEN
1/2 CUP BUTTER OR MARGARINE
3/4 CUP BROWN SUGAR
1/2 CUP MILK

2/3 CUP ALL-PURPOSE FLOUR
1/4 CUP ORANGE JUICE
1 TEASP. VANILLA
1/4 CUP CHOPPED PECANS
ORANGE SLICES

COMBINE ALL INGREDIENTS EXCEPT ORANGE SLICES. PLACE IN A GREASED 8-INCH BAKING
DISH. PLACE ORANGE SLICES ON TOP OF PUDDING. BAKE AT 350 DEGREES FOR 30 MINS. OR
UNTIL SLIGHTLY BROWN AROUND THE EDGES.

AMBROSIA

CUT RIND AND WHITE MEMBRANE FROM JUICY ORANGES, THEN CUT CROSSWISE INTO THIN
SLICES, DISCARDING SEEDS. PUT A GENEROUS LAYER OF ORANGE SLICES IN CRYSTAL BOWL,
SPRINKLE WITH SUGAR AND COVER WITH LAYER OF SHREDDED COCONUT. CONTINUE
LAYERS ENDING WITH COCONUT. CHILL SEVERAL HOURS BEFORE SERVING. MAY ADD
OTHER FRUITS: PINEAPPLE. BANANAS, GRAPES AND BERRIES.

Italian Cream Cake

1/2 CUP CRISCO
1 STICK BUTTER
2 CUPS SUGAR
5 EGGS, SEPARATED
1 TEASP. SODA
2 CUPS FLOUR

1/2 TEASP. SALT
1 CUP BUTTERMILK
1 TEASP. VANILLA
2 CUPS COCONUT, SHREDDED
1 CUP PECANS, CHOPPED

CREAM TOGETHER CRISCO, BUTTER AND SUGAR. ADD 5 EGG YOLKS, ONE AT A TIME, BEATING AFTER EACH ADDITION. ADD DRY INGREDIENTS ALONG WITH BUTTERMILK AND VANILLA. STIR IN COCONUT AND PECANS. BEAT EGG WHITES UNTIL THEY HOLD PEAKS. FOLD IN STIFFLY BEATEN EGG WHITES. BAKE IN 3 GREASED AND FLOURED 9-INCH PANS AT 350 DEGREES FOR 30 MINS.

Icing

1 STICK BUTTER
8 OZ. CREAM CHEESE
1 TEASP. VANILLA

1 TBSP. HOT MILK (OR COFFEE)
1 BOX POWDERED SUGAR
1 CUP PECANS, CHOPPED

CREAM TOGETHER BUTTER AND CREAMED CHEESE. ADD VANILLA AND HOT MILK. ADD POWDERED SUGAR UNTIL DESIRED CONSISTENCY FOR SPREADING. ADD PECANS AND MIX WELL. *VIRGINIA IAQUINTA, OWNER, JULIO'S RESTAURANT, CLARKSBURG, WV.*

Honey Custard

3 EGGS
1 TEASP. VANILLA
GROUND NUTMEG OR CINNAMON

1/4 CUP HONEY OR MAPLE SYRUP
2-1/2 CUPS MILK

BEAT EGGS, HONEY AND VANILLA WITH WIRE WHISK. STIR IN MILK. POUR INTO GLASS BAKING DISH OR 6 CUSTARD CUPS. SPRINKLE WITH SPICE. SET IN PAN OF HOT WATER AND BAKE LARGE DISH AT 325 DEGREES FOR 1 HOUR; BAKING CUPS AT 350 DEGREES FOR 40-45 MINS. CUSTARD IS DONE WHEN KNIFE INSERTED OFF-CENTER COMES OUT CLEAN. SERVE WARM OR COLD. 6 SERVINGS.

Sponge Cake

BEAT 4 EGG YOLKS UNTIL THICK AND LEMON COLOR. ADD 2/3 CUP SUGAR AND BEAT. BEAT IN 1/4 CUP COLD WATER AND 1 TEASP. VANILLA. SIFT 1-1/4 CUPS CAKE FLOUR WITH 1 TEASP. BAKING POWDER, ADD TO EGG YOLKS AND MIX. BEAT EGG WHITES UNTIL STIFF AND FOLD IN 1/3 CUP SUGAR; THEN FOLD INTO OTHER INGREDIENTS. BAKE AT 350 DEGREES FOR 10 MINS.

GLAZED FRESH STRAWBERRY PIE

1 CUP SUGAR
1/4 CUP CORNSTARCH
1 CUP LEMON-LIME CARBONATED
  BEVERAGE
RED FOOD COLORING

1 (9-INCH) BAKED PIE SHELL
3 TO 4 CUPS FRESH WHOLE
  STRAWBERRIES
WHIPPED CREAM

COMBINE SUGAR AND CORNSTARCH. GRADUALLY STIR IN CARBONATED BEVERAGE. COOK OVER LOW HEAT, STIRRING CONSTANTLY, 5 MINS. OR UNTIL SMOOTH AND THICKENED. STIR IN A FEW DROPS OF FOOD COLORING. PLACE STRAWBERRIES IN PIE SHELL; SPOON GLAZE OVER TOP. CHILL. SERVE WITH WHIPPED CREAM. MAKES 6 TO 8 SERVINGS.

APPLE CHEESE DESSERT

6 CUPS PARED, TART, FIRM APPLE SLICES
1 TBSP. LEMON JUICE
1 CUP SUGAR
1/2 CUP SIFTED FLOUR
1/4 TEASP. SALT

1/4 TEASP. CINNAMON
1/4 CUP MARGARINE
2/3 CUP FINELY SHREDDED CHEDDAR
  CHEESE

FILL 9-INCH PIE PAN OR SHALLOW BAKING DISH WITH APPLES. SPRINKLE WITH LEMON JUICE AND 1/2 CUP SUGAR. MIX REMAINING SUGAR, FLOUR, SALT AND CINNAMON. MIX IN BUTTER UNTIL MIXTURE IS CRUMBLY. STIR IN CHEESE. SPREAD OVER APPLES. BAKE AT 350 DEGREES FOR 45 MINS. OR UNTIL APPLES ARE TENDER. SERVE WARM OR COLD. IF DESIRED, TOP WITH ICE CREAM OR WHIPPED CREAM.

CINNAMON APPLES

TAKE 6-8 APPLES, PEEL AND CUT IN HALF, REMOVE CORE. SPRINKLE BOTTOM OF GREASED BAKING DISH WITH 1 TEASP. CINNAMON (OR MORE IF DESIRED), 1 TEASP. LEMON JUICE AND 1 CUP SUGAR. DOT WITH SMALL BITS OF BUTTER. PLACE APPLES HALVES IN DISH, CUT SIDE DOWN. DOT WITH SMALL BITS OF BUTTER AND SPRINKLE WITH MORE SUGAR AND CINNAMON. BAKE AT 350 DEGREES FOR ABOUT 30-35 MINS.

Jellied Coffee Dessert

2 TBSP. GELATIN

3 CUPS HOT COFFEE

1/2 CUP COLD WATER

3/4 CUP SUGAR

Soak the gelatin in cold water 5 mins. and then dissolve in hot coffee. Add sugar and stir until dissolved. Turn into gelatin mold. Chill until set and serve with whipped cream or topping.

Apple Pound Cake

2 CUPS SUGAR

1-1/2 CUPS OIL

3 EGGS

3 CUPS FLOUR

1 TEASP. SODA

1 TEASP. SALT

1 TBSP. VANILLA EXTRACT

3 CUPS DICED APPLES

1 CUP CHOPPED BLACK WALNUTS

1 CUP FLAKED COCONUT

Cream first 3 ingredients in bowl until fluffy. Beat in sifted dry ingredients and vanilla. Fold in apples, walnuts and coconut. Pour into a greased and floured tube pan. Bake at 350 degrees for 1 hour and 20 mins. Serves 16.

West Virginia Skillet Apple Pie

1/2 CUP BUTTER

1 CUP SUGAR

3 LBS. GOLDEN DELICIOUS APPLES

1-1/2 CUPS FLOUR

1/2 TEASP. BAKING POWDER

1 TBSP. SUGAR

1/4 TEASP. SALT

1/4 CUP BUTTER

1 EGG YOLK

4 TBSP. WATER

Peel, core and cut each apple into 16 wedges. In a 10-inch iron skillet, melt 1/2 cup butter. Sprinkle 3/4 cup sugar over the butter. Arrange apple wedges into circles in skillet. Sprinkle remaining 1/4 cup sugar over wedges. Cover pan. Simmer apples over medium heat 15 to 20 mins. until they are tender but hold their shape. Preheat oven to 400 degrees. Mix flour, baking powder, sugar and salt in a bowl. Cut in butter with pastry blender. Stir together egg yolk and water. Sprinkle as much of the yolk-water mixture over flour mixture as is needed to make dough. Roll out into a circle large enough to fit skillet. Press dough firmly to edge of pan to seal. Cut slits in pastry to let steam escape. Bake for 45-60 mins. until pastry is brown. Cover loosely with foil if browning too fast. Let pie cool 5 mins., loosen edges with knife and invert onto a heat-proof serving plate. If apples are not as caramelized as desired, place pie under the broiler for a short time. Be careful, it can burn easily and if too brown will taste bitter.

Mock Apple Pie

PASTRY FOR 2 CRUST PIE
36 RITZ CRACKERS
2 CUPS SUGAR
2 CUPS WATER

2 TEASP. CREAM OF TARTAR
2 TBSP. LEMON JUICE
GRATED RIND OF 1 LEMON
BUTTER AND CINNAMON

BREAK CRACKERS COARSELY INTO PIE SHELL. IN SAUCEPAN, COMBINE WATER, SUGAR AND CREAM OF TARTAR. BOIL GENTLY FOR 15 MINS. ADD LEMON JUICE AND RIND. COOL. POUR SYRUP OVER CRACKERS. DOT WITH BUTTER. SPRINKLE WITH CINNAMON. ADD TOP CRUST, SLIT FOR STEAM TO ESCAPE. BAKE AT 425 DEGREES FOR 30-35 MINS. SERVE WARM. COVER EDGES OF CRUST FOR LAST 10 MINS. IF BROWNING TOO FAST.

Honey Brownies

1/2 CUP BUTTER OR MARGARINE
4 OZ. UNSWEETENED BAKING CHOCOLATE
2/3 CUP HONEY
1 EGG
2 TEASP. VANILLA
1/4 CUP FLOUR

1/2 TO 1 TEASP. GROUND CINNAMON
   (OPTIONAL)
1/4 TEASP. BAKING SODA
DASH SALT
1/2 CUP CHOPPED NUTS (OPTIONAL)
POWDERED SUGAR (OPTIONAL)

MELT BUTTER AND CHOCOLATE; STIR IN HONEY, EGG AND VANILLA. BEAT UNTIL WELL MIXED. COMBINE FLOUR, CINNAMON, SODA AND SALT; MIX WELL. ADD TO HONEY MIXTURE. STIR IN NUTS. POUR INTO PREPARED 9-INCH SQUARE PAN. BAKE AT 350 DEGREES FOR 12 MINS. OR UNTIL WOODEN PICK INSERTED IN CENTER COMES OUT CLEAN.

Old-Fashioned Raisin Cake

1 BOX RAISINS (15 OR 16 OZ.), COOKED
   TENDER, DRAINED AND COOLED
1 CUP LIQUID DRAINED FROM COOKED
   RAISINS
3 CUPS SIFTED ALL-PURPOSE FLOUR
3/4 CUP MARGARINE
2 EGGS

1-3/4 CUPS SUGAR
1/2 TEASP. SALT
1 TEASP. SODA
1-1/4 TEASP. NUTMEG
1-1/4 TEASP. CINNAMON
1-1/4 TEASP. ALLSPICE
1/2 TEASP. GROUND CLOVES

HAVE RAISINS COMPLETELY COOLED BEFORE MAKING CAKE. PREHEAT OVEN TO 350 DEGREES. CREAM MARGARINE AND SUGAR; ADD EGGS ONE AT A TIME. BEAT UNTIL LIGHT AND FLUFFY AFTER EACH ADDITION. SIFT TOGETHER FLOUR, SALT, SODA AND SPICES. ADD ALTERNATELY WITH RAISIN LIQUID, BEATING SMOOTH EACH TIME. STIR IN COOKED RAISINS UNTIL WELL DISTRIBUTED THROUGHOUT BATTER. POUR INTO GREASED AND FLOURED TUBE PAN. BAKE 1 HOUR OR UNTIL DONE.

DOUGHNUTS

1 EGG
1 CUP SUGAR
1 CUP MILK
1 TEASP. SALT

1 TBSP. BUTTER, MELTED
1 TEASP. NUTMEG OR OTHER SPICES
6 TEASP. BAKING SODA

MAKE SOFT DOUGH AND ROLL 1/2-INCH THICK. CUT OUT AND FRY ABOUT 3 MINS. IN DEEP FAT HEATED TO 380-390 DEGREES.

FRESH CRANBERRY CAKE

1 CUP SUGAR
2-1/2 CUPS FLOUR
1/2 TEASP. SALT
1 TEASP. BAKING SODA
1 TEASP. BAKING POWDER
2 CUPS WHOLE CRANBERRIES
1 CUP DATE BITS
1 CUP CHOPPED PECANS

GRATED RIND OF 2 ORANGES
2 EGGS, BEATEN
1 CUP BUTTERMILK
3/4 CUP VEGETABLE OIL
1 TEASP. VANILLA
3/4 CUP ORANGE JUICE
3/4 CUP SUGAR

COMBINE BY SIFTING TOGETHER FIRST 5 INGREDIENTS. ADD NEXT 4 INGREDIENTS. COMBINE BEATEN EGGS WITH BUTTERMILK AND OIL. ADD TO FRUIT MIXTURE. STIR IN VANILLA. SPOON INTO GREASED AND FLOURED TUBE PAN. BAKE AT 325 DEGREES FOR 1 HOUR. COMBINE JUICE AND SUGAR; BRING TO BOIL. POUR OVER HOT CAKE. LET STAND IN PAN 20 MINS. COOL BEFORE SERVING.

BANANA CAKE

1/2 CUP VEGETABLE SHORTENING
2 CUPS SIFTED CAKE FLOUR
1 TEASP. BAKING POWDER
1 TEASP. SODA
3/4 TEASP. SALT
1-1/3 CUPS SUGAR

1/2 CUP BUTTERMILK
1 TEASP. VANILLA
1 CUP MASHED BANANAS (3 OR 4)
2 UNBEATEN EGGS
1/2 CUP CHOPPED NUTS

PREHEAT OVEN TO 375 DEGREES. CREAM SHORTENING UNTIL SOFT. SIFT IN DRY INGREDIENTS AND SUGAR. ADD 1/4 CUP OF THE BUTTERMILK, MASHED BANANAS AND VANILLA. MIX UNTIL ALL FLOUR IS DAMPENED, THEN BEAT FOR 2 MINS. AT LOW SPEED. ADD EGGS, NUTS AND REMAINING 1/4 CUP OF BUTTERMILK; BEAT FOR 1 MORE MIN. AT LOW SPEED. BAKE IN TWO 9-INCH GREASED LAYER PANS FOR 30-35 MINS. OR UNTIL DONE. USE YOUR FAVORITE WHITE FROSTING.

148

West Virginia Apple Black Walnut Cake

4 CUPS RAW APPLES, CHOPPED COARSELY

2 CUPS SUGAR

3 EGGS

3/4 CUP VEGETABLE OIL

2 TEASP. VANILLA

2 CUPS SIFTED ALL-PURPOSE FLOUR

2 TEASP. BAKING SODA

1 TEASP. CINNAMON

1/2 TEASP. NUTMEG

1 TEASP. SALT

1 CUP CHOPPED BLACK WALNUTS

COMBINE APPLES AND SUGAR; LET STAND. BEAT EGGS SLIGHTLY, BEAT IN OIL AND VANILLA. SIFT TOGETHER FLOUR, SALT, SODA AND SPICES. STIR IN ALTERNATELY APPLE MIXTURE AND DRY INGREDIENTS. ADD WALNUTS. POUR INTO GREASED AND FLOURED 9x13x2 PAN. BAKE AT 350 DEGREES FOR ABOUT AN HOUR OR UNTIL DONE. COOL, THEN COVER WITH LEMON BUTTER FROSTING.

Lemon Butter Frosting

3 CUPS CONFECTIONER'S SUGAR

4 TBSP. BUTTER OR MARGARINE

2 TBSP. LEMON JUICE

1 OR 2 TBSP. COLD WATER

1 TEASP. LEMON EXTRACT

FEW GRAINS OF SALT

CREAM BUTTER, ADD SUGAR GRADUALLY, CREAMING THOROUGHLY. BEAT IN LEMON JUICE, LEMON EXTRACT ADN ENOUGH WATER TO MAKE SPREADING CONSISTENCY. SPREAD ON COOL CAKE. MAKES ABOUT 3-1/2 CUPS FROSTING.

Blackberry Pie

3/4 CUP SUGAR

1/4 CUP ALL-PURPOSE FLOUR

1/2 TEASP. GROUND CINNAMON

1/4 TEASP. GROUND NUTMEG

1/2 TEASP. FINELY GRATED LEMON PEEL

1/8 TEASP. SALT

5 CUP FRESH BLACKBERRIES, RINSED
  AND DRAINED WELL

1 TBSP. BUTTER

1-1/2 CUPS SOUR CREAM

TOSS TOGETHER ALL INGREDIENTS EXCEPT BUTTER.

Crust

2 CUPS ALL-PURPOSE FLOUR

1 TEASP. SALT

3/4 CUP SHORTENING

5 TO 6 TBSP. COLD WATER

PREHEAT OVEN TO 425 DEGREES. MIX WITH FORK. ROLL OUT HALF OF DOUGH FOR 9-INCH BOTTOM CRUST. POUR IN MIXTURE, DOT WITH BUTTER. ROLL OUT TOP CRUST; PLACE OVER FILLING. SEAL EDGES, CUT A FEW SLASHES FOR STEAM TO ESCAPE. BAKE FOR 50 MINS. OR UNTIL CRUST IS GOLDEN BROWN.

RHUBARB-STRAWBERRY PIE

2 CUPS STRAWBERRIES, WASHED, HALVED
3 CUPS RHUBARB, CUT IN SMALL PIECES
1-1/2 CUPS SUGAR

4 TBSP. QUICK-COOKING TAPIOCA
2 TBSP. BUTTER

PREHEAT OVEN TO 350 DEGREES. MIX STRAWBERRIES, RHUBARB, TAPIOCA AND SUGAR. POUR MIXTURE INTO 9-INCH UNBAKED PIE SHELL. DOT WITH BUTTER. BAKE FOR 35 MINS. OR UNTIL RHUBARB IS TENDER BUT NOT MUSHY WHEN TESTED WITH FORK. COOL PIE BEFORE SERVING, TO ALLOW JUICE TO THICKEN. FOR BEST FLAVOR DO NOT CHILL.

VIRGINIA POUND CAKE

8 LARGE EGGS, SEPARATED
1-1/2 TEASP. CREAM OF TARTAR
2-1/4 CUPS SUGAR
2-1/4 CUPS ALL-PURPOSE FLOUR
1-1/2 CUPS BUTTER OR MARGARINE, SOFTENED
2 TBSP. LEMON JUICE

2-1/4 TEASP. VANILLA EXTRACT
1/4 TEASP. BAKING SODA
1/4 TEASP. SALT
1 CUP WALNUTS, CHOPPED
CONFECTIONER'S SUGAR (OPTIONAL)

PREHEAT OVEN TO 325 DEGREES. GREASE AND FLOUR 10-INCH BUNDT PAN. IN LARGE BOWL, WITH MIXER AT HIGH SPEED, BEAT EGG WHITES AND CREAM OF TARTAR UNTIL SOFT PEAKS FORM. GRADUALLY SPRINKLE IN 1 CUP SUGAR, 2 TBSP. AT A TIME, BEATING WELL AFTER EACH ADDITION UNTIL SUGAR DISSOLVES AND WHITES STAND IN STIFF PEAKS. IN ANOTHER LARGE BOWL, COMBINE EGG YOLKS, FLOUR, BUTTER OR MARGARINE, LEMON JUICE, VANILLA EXTRACT, BAKING SODA, SALT AND REMAINING 1-1/4 CUPS SUGAR. WITH SAME BEATERS AND WITH MIXER AT LOW SPEED, BEAT INGREDIENTS UNTIL WELL MIXED, CONSTANTLY SCRAPING BOWL WITH SPATULA. STIR IN CHOPPED WALNUTS. FOLD IN EGG WHITES, 1/3 AT A TIME; SPOON INTO PAN. BAKE 1 HOUR AND 10 MINS. OR UNTIL TOOTHPICK INSERTED IN CENTER OF CAKE COMES OUT CLEAN. COOL CAKE IN PAN ON WIRE RACK 15 MINS. REMOVE CAKE FROM PAN; COOL COMPLETELY ON RACK. TO SERVE, SPRINKLE WITH CONFECTIONER'S SUGAR. MAKES 16 SERVINGS.

CARROT FUDGE

3-1/2 CUPS SUGAR
1-1/2 CUPS GRATED RAW CARROTS
1/2 CUP SWEETENED CONDENSED MILK

1/2 CUP WATER
1 TEASP. LEMON EXTRACT

COMBINE FIRST 4 INGREDIENTS. BOIL UNTIL A LITTLE BIT OF MIXTURE FORMS A FIRM BALL WHEN DROPPED IN COLD WATER. ADD EXTRACT AND BEAT UNTIL CREAMY. POUR INTO A BUTTER PAN. CUT WHEN COOLED.

CRACKER CAKE

42 SODA CRACKERS, CRUMBLED
2-1/4 CUPS CHOPPED WALNUTS
3 TEASP. BAKING POWDER
9 EGG WHITES

3 CUPS SUGAR
1 TBSP. VANILLA
1 LARGE CONTAINER WHIPPED TOPPING

MIX TOGETHER CRACKERS, NUTS AND BAKING POWDER. IN SEPARATE BOWL, BEAT EGG WHITES, ADDING SUGAR GRADUALLY UNTIL STIFF. FOLD EGG MIXTURE INTO CRACKER MIXTURE. ADD VANILLA. POUR INTO 9x13 BUTTER PAN. BAKE AT 325 DEGREES FOR 45 MINS. COVER COMPLETELY COOLED CAKE WITH WHIPPED TOPPING. REFRIGERATE OVERNIGHT BEFORE SERVING.

PINEAPPLE UPSIDE-DOWN CAKE

3 TBSP. BUTTER OR MARGARINE
1 No. 2 CAN (2-1/2 CUPS) PINEAPPLE
   TIDBITS OR CRUSHED PINEAPPLE
MARASCHINO CHERRIES
WALNUT HALVES
2/3 CUP BROWN SUGAR
1/3 CUP SHORTENING

1/2 CUP GRANULATED SUGAR
1 EGG
1 TEASP. VANILLA
1-1/4 CUPS SIFTED CAKE FLOUR
1-1/2 TEASP. BAKING POWDER
1/2 TEASP. SALT

PREHEAT OVEN TO 350 DEGREES. MELT BUTTER IN 9x1-1/2 ROUND PAN. DRAIN PINEAPPLES, RESERVING 1/2 CUP SYRUP. ARRANGE CHERRIES AND NUTS IN BOTTOM OF PAN. COVER WITH BROWN SUGAR, THEN PINEAPPLE. CREAM TOGETHER SHORTENING AND GRANULATED SUGAR; ADD EGG AND VANILLA AND BEAT UNTIL FLUFFY. SIFT TOGETHER DRY INGREDIENTS AND ADD ALTERNATING WITH RESERVED SYRUP; BEATING AFTER EACH ADDITION. SPREAD OVER PINEAPPLE. BAKE IN MODERATE 350 DEGREE OVEN FOR 45-50 MINS. LET STAND 5 MINS. AND INVERT ON PLATE. SERVE WARM.

SNICKERDOODLE BARS

1-1/2 CUPS FLOUR
1 TEASP. BAKING POWDER
1/4 TEASP. SALT
1 CUP SUGAR
5 TBSP. VEGETABLE SHORTENING

1 TEASP. VANILLA
2 EGGS, BEATEN, WITH MILK TO MAKE
   1 CUP
CHOPPED NUTS
SUGAR AND CINNAMON

SIFT AND MEASURE FLOUR, BAKING POWDER, SALT AND SUGAR. MIX LIQUIDS TOGETHER. COMBINE THE TWO MIXTURES. POUR INTO 8x8x2 OR 7x12 PAN. SPREAD WITH CINNAMON MIXTURE, SPRINKLE WITH CHOPPED NUTS. BAKE AT 350 DEGREES FOR ABOUT 20 MINS. COOL AND CUT INTO BARS.

Easy Apple Cake

3/4 CUP MARGARINE, ROOM TEMPERATURE
2 CUPS SUGAR
2 EGGS
2-1/4 CUPS FLOUR
1/2 TEASP. SALT

1/2 TEASP. NUTMEG
1 TEASP. CINNAMON
1-1/2 TEASP. SODA
1 TEASP. VANILLA
2 CUPS CHOPPED APPLES

CREAM BUTTER AND SUGAR. ADD EGGS, ONE AT A TIME, BEATING AFTER EACH ADDITION. ADD CHOPPED APPLES, THEN THE DRY INGREDIENTS WHICH HAVE BEEN SIFTED TOGETHER. POUR INTO 8x14 PAN AND BAKE AT 350 DEGREES FOR 45 MINS.

Topping

1 CUP BROWN SUGAR
1 CUP COCONUT
6 TBSP. MARGARINE OR BUTTER

1/2 CUP EVAPORATED MILK
1 TEASP. VANILLA

COMBINE ALL INGREDIENTS. SPREAD ON BAKED CAKE AND PUT UNDER BROILER UNTIL CAKE BUBBLES.

Dried Apple Pie

2-1/2 CUPS MASHED, COOKED APPLES
   THAT HAVE BEEN DRIED
1/2 CUP BROWN SUGAR
1/2 CUP WHITE SUGAR

1/2 TEASP. NUTMEG
1/4 TEASP. CINNAMON
1/2 TEASP. GROUND CLOVES
PIE CRUST FOR DOUBLE CRUST PIE

COMBINE NUTMEG, SUGARS, CLOVES, CINNAMON AND MIX WITH APPLES. FILL THE PIE CRUST, CUT SMALL VENT HOLES IN TOP CRUST, FLUTE EDGES AND BAKE AT 350 DEGREES FOR 50 MINS. OR UNTIL THE CRUST IS BROWN AND THE APPLES OOZE FROM THE VENT HOLES.

Seed Cake

1/2 LB. FLOUR
2 TEASP. BAKING POWDER
6 OZ. BUTTER OR MARGARINE
6 OZ. CASTER CONFECTIONER'S SUGAR

1 OZ. CARAWAY SEEDS
3 OZ. MIXED ORANGE/LEMON PEEL
2 EGGS
1 TBSP. WATER

PREHEAT OVEN TO 325 DEGREES. LINE ROUND 6-INCH CAKE TIN WITH GREASED PAPER. SIEVE FLOUR AND BAKING POWDER. CREAM BUTTER AND SUGAR AND BEAT IN EGGS. STIR IN FLOUR, CARAWAY SEEDS, MIXED PEELS AND WATER. BAKE IN CENTER OF THE OVEN FOR 1-1/4 TO 1-1/2 HOURS.

Rich White Cake with Strawberry Frosting

1/2 cup butter or margarine, softened	1 tbsp. plus 1 teasp. baking powder
1/2 cup shortening	1 teasp. salt
2 cups sugar	2 teasp. vanilla extract
2/3 cup water	1 teasp. almond extract
2/3 cup milk	6 egg whites
3 cups sifted cake flour	Strawberry frosting

Cream butter and shortening; gradually add sugar, beating at medium speed. Combine water and milk; set aside. Combine flour, baking powder and salt; add to creamed mixture alternately with milk mixture, beginning and ending with flour. Stir in flavorings. Beat egg whites (at room temperature) until stiff peaks form. Gently fold into batter. Pour into three greased and floured 9-inch round cake pans. Bake at 350 degrees for 20 mins. or until a wooden pick inserted in center comes out clean. Cool in pans 10 mins. Remove from pans and cool completely on wire racks. Spread strawberry frosting between layers and on top and sides of cake.

Strawberry Frosting

2-1/4 cups whole unsweetened frozen strawberries	2 egg whites
1 cup sugar	Dash of salt

Thaw strawberries; place in a strainer. Slightly mash, and let drain to measure 2/3 cup strawberry pulp. Combine pulp and remaining ingredients in top of a double boiler. Place over boiling water, beat at high speed of electric mixer 7 mins. Remove from heat. Yields enough frosting for one 3-layer cake.

Garnish with whole fresh strawberries

Overnight Apples (per serving)

1 apple	Sour cream
Pinch ground cloves	1/4 cup raisins
Pinch dried ground orange peel	Dash ground nutmeg and
1/4 teasp. butter	cinnamon
Reconstituted orange juice	1/4 teasp. brown sugar

Core apples and set upright in Dutch oven. In center of each apple layer raisins, cloves, nutmeg, cinnamon, orange peel, brown sugar and butter. pour reconstituted orange juice (fresh won't work) to fill pot up to middle of apples. Cook in 200 degree oven overnight. (May be done in crock pot set on low overnight.) Serve with dollop of sour cream.

Raisin Pie with Meringue

2 EGG YOLKS
1 CUP SUGAR
1 LEMON, JUICE AND RIND

1 CUP SEEDLESS RAISINS
PINCH SALT
1/3 CUP WATER

COOK RAISINS FOR A FEW MINUTES IN THE WATER. ADD SUGAR, LEMON, SALT AND BEATEN YOLKS. POUR IN PAN LINED WITH UNBAKED PASTRY AND BAKE UNTIL SET IN MODERATE OVEN. COVER WITH MERINGUE MADE WITH 2 WHITES.

Poor Man's Pecan Pie

1/2 CUP GRAPE NUTS
1/2 CUP LUKEWARM WATER
1 CUP BROWN SUGAR
1 CUP CORN SYRUP
1/4 CUP BUTTER

1/8 TEASP. SALT
3 EGGS (OR 2 EGGS AND 1 TEASP. CORNSTARCH)
1 TEASP. VANILLA
1 UNBAKED PIE SHELL

SOAK GRAPE NUTS IN 1/2 CUP WARM WATER UNTIL WATER IS ABSORBED. COMBINE SUGAR, CORN SYRUP, BUTTER AND SALT IN PAN. BRING TO A BOIL QUICKLY, STIRRING UNTIL SUGAR IS DISSOLVED. REMOVE FROM HEAT. BEAT EGGS UNTIL FOAMY. ADD SMALL AMOUNT OF HOT SYRUP MIXTURE TO EGGS BEATING WELL. ADD THE REMAINING AMOUNT TO HOT SYRUP MIXTURE, MIXING WELL. STIR IN SOFTENED GRAPE NUTS AND VANILLA. POUR INTO PASTRY LINED PAN. BAKE AT 375 DEGREES FOR 45-50 MINS. SERVE WITH WHIPPED CREAM IF DESIRED.

Pinto Bean Pie

1-1/4 CUPS SUGAR
1 STICK BUTTER, SOFTENED
3 EGGS, BEATEN
1/2 CUP PINTO BEANS, COOKED SOFT (MASH)

1 TEASP. VANILLA
1 CUP COCONUT OR PECANS, CHOPPED, OR 1/2 CUP COCONUT AND 1/2 CUP PECANS, CHOPPED

MIX ALL INGREDIENTS TOGETHER AND POUR INTO THE FOLLOWING CRUST:

1-1/2 CUPS FLOUR
1-1/2 TEASP. SUGAR (MIX WITH FLOUR)

1/2 CUP VEGETABLE OIL
2 TEASP. MILK (WHIPPED WITH THE OIL)

MIX ALL INGREDIENTS IN BOWL UNTIL FLOUR IS ALL DAMPENED. PRESS FIRMLY INTO GLASS PIE PLACE, BOTTOM AND SIDES. POUR IN BEAN MIXTURE. BAKE ON BOTTOM RACK OF 400 DEGREES OVEN FOR 15 MINS. REDUCE HEAT TO 350 DEGREES AND BAKE 45 MINS. LONGER.

Raisin Pie

1-1/2 cups seeded raisins
1-1/2 cups boiling water
1 tbsp. flour
1/2 cup sugar

1/2 cup finely chopped walnuts
1 tbsp. lemon juice
grated rind of 1/2 lemon

Wash the raisins carefully and cook in the boiling water until tender. Mix flour and sugar; add to cooked raisins. Add the lemon gratings and walnuts. Cool slightly and bake in a double crust pie.

Grape Nuts Raisin Pie

3/4 cup Grape Nuts
3/4 cup brown sugar, firmly packed
1/4 cup vinegar
3/4 cup raisins, chopped

2-1/4 cups hot water
3 tbsp. butter
1 recipe for 9-inch double crust pie

Combine Grape Nuts, raisins, sugar, water, vinegar and butter. Cook 10 mins. Cool. Line pie plate with crust. Fill with Grape Nuts mixture. Arrange lattice of pastry strips across top. Moisten edges of pie with cold water. Bake in hot oven (425 degrees) for 10 mins., then decrease heat to 350 degrees and bake 30 mins. longer.

Tipsy Pudding

4 oz. breadcrumbs
4 oz. raisins
4 oz. currants
4 oz. chopped apples
1/2 teasp. salt

4 oz. brown sugar
4 eggs
1 teasp. ground ginger
1/2 teasp. grated nutmeg
1 sherry glass of brandy

Mix all ingredients together and steam in well-greased pan set in a pan of water for 3 hours. Serve with Brandy Sauce.

Brandy Hard Sauce

5 tbsp. butter (no substitute)
1 cup Confectioner's sugar

2 tbsp. brandy

Cream butter, slowly add sugar, beating well until creamy and pale yellow. Add Brandy and blend well. Cover and refrigerate. Serve cool, but not chilled.

TEA CAKE

3 CUPS GOLDEN RAISINS

2 CUPS BROWN SUGAR, FIRMLY PACKED

3 CUPS DARK RAISINS

1 CUP COLD BREAKFAST TEA

1/2 CUP IRISH WHISKEY

1 TBSP. HONEY, DISSOLVED IN A LITTLE
WARM WATER FOR GLAZING

3 EGGS, BEATEN

3 TEASP. BAKING POWDER

GRATED RIND OF 1 LEMON

1 TEASP. GRATED NUTMEG

1 TEASP. GRATED ALLSPICE

4 CUPS UNBLEACHED WHITE FLOUR

PUT RAISINS, BROWN SUGAR, TEA AND WHISKEY IN A BOWL AND SOAK OVERNIGHT, OR AT LEAST 12 HOURS. PREHEAT OVEN TO 300 DEGREES. ADD FLOUR, EGGS, BAKING POWDER, GRATED LEMON RIND AND SPICES TO RAISIN MIXTURE. MIX WELL WITH WOODEN SPOON. PLACE MIXTURE IN 10-INCH ROUND CAKE PAN AND BAKE FOR 1-1/2 HOURS UNTIL NICELY BROWNED. COOL ON WIRE RACK. WHEN COOL, BRUSH WITH WARM HONEY MIXTURE FOR A SHINY GLAZE. SERVE WARM WITH BUTTER.

BLUEBERRY SHORTCAKE

3-1/2 CUPS SIFTED ALL-PURPOSE FLOUR

1 TBSP. BAKING POWDER

1/2 TEASP. SALT

1/2 CUP (1 STICK) BUTTER

1 EGG

3/4 CUP MILK

1 PINT BLUEBERRIES

1/2 CUP SUGAR

PREHEAT OVEN TO 400 DEGREES. SIFT TOGETHER FLOUR, BAKING POWDER AND SALT. CUT IN BUTTER WITH PASTRY BLENDER OR TWO FORKS UNTIL MIXTURE IS LIKE CORN MEAL. IN A SEPARATE BOWL, BEAT EGGS THOROUGHLY, THEN STIR IN MILK. STIR THIS MIXTURE INTO FLOUR WITH A FORK. DIVIDE DOUGH IN HALF AND ROLL ONE PORTION TO FIT BOTTOM OF 9-INCH PIE PAN. COVER WITH BLUEBERRIES, THEN SPRINKLE WITH SUGAR. COVER WITH REMAINING DOUGH (IN CIRCLE). BAKE FOR 30 MINS. OR UNTIL DOUGH IS GOLDEN BROWN. SERVE WITH CREAM, WHIPPED CREAM OR ICE CREAM. SERVES 6.

BAKED HONEY CUSTARD

2 CUPS MILK

4 TBSP. HONEY

3 EGGS

1/4 TEASP. SALT

MACE OR NUTMEG

PREHEAT OVEN TO 375 DEGREES. SCALD MILK, THEN STIR IN HONEY. BEAT EGGS AND SALT TOGETHER, THEN SLOWLY BEAT IN LITTLE OF HOT MILK MIXTURE. COMBINE THE TWO AND POUR INTO 6 CUSTARD CUPS, SPRINKLE WITH MACE OR NUTMEG. SET CUPS IN PAN OF HOT WATER AND BAKE FOR 30-40 MINS. WHEN KNIFE INSERTED IN CENTER COMES OUT DRY, CUSTARD IS COOKED. REMOVE CUPS FROM WATER IMMEDIATELY AND SERVE COLD. YIELDS: 6 SERVINGS.

BERRY FOOL

1 QUART RIPE GOOSEBERRIES, STRAWBER-
   RIES, BLACKBERRIES OR RASPBERRIES
1-1/2 TEASP. GRATED LEMON RIND

1-1/2 CUPS HEAVY CREAM
1 CUP SUGAR
1/2 CUPS CRUMBLED MACAROONS

COMBINE BERRIES WITH 1/4 CUP WATER IN SAUCEPAN. COOK OVER A LOW HEAT UNTIL FRUIT IS EXTREMELY TENDER. REMOVE FROM HEAT AND PUREE IN BLENDER. WHILE HOT, STIR IN SUGAR AND LEMON RIND. SET ASIDE TO COOL. WHIP CREAM UNTIL IT HOLDS SHAPE, THEN FOLD INTO COOL FRUIT PUREE. SPOON INTO SERVING BOWL, SPRINKLE SURFACE WITH MACAROON CRUMBS AND CHILL THOROUGHLY. SERVES 6.

PUMPKIN PUDDING

2 CUPS ALL-PURPOSE FLOUR
1/4 TEASP. BAKING SODA
1-1/2 TEASP. CINNAMON
1/4 TEASP. GINGER
1/2 CUP SWEET BUTTER, SOFTENED
3/4 CUP BROWN SUGAR, FIRMLY PACKED
3/4 CUP COOKED PUMPKIN
1 CUP WALNUTS, FINELY CHOPPED

1-1/2 TEASP. BAKING POWDER
1 TEASP. SALT
1/4 TEASP. CLOVES
1/8 TEASP. NUTMEG
1/4 CUP GRANULATED SUGAR
2 EGGS
1/4 CUP LIGHT MOLASSES

SIFT THE FLOUR ALONG WITH THE BAKING POWDER, SODA, SALT, CINNAMON, CLOVES, GINGER AND NUTMEG; SET ASIDE. IN A LARGE MIXING BOWL, BEAT BUTTER WITH SUGARS. ADD EGGS, BEAT UNTIL LIGHT AND FLUFFY. IN A SMALL BOWL, COMBINE PUMPKIN AND MOLASSES. INTO THE SUGAR MIXTURE, BEAT THE PUMPKIN MIXTURE ALTERNATELY WITH FLOUR MIXTURE, STARTING AND ENDING WITH FLOUR. STIR IN WALNUTS. TURN BATTER INTO WELL-GREASED 1-1/2 QUART PUDDING MOLD OR PAN. COVER WITH FOIL AND TIE WITH STRING TO KEEP IN PLACE. PLACE ON A TRIVET IN A DEEP KETTLE. ADD BOILING WATER TO COME HALFWAY UP MOLD. COVER KETTLE. BRING TO BOILING REDUCE HEAT AND SIMMER 2-1/2 HOURS. AFTER COOLING FOR ABOUT 5 MINS., TURN PUDDING OUT ONTO A SERVING PLATE. SERVE WARM WITH VANILLA ICE CREAM. SERVES 6-8.

FRESH PEACH PIE

2 CUPS WATER
2 TBSP. CORNSTARCH
4 CUPS RIPE SLICED PEACHES
WHIPPED TOPPING

1 CUP SUGAR
1 (3 OZ.) PACKAGE APRICOT OR PEACH
   GELATIN
1 BAKED PIE SHELL

HEAT WATER, SUGAR AND CORNSTARCH TO BOILING AND COOK UNTIL THICKENED. REMOVE FROM HEAT AND ADD GELATIN. COOL. ADD SLICED PEACHES AND POUR INTO BAKED PIE SHELL. CHILL. GARNISH WITH WHIPPED TOPPING BEFORE SERVING. IF PEACHES ARE VERY JUICY, REDUCE WATER BY 1/4 CUP.

A SURE MONEY-MAKER AT MANY WEST VIRGINIA COUNTY FAIRS. I ATE MY FIRST
FUNNEL CAKE AT THE WEST VIRGINIA STATE FAIR AT LEWISBURG.

FUNNEL CAKES I

2-1/2 CUPS SELF-RISING FLOUR
1/4 CUP SUGAR
1-1/3 CUPS MILK

2 EGGS, SLIGHTLY BEATEN
VEGETABLE OIL
SIFTED POWDERED SUGAR (OPTIONAL)

STIR ALL BUT POWDERED SUGAR TOGETHER. FUNNEL INTO DEEP OIL (375 DEGREES) 1/4
CUP AT A TIME. FRY ABOUT A MINUTE UNTIL GOLDEN. DUST WITH POWDERED SUGAR.

FUNNEL CAKES II

3 EGGS
2 CUPS MILK
1/4 CUP SUGAR

3 TO 4 CUPS FLOUR
1/2 TEASP. SALT
2 TEASP. BAKING POWDER

BEAT EGGS; ADD SUGAR AND MILK. SIFT HALF THE FLOUR, SALT AND BAKING POWDER
TOGETHER AND ADD TO MILK AND EGG MIXTURE. BEAT THE BATTER SMOOTH AND ADD
ONLY AS MUCH MORE FLOUR AS NEEDED. BATTER SHOULD BE THIN ENOUGH TO RUN
THROUGH A FUNNEL. DROP FROM FUNNEL INTO DEEP HOT FAT (375 DEGREES). SPIRALS
AND INTRICATE SHAPES CAN BE MADE BY SWIRLING AND CRISS-CROSSING WHILE CONTROL-
LING THE FUNNEL SPOUT WITH YOUR FINGER. SERVE HOT WITH MOLASSES, JELLY OR JAM,
OR SPRINKLE WITH POWDERED SUGAR.

APPLE FUNNEL CAKES

1-1/4 CUPS FLOUR
3/4 CUP APPLE JUICE
1 EGG

1 TEASP. BAKING POWDER
1 TEASP. ALMOND FLAVORING
1/8 TEASP. SALT

ABOUT 30 MINS. BEFORE SERVING, HEAT A 12-INCH SKILLET OVER MDEIUM HEAT WITH 3/
4-INCH OF OIL TO ABOUT 325 DEGREES OR USE ELECTRIC SKILLET. IN MEDIUM BOWL WITH
WIRE WHIP, ADD FLOUR, BAKING POWDER, ALMOND FLAVORING, SALT, EGG AND APPLE
JUICE. POUR 1/4-CUP BATTER INTO FUNNEL WHILE HOLDING END WITH FINGER. LET BATTER
RUN IN A 6-INCH SPIRAL INTO OIL. FRY 3 TO 5 MINS. UNTIL BROWN. DRAIN ON PAPER TOWEL.
MIX 2 TBSP. CONFECTIONERS SUGAR AND 1/4 TEASP. CINNAMON AND SPRINKLE OVER
CAKES. YIELDS 7 CAKES.

Quick Peach Dumplings

1 QUART FRESH PEACHES, SLICED
4 TBSP. BUTTER
1/4 TEASP. SALT
2 TBSP. BUTTER OR SHORTENING

2/3 CUP SUGAR
1 CUP FLOUR
1-1/2 TEASP. BAKING POWDER
1/3 TO 1/2 CUP MILK

PUT SLICED PEACHES, SUGAR AND BUTTER IN HEAVY PAN WITH TIGHT LID. BRING PEACHES TO A BOIL. SIFT FLOUR, SALT AND BAKING POWDER TOGETHER. CUT BUTTER INTO FLOUR MIXTURE UNTIL CRUMBLY. ADD ENOUGH MILK TO MAKE A DROP BISCUIT DOUGH. DROP PIECES OF THE DOUGH (SIZE OF PECANS) OVER BOILING PEACHES. REDUCE HEAT, COVER TIGHTLY AND SIMMER FOR 15 TO 20 MINS. UNTIL DUMPLINGS ARE COOKED THROUGH. SERVE HOT WITH WHIPPED CREAM OR ICE CREAM.

Mountain Strawberry Shortcake

1-1/2 QUARTS OF WEST VIRGINIA STRAW-
BERRIES
1/2 CUP SHORTENING
3 CUPS ALL-PURPOSE FLOUR
1/4 TEASP. SALT
1-1/2 CUPS MILK

1-1/2 CUPS SUGAR
2 EGGS, WELL BEATEN
1-1/2 TBSP. BAKING POWDER
1-1/2 TEASP. VANILLA EXTRACT
1-1/2 CUPS HEAVY CREAM

PREHEAT OVEN TO 375 DEGREES. WASH STRAWBERRIES. SLICE ONE QUART, LEAVING REMAINDER WHOLE. CREAM SUGAR AND SHORTENING TOGETHER IN A LARGE BOWL. ADD BEATEN EGGS. MIX WELL. SIFT TOGETHER FLOUR, BAKING POWDER AND SALT. STIR VANILLA EXTRACT INTO MILK. ADD PART OF FLOUR MIXTURE ALTERNATELY WITH PART OF MILK MIXTURE, STIRRING AFTER EACH ADDITION UNTIL BOTH ARE USED UP. OIL A SHALLOW OBLONG BAKING PAN, ABOUT 10x13 AND POUR IN BATTER. BAKE 20-30 MINS. WHIP THE HEAVY CREAM WITH JUST ENOUGH SUGAR TO SWEETEN. COOL SHORTCAKE; CUT INTO SERVING PIECES AND SPLIT EACH. SPREAD WHIPPED CREAM AND SLICED STRAWBERRIES BETWEEN LAYERS. TOP WITH MORE CREAM AND WHOLE BERRIES. SERVES 6-8.

Pan Fried Peaches

6 PEACHES
1 TBSP. SUGAR

3 TBSP. BUTTER OR MARGARINE
1/4 TO 1/2 TEASP. CINNAMON

WASH, PEEL, HALVE AND PIT PEACHES. SLICE 1/2-INCH THICK. MELT BUTTER IN FRYING PAN. FRY PEACHES OVER MODERATELY LOW HEAT UNTIL TENDER, TURNING TO BROWN EVENLY (ABOUT 12-15 MINS.) SPRINKLE WITH MIXTURE OF SUGAR AND CINNAMON. SERVE OVER HOT BISCUITS OR VANILLA ICE CREAM. 6 SERVINGS.

SOUR CREAM COFFEE CAKE CUPCAKES

1 CUP BUTTER	2 CUPS PLUS 4 TEASP. SUGAR
2 EGGS	1 CUP SOUR CREAM
1 TEASP. VANILLA	2 CUPS FLOUR
1 TEASP. BROWN SUGAR	1 TEASP. SALT
1 CUP CHOPPED BLACK WALNUTS	1 TEASP. CINNAMON

CREAM BUTTER AND 2 CUPS SUGAR UNTIL LIGHT AND FLUFFY. ADD EGGS, ONE AT A TIME, BEATING WELL AFTER EACH ADDITION. FOLD IN SOUR CREAM AND VANILLA. SIFT FLOUR, BROWN SUGAR, SALT; ADD TO BATTER. IN A SMALL BOWL, COMBINE 4 TEASP. SUGAR, CINNAMON AND NUTS. FILL CUPCAKE LINERS 1/3 FULL WITH BATTER; SPRINKLE GENEROUSLY WITH CINNAMON-NUT MIXTURE. ADD MORE BATTER UNTIL LINERS ARE 2/3 FULL. SPRINKLE AGAIN WITH CINNAMON-NUT MIXTURE. BAKE AT 350 DEGREES FOR 25-30 MINS. *(A 1987 BLACK WALNUT CONTEST WINNING RECIPE FOR MARIE BAILEY OF SPENCER, W.VA.)*

CRUSTLESS SWEET POTATO PIE

4 CUPS GRATED RAW SWEET POTATOES	1 CUP MILK
1 CUP SELF-RISING FLOUR	3/4 CUP BUTTER OR MARGARINE
1 TEASP. GROUND CINNAMON OR VANILLA	2 CUPS SUGAR
EXTRACT	4 EGGS, BEATEN

PREHEAT OVEN TO 350 DEGREES. GRATE SWEET POTATOES. MELT BUTTER. MIX FLOUR, SUGAR, CINNAMON OR VANILLA. THEN ADD EGGS AND MELTED BUTTER. ADD MILK AND BEAT WELL. MIX IN SWEET POTATOES; BEAT AGAIN. POUR INTO 9x13 PAN AND BAKE 35-40 MINS. SWEET POTATOES WILL FORM CRUNCHY TOPPING FOR CUSTARD PIE.

CORNMEAL POUND CAKE

6 TBSP. BUTTER	1 CUP SUGAR
4 EGGS	1-1/4 CUPS SIFTED PASTRY FLOUR
3/4 TEASP. BAKING POWDER	1/4 CUP SIFTED WHITE CORNMEAL
1/8 TEASP. FRESHLY GRATED NUTMEG	1/4 TEASP. CINNAMON
OR 1/4 TEASP. DRIED NUTMEG	2 TBSP. APPLE BRANDY (OR REGULAR)
1/2 TEASP. VANILLA	

THOROUGHLY CREAM BUTTER AND SUGAR UNTIL FLUFFY. BEAT IN EGGS, ONE AT A TIME. SIFT TOGETHER FLOUR, BAKING POWDER AND CORNMEAL. COMBINE SPICES WITH FLOUR MIXTURE. BLEND DRY INGREDIENTS INTO THE BATTER **BY HAND**, ALTERNATING WITH BRANDY AND VANILLA. POUR INTO GREASED SHALLOW CAKE PAN, AN 8-INCH SQUARE PAN OR 10x6 PAN. THE PAN SHOULD BE LINED WITH WAXED PAPER. BAKE AT 325 DEGREES FOR 1-1/2 HOURS. REMOVE FROM OVEN AND COOL FOR 10 MINS. INVERT ON CAKE RACK AND STRIP OFF WAX PAPER.

APPLE WALNUT CAKE

4 CUPS COARSELY CHOPPED APPLES

2 CUPS SUGAR

2 EGGS

1/2 CUP VEGETABLE OIL

2 TEASP. VANILLA

2 CUPS SIFTED ALL-PURPOSE FLOUR

2 TEASP. BAKING SODA

2 TEASP. CINNAMON

1 TEASP. SALT

1 CUP CHOPPED WALNUTS

COMBINE APPLES AND SUGAR AND LET STAND. BEAT EGGS SLIGHTLY, BEAT IN OIL AND VANILLA. MIX AND SIFT FLOUR, BAKING SODA, CINNAMON AND SALT. ALTERNATELY STIR APPLE MIXTURE AND FLOUR MIXTURE INTO EGGS. ADD WALNUTS. POUR INTO GREASED AND FLOURED 13x9x2 OBLONG PAN. BAKE AT 350 FOR 1 HOUR, OR UNTIL CAKE TESTS DONE. LET STAND IN PAN UNTIL COOL. TURN OUT ON WIRE RACK TO CONTINUE COOLING. FROST WITH LEMON BUTTER FROSTING AND DECORATE WITH WHOLE WALNUTMEATS. CUT IN SQUARES TO SERVE. SERVES 12 TO 15.

LEMON BUTTER FROSTING

4 TBSP. BUTTER OR MARGARINE

3 CUPS CONFECTIONER'S SUGAR

PINCH OF SALT

2 TBSP. LEMON JUICE

1-2 TBSP. COLD WATER

CREAM BUTTER OR MARGARINE. ADD SUGAR GRADUALLY, CREAMING THOROUGHLY. BEAT IN LEMON JUICE AND ENOUGH COLD WATER TO MAKE OF SPREADABLE CONSISTENCY. BEAT IN SALT. SPREAD ON THOROUGHLY COOLED CAKE. MAKES ABOUT 3-1/2 CUPS FROSTING.

EGGLESS, MILKLESS, BUTTERLESS CAKE

2 CUPS BROWN SUGAR

2 CUPS HOT WATER

2 TBSP. SHORTENING

1 TEASP. SALT

1 TEASP. SODA

1 PACKAGE SEEDLESS RAISINS

1 TEASP. CINNAMON

1 TEASP. CLOVES

3 CUPS SIFTED FLOUR

1 TEASP. HOT WATER

BOIL TOGETHER SUGAR, WATER, SHORTENING, SALT, RAISINS AND SPICES FOR 5 MINS. REMOVE FROM HEAT AND, WHEN COLD, ADD THE FLOUR AND THE BAKING SODA DISSOLVED IN 1 TEASPOON OF HOT WATER. POUR INTO TWO LOAF PANS AND BAKE AT 325 DEGREES ABOUT 45 MINS. THESE CAKES STAY MOIST FOR A LONG TIME AND ARE GOOD FOR LUNCHBOXES.

Chocolate Peanut Butter Cake

1-1/2 cups sugar
1 cup vegetable shortening
2 eggs
1 tbsp. peanut butter
1 teasp. vanilla
1 cup buttermilk
1/2 cup boiling water

2-1/4 cups sifted flour
1 teasp. soda
1 teasp. baking powder
1/2 teasp. salt
1/2 cup cocoa
peanut butter
icing

Mix sugar, shortening and 1 tbsp. peanut butter. Mix cocoa with boiling water and add to peanut butter mixture. Add vanilla and beaten eggs. Add buttermilk; stir. Add flour, baking powder, soda and salt. Beat mixture until smooth and fluffy. Pour into 9x13 pan and bake at 350 degrees for 35-40 mins. While cake is still hot, spread with layer of peanut butter, then top with icing.

Icing

1 lb. box confectioner's sugar
2 tbsp. cocoa
pinch of salt

1 stick margarine
1 teasp. vanilla
4 tbsp. evaporated milk

Mix together sugar, margarine, cocoa and salt. Heat milk; pour over sugar mixture. Stir in vanilla. Beat until smooth and creamy. If too stiff, add more milk. Spread over cake.

Apple Tube Cake

2 cups sugar
3 eggs
1-1/2 teasp. baking soda
1 teasp. each cinnamon, allspice, nutmeg
1-1/2 cups peeled and chopped apples
1 cup walnuts

1 cup vegetable oil
2-1/4 cups all-purpose flour,
  sifted
1/2 teasp. salt
1 cup buttermilk
1 teasp. vanilla

Beat sugar, oil and eggs on medium speed, about 5 mins. Add flour, spices, soda, salt and buttermilk; mix well. Then add apples, nuts and vanilla. Bake in tube pan at 350 degrees for about 1 hour or 70 mins.

Orange Glaze

1/4 cup orange juice
2 tbsp. melted butter

1/2 box (4 oz.) powdered sugar

Mix all ingredients well and pour over Apple Tube Cake while still warm. Let set in tube pan until thoroughly cooled.

OLD-FASHIONED DEVIL'S FOOD CAKE

2 EGGS
3/4 CUP COCOA
2 CUPS SUGAR
1 CUP BOILING WATER
2 TEASP. SODA

1 CUP SHORTENING
3 CUPS FLOUR
1 CUP SOUR CREAM
2 TEASP. VANILLA

MIX ALL INGREDIENTS TOGETHER. POUR INTO GREASED AND FLOURED LOAF PAN. BAKE IN SLOW OVEN (250 DEGREES) FOR 30 MINS., OR UNTIL CAKE TESTS DONE.

OLD-FASHIONED SPONGE CAKE

8 EGGS
2 CUPS SUGAR
1 SCANT TBSP. VANILLA

2 CUPS SIFTED FLOUR
1-1/2 TEASP. VINEGAR

SEPARATE EGGS AND BEAT IN DIFFERENT BOWLS, ADDING 1 CUP OF SUGAR TO EACH MIXTURE. PUT TOGETHER AND ADD THE VINEGAR AND SIFTED FLOUR. ADD VANILLA AND MIX WELL. BAKE IN 250 DEGREE OVEN FOR ABOUT 30 MINS. IN ANGEL FOOD CAKE (TUBE) PAN.

LAZY DAISY OATMEAL CAKE

1-1/4 CUPS BOILING WATER
1/2 CUP SOFT BUTTER OR MARGARINE
1 CUP BROWN SUGAR
2 EGGS
1 TEASP. BAKING SODA
3/4 TEASP. CINNAMON

1 CUP OATMEAL
1 CUP WHITE SUGAR
1 TEASP. VANILLA
1-1/2 CUPS FLOUR
1/2 TEASP. SALT

POUR WATER OVER OATS AND LET STAND 20 MINS. MIX ALL INGREDIENTS WELL. BAKE AT 350 DEGREES FOR 50-55 MINS.

ICING:

1/4 CUP MELTED BUTTER
1/2 CUP BROWN SUGAR
1/3 CUP NUTS

3 TBSP. CONDENSED MILK OR
    HALF AND HALF
3/4 CUP COCONUT.

COMBINE ALL THESE INGREDIENTS, MIX WELL. SPREAD OVER COOLED CAKE. PLACE IN OVEN UNDER BROILER UNTIL ICING BUBBLY. *BETTY DUNLAP*

163

BREAD PUDDING WITH RUM SAUCE*

12-15 CUPS OF COARSE **HOMEMADE**
   BREADCRUMBS
3 CUPS SUGAR
1 TBSP. CINNAMON
1 TBSP. NUTMEG
1 TBSP. VANILLA

9 LARGE EGGS (IF HALVING RECIPE
   USE 6 EGGS)
1 LB. BUTTER (NOT MARGARINE),
   MELTED
6 OZ. DARK RUM
1 TEASP. RUM FLAVORING (OPTIONAL)

MIX ALL INGREDIENTS TOGETHER AND BAKE UNCOVERED IN A WATER BATH AT 350 DEGREES UNTIL SET. USE A PAN AT LEAST 3 INCHES DEEP AS PUDDING PUFFS UP WHILE COOKING, THEN SETTLES AS IT COOLS.

RUM SAUCE

6 CUPS WATER
2 CUPS SUGAR
1/2 CUP DARK RUM
1 LB. BUTTER (NO SUBSTITUTE)

8 TBSP. CORN STARCH
1 TEASP. CINNAMON
1 TEASP. NUTMEG
1 TEASP. VANILLA

BRING 4 CUPS WATER AND THE SUGAR TO A BOIL, THEN TAKE 2 CUPS OF COLD WATER AND ADD TO CORN STARCH, MIXING WELL. ADD TO THE SUGAR/WATER, WITH SPICES AND STIR UNTIL IT THICKENS. THEN ADD RUM AND BUTTER AND MIX THOROUGHLY. POUR OVER PUDDING.

*THIS RECIPE MAKES 20-30 SERVINGS BUT MAY BE HALVED SUCCESSFULLY. FROM *ASHBY BERKELEY, OWNER/CHEF AT THE RIVERSIDE INN AND PENCE SPRINGS RESORT, PENCE SPRINGS, WV.*

SCRIPTURE CAKE

4-1/2 CUPS (1ST KINGS 4-22) FLOUR
1 CUP (JUDGES 5-25 LAST CLAUSE) BUTTER
2 CUPS (JEREMIAH 6-20) SUGAR
2 CUPS (1ST SAMUEL 30-12) RAISINS
2 CUPS (NAHUM 3-12) FIGS
2 CUPS (NUMBER 17-18) ALMONDS
2 TBSP. (1ST SAMUEL 14-13) HONEY

1 PINCH (LEVITICUS 2-13) SALT
6 (JEREMIAH 17-11) EGGS
1/2 CUP (JUDGES 4-19 LAST CLAUSE)
   MILK
2 TBSP. (AMOS 4-5) LEAVEN [BAKING
   POWDER]

MIX LIKE A FRUIT CAKE, SEASON TO TASTE WITH (2ND CHRONICLES 9-9) SPICES. BAKE IN 325 DEGREE OVEN UNTIL DONE.

Baked Apple Dumplings

1-1/2 RECIPES OF SHORTCAKE BISCUIT
6 BAKING APPLES SMALL- TO MEDIUM-SIZED
3/4 CUP FIRMLY PACKED BROWN SUGAR
1/3 CUP CHOPPED NUTS

1-1/2 TBSP. BUTTER
1 TEASP. CINNAMON
2 TBSP. LEMON JUICE

Shortcake Biscuit

2 CUPS FLOUR
1 TEASP. SALT
6 TO 8 TBSP. SHORTENING

3 TEASP. BAKING POWDER
2 TO 4 TBSP. SUGAR
APPROXIMATELY 2/3 CUP MILK

SIFT FLOUR; MEASURE. ADD BAKING POWDER, SALT AND SUGAR. SIFT AGAIN. CUT IN SHORTENING WITH PASTRY BLENDER OR 2 KNIVES, UNTIL MIXTURE RESEMBLES COARSE CORNMEAL. STIRRING IT IN WITH A FORK, ADD ENOUGH MILK TO MAKE A SOFT DOUGH; CONTINUE STIRRING UNTIL ALL OF THE FLOUR DISAPPEARS. TURN ONTO FLOURED BOARD; KNEAD LIGHTLY FOR ABOUT 30 SECS. TURN SMOOTH SIDE UP AND PAT DOUGH OR ROLL OUT ABOUT 1/4-INCH THICK. CUT INTO 6 SQUARES. PEEL AND CORE APPLES. PLACE EACH ON A SQUARE OF BISCUIT DOUGH. FILL CENTERS WITH MIXTURE OF BROWN SUGAR, CINNAMON AND CHOPPED NUTS. SPRINKLE WITH LEMON JUICE AND DOT WITH BUTTER. BRING OPPOSITE CORNERS OF THE DOUGH TOGETHER ON TOP OF APPLES. MOISTEN EDGES OF SIDES AND SEAL. MAKE SEVERAL GASHES IN EACH WITH SHARP KNIFE. BAKE AT 375 DEGREES FOR 40 MINS. OR UNTIL APPLES ARE TENDER AND SHORTCAKE IS BROWN. SERVES 6. GOOD SERVED WITH WHIPPED CREAM.

IF SWEETER DUMPLINGS ARE DESIRED, AFTER THEY HAVE BEGUN TO BROWN, BASTE THEM WITH SYRUP MADE BY BOILING TOGETHER FOR 3 MINS.: 1/2 CUP SUGAR, 1 CUP WATER, 1 TBSP. BUTTER AND 1/2 TEASP. CINNAMON.

Honey Shortbread

1 CUP BUTTER
1/3 CUP HONEY
1 TEASP. VANILLA

2-1/2 CUPS ALL-PURPOSE FLOUR
3/4 CUP CHOPPED PECANS

WITH AN ELECTRIC MIXER BEAT BUTTER, HONEY AND VANILLA TOGETHER UNTIL MIXTURE IS LIGHT AND FLUFFY. ADD FLOUR, A CUP AT A TIME, BEATING WELL AFTER EACH ADDITION. IF DOUGH BECOME TOO STIFF, KNEAD IN REMAINING FLOUR BY HAND. WORK IN NUTS. PAT DOUGH INTO SHORTBREAD MOLD OR UNGREASED 9-INCH CAST-IRON SKILLET. SCORE THE SURFACE WITH A KNIFE SO IT CAN BE DIVIDED INTO 24 WEDGES; WITH A FORK, PRICK DEEPLY INTO THE KNIFE SCORES. BAKE AT 300 DEGREES FOR 35-40 MINS. COOL 10 MINS. AND REMOVE FROM PAN. CUT INTO WEDGES WHILE WARM. MAKES 24 WEDGES.

Prune Cake

1-1/2 cups sugar
1 cup vegetable oil
3 eggs, beaten
1 cup buttermilk
1 cup chopped nuts
2 cups flour
1 teasp. soda

1 teasp. cinnamon
1 teasp. nutmeg
1 teasp. allspice
1/2 teasp. salt
1 cup cooked prunes, seeded and
   chopped fine
2 teasp. vanilla

Blend sugar and oil; add eggs and beat well. Sift dry ingredients together three times; add alternately with buttermilk, beating well after each addition. Add nuts, prunes and vanilla. Stir to distribute through batter. Pour batter into greased and floured 9x13x2 cake pan. Bake at 350 degrees for 35-40 mins. or until cake tests done. While cake is baking, prepare sauce and pour it over cake while it is hot. Leave in pan.

Sauce

1 cup sugar
1/2 cup buttermilk
1/2 teasp. soda

2 teasp. vanilla
1/4 to 1/2 cup butter

Combine all ingredients in saucepan. Boil for 1 min. Pour immediately over cake while it is hot.

Grape Pie

Prepare your favorite two-crust pastry.

1 lb. green seedless grapes
1/2 cup brown sugar

1/2 cup molasses

Place bottom pastry into 9-inch pie pan. Fill with whole grapes, then sprinkle with the brown sugar and cover with the molasses. Add top crust and bake for 35 mins. in moderate (350-375 degree) oven.

BUTTERHORNS

PASTRY:

1 CUP BUTTER
1 EGG YOLK, BEATEN

2 CUPS FLOUR
1/2 CUP SOUR CREAM

WITH FORK, CUT BUTTER INTO FLOUR UNTIL IT RESEMBLES CRUMBS. COMBINE EGG YOLK AND SOUR CREAM. BLEND INTO FLOUR MIXTURE. CHILL OVERNIGHT, OR IN FREEZER FOR A FEW HOURS.

FILLING:

3/4 CUP SUGAR
3/4 CUP MINCED NUTS
1 TEASP. CINNAMON

EGG WHITE TO BRUSH PASTRY BEFORE
BAKING

DIVIDE PASTRY DOUGH INTO 4 PARTS ON LIGHTLY FLOURED BOARD. ROLL EACH PART INTO 10-INCH CIRCLE. SPRINKLE WITH 1/4 OF FILLING AND CUT INTO 12-16 PIE-SHAPED WEDGES. ROLL UP EACH WEDGE FROM WIDE END, PLACE ON LIGHTLY GREASED COOKIE SHEET. BRUSH WITH EGG WHITE. BAKE AT 350 DEGREES FOR 20 MINS. OR UNTIL LIGHTLY BROWNED. MAKES 4 DOZEN. *MARY JO ZSOLDAS*

WILD FOODS

     While in most areas of the United States gathering wild foods to cook, or killing game for the table, may be almost extinct - not so in West Virginia.

     The National Wild Foods Association, headquartered in Parkersburg, W.Va., boasts members from all over the nation, and has hosted the annual North Bend (State Park) Nature Wonder Weekend, the 3rd weekend of September, for some 30 years.

     There is plenty of small game and fish to be had in West Virginia. In a poll taken in 1992, 52 percent of the State's population said they hunted wild animals, and 39 percent said the primary reason was **for food**.

     By far, however, the most popular game meat is venison. Many men traditionally take off work the first week of deer season, and in some rural counties schools are closed. An estimated 375,000 deer hunters go after the 900,000 to 1 million ungulates still roaming the State.

VENISON STEAKS OR CHOPS

8 VENISON STEAKS OR CHOPS,
   1-1/2 INCH THICK
DRY RED WINE
FRESHLY GROUND PEPPER
SEASONED ALL-PURPOSE FLOUR

1 SMALL ONION, MINCED
BUTTER
1/2 LB. MUSHROOMS, SLICED
3 SLICES BACON, CUT INTO SMALL PIECES
1/2 CUPS DICED CELERY

PLACE STEAKS/CHOPS IN A SHALLOW DISH AND POUR WINE OVER THE TOP TO COVER MEAT.
SPRINKLE LIBERALLY WITH PEPPER. LET STAND OVERNIGHT, TURNING OCCASIONALLY.
REMOVE STEAKS FROM MARINADE AND PAT DRY. DREDGE IN SEASONED FLOUR. HEAT
ENOUGH BUTTER IN HEAVY SKILLET TO COVER BOTTOM. ADD STEAKS AND COOK UNTIL
BROWNED ON BOTH SIDES AND TENDER. WHILE STEAKS ARE COOKING, MELT 2 TBSP. BUTTER
IN ANOTHER SKILLET. ADD MUSHROOMS, BACON, ONION AND CELERY; COOK SLOWLY UNTIL
ONION IS TENDER. STIR IN ABOUT 1/4 CUP WINE, BRING TO A BOIL, SIMMER 2 MINS. SERVE
STEAKS TOPPED WITH WINE SAUCE. SERVES 8.

FRIED RABBIT

TENDER RABBIT CAN BE FRIED AND SERVED JUST LIKE CHICKEN,
THE FLAVOR IS MUCH THE SAME.

1 (3 TO 3-1/2 LB.) RABBIT, CUT UP
1/4 CUP ALL-PURPOSE FLOUR
1-1/2 TEASP. SALT
1 TEASP. PAPRIKA

1/4 TEASP. FRESHLY GROUND BLACK
   PEPPER
2 TO 3 TBSP. VEGETABLE OIL OR
   SHORTENING

WASH RABBIT AND PAT DRY WITH PAPER TOWELS. COMBINE FLOUR, SALT, PAPRIKA AND
PEPPER IN A PAPER OR PLASTIC BAG. DREDGE RABBIT PIECES, A FEW AT A TIME, UNTIL
THOROUGHLY COATED. IN A LARGE HEAVY SKILLET, HEAT OIL OR SHORTENING. ADD
RABBIT. COOK OVER MEDIUM HEAT 10 TO 15 MINS., TURNING PIECES TO BROWN EVENLY.
REDUCE HEAT AND COVER. COOK 30 MINS. UNCOVER AND COOK 25-35 MINS. LONGER OR
UNTIL MEAT IS TENDER. SERVES 6.

GRILLED TROUT

1 LARGE, FRESH TROUT

SALT, PEPPER, MELTED BUTTER

PREHEAT BROILER TO 450 DEGREES. CUT THE CLEANED TROUT SO IT WILL LIE FLAT WHEN
OPENED AND REMOVE BACKBONE. PLACE, SKIN SIDE DOWN IN WELL-OILED BROILING PAN.
SPRINKLE WITH SALT AND PEPPER AND BRUSH GENEROUSLY WITH BUTTER. BROIL 3-INCHES
FROM TIP OF UNIT FOR 8-10 MINS. OR UNTIL FISH FLAKES EASILY WITH FORK. DO NOT
OVERCOOK.

Wild Onions and Eggs

4 bunches of wild onions or
   green onions
6 eggs

2-3 tbsp. bacon fat
1 teasp. salt

Wash onions and chop both bulb and green tops finely. Cook in heated bacon fat with 1 tbsp. water added until onions are tender. Season eggs with salt and beat until yolks and whites are well blended. Pour over onions and scramble. Serves 4.

===============

Onion Stuffed Rabbit

1 rabbit (about 2 lbs.)
1-1/2 teasp. salt
1/8 teasp. pepper

1-1/2 cups sliced onion
3 bacon slices

Rub salt and pepper inside rabbit. Stuff with onion slices. Truss. Lay strips of bacon over rabbit. Wrap in aluminum foil, place in shallow baking pan and bake at 350 degrees for 1-1/2 hours. Serves 4.

===============

Violet Jelly

Gather about two cups of violets, no stems, just heads. Put blossoms in a shallow and look for bugs. Rinse violets in cold water and place in a quart jar. Cover with boiling water, put the lid on, and let stand 24 hours. Next day, strain out blossoms, and to 3 cups of violet water add the juice of 1 lemon, plus 1 package of powdered pectin. Bring to boil. Add 4 cups sugar, bring to boil again, and boil hard for 1 min. Pour into hot glasses and seal.

This is very sweet and tastes like violets. Not to be served spread thickly on toast, but with crackers or on small squares of toast with tea. Makes a different gift.

===============

Wild Greens

Pick such "weeds" as pokeweed (while very young), lamb's quarter, mustard or dandelion. Wash thoroughly, parboil for about 45 mins. in salt water, drain, and serve with vinegar. May also add garden greens such as young rhubarb, beet or spinach leaves.

BREADED DANDELION BLOSSOMS

1/4 CUP MILK	PINCH SALT
2 TBSP. POWDERED MILK	16 LARGE, FRESH DANDELION
1 TBSP. BAKING POWDER	BLOSSOMS
1 EGG	SHORTENING
1/2 CUP FLOUR	

MIX ALL INGREDIENTS EXCEPT BLOSSOMS AND SHORTENING. WASH BLOSSOMS LIGHTLY, DRAIN. DO NOT ALLOW TO WILT. DIP BLOSSOMS INTO BATTER, FRY IN DEEP FAT UNTIL GOLDEN BROWN. SERVES 4-5.

COOKED DRESSING FOR DANDELION GREENS

1/2 CUP CREAM	2 EGGS
1 TBSP. SUGAR	1 TEASP. SALT
4 TBSP. VINEGAR	1/2 CUP BUTTER
4 SLICES BACON, CUT INTO CUBES	PEPPER TO TASTE

WASH, PAT DRY DANDELION GREENS AND PUT IN BOWL. PLACE IN WARM PLACE. FRY BACON PIECES UNTIL BROWN AND CRUMBLY. DROP OVER LEAVES. PLACE BUTTER AND CREAM IN A SKILLET AND MELT BUTTER. BEAT EGGS; ADD SALT, PEPPER, SUGAR AND VINEGAR; THEN MIX WITH WARM CREAM MIXTURE. POUR INTO SKILLET AND INCREASE HEAT, STIRRING UNTIL DRESSING BECOMES THICK LIKE CUSTARD. POUR PIPING HOT OVER DANDELION LEAVES AND STIR THOROUGHLY. NEVER USE DANDELION LEAVES AFTER THEY BLOSSOM AS THEY WILL BE BITTER.

BAKED GROUSE

SOAK CLEANED BIRD FOR 6-8 HOURS IN SALT WATER (1 TBSP. PER PINT OF WATER), MAKING SURE BIRD IS TOTALLY COVERED WITH THIS BRINE. REMOVE FROM BRINE AND RINSE BIRD THOROUGHLY. STUFF WITH YOUR FAVORITE DRESSING OR:

4 CUPS CHOPPED ONION	SAGE TO TASTE
3 TBSP. CHOPPED ONION	1/4 CUP MELTED MARGARINE
3 TBSP. CHOPPED CELERY	HOT WATER
1 TEASP. SALT	1/4 TEASP. POULTRY SEASONING

PREHEAT OVEN TO 325 DEGREES. MIX ALL INGREDIENTS WELL AND USE TO STUFF BIRD. WRAP GROUSE IN ALUMINUM FOIL TO ROAST. BAKE FOR 30 MINS. PER POUND. ONE BIRD WILL SERVE TWO ADULTS.

VENISON ROAST

COVER DEER ROAST COMPLETELY WITH BUTTERMILK AND LET SOAK FOR 8-10 HOURS, TURNING OCCASIONALLY. WIPE BUTTERMILK FROM VENISON WITH PAPER TOWELS. DO NOT WASH. BROWN ON EACH SIDE IN SHORTENING. ADD ENOUGH WATER TO HAVE A DEPTH OF AN INCH OR SO. ADD ENOUGH SALT AND PEPPER FOR SIZE OF ROAST. COVER AND COOK SLOWLY (300-325 DEGREES) UNTIL TENDER, ADDING MORE WATER AS NEEDED. TOWARDS END OF COOKING TIME ADD 1 CUP RED WINE FOR EACH 2 LBS. OF MEAT, BASTING OFTEN UNTIL DONE.

DANDELION JELLY

ONE QUART OF DANDELION BLOSSOMS GATHERED IN THE MORNING WHEN THEY ARE FRESH AND FULL. RINSE THE YELLOW BLOSSOMS SEVERAL TIMES IN COLD WATER. CUT THE GREEN PORTION FROM THE BASE OF THE BLOSSOMS. PUT BLOSSOMS IN A PAN AND ADD 1 QUART OF WATER. BOIL FOR EXACTLY 3 MINS. DRAIN OFF LIQUID THROUGH A COLANDER. YOU SHOULD HAVE ABOUT 3 CUPS OF LIQUID. ADD 1 PACKAGE OF FRUIT PECTIN, 1 TEASP. ORANGE OR LEMON EXTRACT AND 4-1/2 CUPS OF SUGAR. BOIL THIS MIXTURE EXACTLY 3 MINS., STIRRING CONSTANLY. PLACE IN STERILIZED JARS.

ROSE HIP JELLY

1 QUART CLEAN ROSE HIPS
5 TART APPLES, UNPEELED
1 LEMON
1 TEASP. CLOVES

GATHER ROSE HIPS (BULBOUS PART LEFT ON STEM AFTER PETALS DROP) IN FALL WHEN THEY HAVE TURNED A REDDISH-BROWN COLOR. COOK ALL INGREDIENTS TOGETHER UNTIL TENDER. CRUSH AND STRAIN IN JELLY BAG. ADD 1 CUP SUGAR TO EACH CUP OF LIQUID. BOIL UNTIL IT JELLIES AND PUT INTO STERILIZED JARS. SEAL WITH WAX.

POKE "SALLET"

2 LBS. FRESH YOUNG POKE WITH
  LEAVES, WASHED
2 TBSP. BACON DRIPPINGS
5-6 TOPS OF GREEN ONIONS, CHOPPED
1 BEATEN EGG
SALT AND PEPPER TO TASTE

PARBOIL POKE FOR 15 MINS. AND THEN THROW OUT WATER. ADD NEW WATER AND BOIL AGAIN FOR 10 MINS. WITH ONION TOPS, SALT AND PEPPER. HEAT BACON DRIPPINGS IN LARGE IRON SKILLET AND ADD DRAINED POKE AND STIR FOR 5 MINS. OVER MEDIUM HEAT. ADD BEATEN EGG AND SCRAMBLE WITH POKE. SERVE HOT.

Frog Legs

Sprinkle 12 pairs of frog legs with lemon juice. Cover with ice and place in refrigerator for several hours. Dry, roll in cracker crumbs or flour, dip in beaten egg and roll in crumbs again. Fry in deep butter until golden brown. Serve with lemon quarters and tartar sauce.

Fruited Squirrel

2 squirrels, cut into serving pieces
12 prunes
1/4 cup raisins
3 tbsp. vinegar
6 gingersnaps, crumbled
1/2 teasp. salt

pinch of mixed whole pickling spices
1 medium onion, diced
3 tbsp. brown sugar
1 tbsp. butter
2 tbsp. flour, browned

Cook squirrel in salted water until tender. Remove meat. To liquid, add all ingredients except flour and simmer a few mins. Thicken with flour dissolved in 1/4 cup cold water. Add meat, heat thoroughly. Serve 4.

Deer Salami

5 lbs. deer burger
2-1/2 teasp. whole mustard seed
2-1/2 teasp. garlic powder
2-1/2 teasp. coarse pepper

3 teasp. cayenne powdered pepper (optional)
1 bottle liquid smoke

Mix ingredients in large bowl. Refrigerate, mixing once a day for 4 days. On day 4, roll into slices (10) and coat with liquid smoke. Bake on cookie sheet at 150 degrees for 8 hours. turning every 2 hours.

Venison Meat Loaf

1/2 lb. ground venison
1/2 lb. sausage
3 eggs
1 cup bread- or cracker crumbs
1 cup milk

1/2 cup onion, minced
1/4 teasp. thyme
1 teasp. salt
1/4 teasp. pepper

Mix venison and sausage thoroughly with other ingredients. Place in loaf pan and bake in 350 degree oven for approximately 1 hour.

SQUIRREL AND GRAVY

CLEAN SQUIRREL AND CUT INTO SERVING PIECES. SOAK AT LEAST ONE HOUR IN SALTED WATER. REMOVE MEAT, DRAIN AND PLACE IN HEAVY DUTCH OVEN. COVER WITH FRESH WATER. COOK ON MODERATE HEAT UNTIL MEAT IS TENDER. PUT 1/2 CUP FLOUR INTO A SMALL AMOUNT OF WATER AND STIR UNTIL IT MAKES A THICK PASTE. ADD TO POT AND STIR UNTIL WELL MIXED. LET COOK A SHORT TIME LONGER UNTIL ALL IS WELL BLENDED. SERVE WITH GOOD HOMEMADE BISCUITS OR CORNBREAD TO "SOP THE GRAVY."

VENISON CHILI

2 LBS. VENISON, CUT INTO 1/2-INCH CUBES
1 LB. GROUND BEEF
2 LARGE RED ONIONS, CHOPPED
2 (15-1/2 OZ.) CANS KIDNEY BEANS, UNDRAINED

3 (8 OZ.) CANS TOMATO SAUCE
1 (6 OZ.) CAN TOMATO PASTE
1 CUP WATER
3-4 TBSP. CHILI POWDER

COMBINE VENISON, GROUND BEEF AND ONION IN DUTCH OVEN; COOK UNTIL BROWNED, STIRRING TO CRUMBLE BEEF. DRAIN OFF PAN DRIPPINGS. STIR IN REMAINING INGREDIENTS. COVER AND SIMMER 1/2 HOUR OR UNTIL VENISON IS TENDER, ADDING WATER AS NEEDED. YIELDS ABOUT 7 CUPS.

VENISON SAUSAGE

4 LBS. VENISON
1 LB. FRESH PORK
5 TEASP. SALT

2-1/2 TEASP. GROUND PEPPER
1/2 TEASP. SUGAR
5 TEASP. SAGE

TRIM EXCESS FAT, IF ANY, FROM VENISON. CUT INTO PIECES AND PUT THROUGH MEAT GRINDER WITH FRESH PORK. ADD OTHER INGREDIENTS AND MIX THOROUGHLY. FORM INTO PATTIES FOR COOKING. MAKES 5 LBS. OF SAUSAGE.

VENISON BURGERS

2-1/2 LBS. GROUND VENISON
1/2 CUP MINCED ONION
1 CLOVE GARLIC, MINCED
4 TBSP. CHOPPED PARSLEY

2/3 CUP DRY RED WINE
2 TBSP. SOY SAUCE
SALT AND PEPPER TO TASTE

MIX ALL INGREDIENTS; FORM INTO THICK PATTIES. BROIL 10 MINS. ON EACH SIDE (LESS FOR RARE). SERVE IMMEDIATELY IN HOT BURGER BUNS. SERVES 8-10.

Roast Pheasant

1 (2/12 LB.) PHEASANT	1/2 LARGE ONION, CHOPPED
3 STRIPS BACON	1/2 CUP OIL
1/2 STALK CELERY, CHOPPED	1/2 TEASP. ROSEMARY LEAVES
1/2 CUP WHITE WINE	SALT AND PEPPER

PREHEAT OVEN TO 350 DEGREES. SEASON CAVITY OF PHEASANT WITH SALT AND PEPPER, PINCH OF ROSEMARY AND ONE SLICE OF BACON. COAT ROASTING PAN WITH OIL. PLACE PHEASANT IN PAN, BREAST UP. SPRINKLE WITH ROSEMARY, SALT AND PEPPER. PLACE REMAINING BACON SLICES OVER BREAST. ADD CHOPPED CELERY, ONIONS AND WHITE WINE. COVER WITH ALUMINUM FOIL FOR FIRST HOUR, THEN UNCOVER FOR BROWNING. ADD 1 CUP WATER AND COOK FOR AN ADDITIONAL HOUR, OR UNTIL DONE. SERVES 2. *THE BAVARIAN INN, SHEPHERDSTOWN, W.VA.*

Wild Roast Turkey

1 WILD TURKEY (10-12 LBS.)	SALT AND PEPPER
1 CHOPPED ONION	1 LB. PORK SAUSAGE
1-1/2 QUARTS SOFT BREADCRUMBS	1/4 TEASP. PEPPER
2 TEASP. SALT	3 TBSP. CHOPPED PARSLEY
BACON OR MELTED BACON FAT	

DRESS TURKEY, SEASON WITH SALT AND PEPPER INSIDE AND OUT AND WEIGH TO DETERMINE COOKING TIME (20-25 MINS. PER POUND). MAKE STUFFING FROM OTHER INGREDIENTS: COOK ONION WITH SAUSAGE FOR 5 MINS.; THEN ADD BREADCRUMBS, PEPPER, SALT AND PARSLEY. MOISTEN WITH A LITTLE HOT WATER IF TOO DRY. PLACE TURKEY, BREAST DOWN, IN UNCOVERED PAN. STUFF AND ROAST FOR HALF THE TOTAL REQUIRED TIME. TURN BIRD BREAST UP. LAY STRIPS OF BACON OVER BREAST OR COVER WITH A PIECE OF CLOTH DIPPED IN BACON FAT. FINISH ROASTING. IF CLOTH IS USED, REMOVE TOWARDS THE END OF COOKING TIME FOR BROWNING BIRD. SERVES 6-8.

One-Dish Rabbit

1 RABBIT, CUT INTO SERVING PIECES	2 MEDIUM ONIONS, SLICED 1/2-INCH
SALT AND PEPPER	THICK
FLOUR	4-5 SMALL POTATOES, QUARTERED
OIL	1 CAN (16 OZ.) TOMATOES

SPRINKLE RABBIT WITH SALT, PEPPER AND FLOUR. FRY IN OIL UNTIL LIGHTLY BROWNED. LAYER, RABBIT, ONIONS AND POTATOES IN GREASED CASSEROLE. COVER WITH TOMATOES. BAKE IN 350 DEGREE OVEN FOR 2 HOURS. SERVE ON HOT BISCUITS. SERVES 4-6.

FLOUNDER DIANNA*

4 (6-8 OZ.) FLOUNDER FILETS
1/2 CUP SLICED RAMPS OR SPRING ONIONS
1/4 CUP PINE NUTS
1/4 CUP WHITE WINE
SALT, PEPPER AND THYME TO TASTE

FRESH DANDELION GREENS TO MAKE 2
CUPS, BLANCHED AND CHOPPED
1/4 LB. BUTTER
JUICE OF ONE LEMON

BLANCH DANDELION GREENS IN SALTED WATER. RINSE IN ICE WATER; CHOP. MIX IN TOASTED PINE NUTS AND LEMON JUICE. SAUTÉ RAMPS SEASONED WITH SALT, PEPPER AND THYME. COMBINE ALL INGREDIENTS. SPREAD AS A FILLING ON FLOUNDER FILETS. ROLL LARGE END OF FISH TO TAIL AND PLACE IN CASSEROLE. BAKE AT 350 DEGREES UNTIL DONE (ABOUT 15 MINS.).

*WILD FOODS PRIZE-WINNING RECIPE FROM NORTH BEND NATURE WONDER WEEKEND IN 1986 BY MERV MINNICH OF CHARLESTON, S.C.

APPLE-ROASTED WILD DUCK

2 WILD DUCKS
1 CUP RAISINS
1 CUP APPLE JUICE
2 TEASP. SALT

2 CUPS APPLE QUARTERS
1 CUP BREADCRUMBS
1 SLICE ONION
1/4 TEASP. PEPPER

CLEAN AND WASH DUCKS WELL. MIX APPLES, RAISINS AND BREADCRUMBS. POUR IN 1/2 TO 3/4 CUP APPLE JUICE AND MIX UNTIL MOIST. FILL DUCKS WITH MIXTURE. RUB DUCKS WITH THE SLICE OF ONION, SALT AND PEPPER. ROAST IN 325 DEGREE OVEN BREAST SIDE DOWN, 2-1/2 TO 3 HOURS. BASTE WITH REMAINING APPLE JUICE DURING COOKING. SERVES 6.

SQUIRREL STEW

2 SQUIRRELS
1 LARGE ONION, MINCED
1 CAN CREAM STYLE CORN
1 TBSP. SALT
1 LARGE POTATO, QUARTERED
4 TBSP. SUGAR

3 QUARTS WATER
2 CUPS DRIED LIMA BEANS, SOAKED
1/2 LB. BUTTER
1/2 TEASP. PEPPER
1 (No. 2) CAN TOMATOES, SLICED

DISJOINT SQUIRRELS AND PLACE IN DEEP KETTLE WITH WATER, ONION, LIMA BEANS, CORN, 1/4 LB. BUTTER, 1 TBSP. SALT, 1/2 TEASP. PEPPER AND ANY OF YOUR OTHER FAVORITE SEASONINGS (GARLIC, CELERY SEED, ETC.). COVER AND SIMMER 2 HOURS. ADD POTATOES, TOMATOES AND SUGAR. SIMMER 1 HOUR MORE. ABOUT 15 MINS. BEFORE STEW IS COOKED, ADD ANOTHER 1/4 LB. BUTTER AND MIX WELL. SERVES 4.

WILD GRAPE SAUCE

4 CUPS WILD GRAPES
1/4 CUP SHERRY
1 TBSP. LEMON JUICE

4 TBSP. BUTTER
3 WHOLE CLOVES
1 TBSP. GRATED LEMON RIND

WASH GRAPES, COVER WITH BOILING WATER AND SIMMER 5 MINS. DRAIN. PUT THROUGH A SIEVE. MELT BUTTER IN A SAUCEPAN AND ADD SHERRY, CLOVES AND LEMON JUICE. SIMMER 5 MINS. REMOVE CLOVES AND ADD GRAPE PUREE AND LEMON RIND. HEAT THROUGH. SERVE WITH ANY GAME BIRD.

BEVERAGES

MINT JULEPS

SHOULD BE SERVED IN FROSTED STERLING SILVER JULEP CUPS, BUT IF UNAVAILABLE, CHILL IN FREEZER-HEAVY 10-OZ. TUMBLERS.

12 JULEP CUPS OR GLASSES
CRUSHED ICE
3 CUPS GRANULATED SUGAR
24 OZ. OF 100-PROOF BOURBON

12 MINT SPRIGS FOR GARNISH
1-1/2 CUPS WATER
HANDFUL OF MINT SPRIGS

CHILL CUPS/GLASSES IN FREEZER FOR SEVERAL HOURS. FILL CUPS WITH CRUSHED ICE AND RETURN TO FREEZER OVERNIGHT. MAKE A SYRUP BY BRINGING SUGAR AND WATER TO A BOIL. REDUCE HEAT AND SIMMER FOR 5-10 MINS. UNTIL CLEAR AND THICK. WHILE STILL HOT, STIR IN A HANDFUL OF MINT SPRIGS, ALLOW TO COOL. STRAIN SYRUP, DISCARDING MINT. REMOVE CUPS FROM FREEZER 15 MINS. BEFORE SERVNG. POUR 2 OZ. OF BOURBON AND 2 OZ. OF SYRUP OVER ICE. DECORATE WITH SPRIG OF MINT. MAKES 12.

FIRST MINT JULEPS SERVED AT *THE GREENBRIER, WHITE SULPHUR SPRINGS, W.VA.*

CATNIP TEA

POUR PINT OF BOILING WATER OVER ABOUT 1/2 CUP OF BROKEN STEMS AND LEAVES. LET STAND SEVERAL MINS., THEN STRAIN. BEST TO GATHER IN SPRING WHEN FLOWERING. CATNIP TEA WILL INDUCE SLEEP.

SASSAFRAS TEA

IN THE SPRING GATHER ROOTS AND TENDER TWIGS. POUND THE ROOTS TO A PULP IF THEY ARE LARGE AND WASH. PARE OUTER BARK FROM TWIGS. BOIL UNTIL DARK IN COLOR. STRAIN AND SWEETEN WITH HONEY. USE 4 AVERAGE-SIZED ROOTS TO EACH GALLON OF WATER MAKING 1 GALLON OF TEA.

GINGER WATER

1/2 TO 3/4 CUP PACKED BROWN SUGAR
1 TEASP. POWDERED GINGER

1/2 CUP CIDER VINEGAR

DISSOLVE BROWN SUGAR AND GINGER IN VINEGAR BY SHAKING OR STIRRING. ADD 1 QUART COLD WATER AND MIX. CHILL WELL AND SERVE. SERVES 6.

FORERUNNER OF GINGER ALE - GOOD THIRST QUENCHER.

Mint Tea

Gather mint leaves in the summer when plants are young, just before or just after blooming. Boil the leaves in water, strain and sweeten with honey. Good cold remedy.

East Indian Tea

2 cups milk
2 cinnamon sticks
1 teasp. whole coriander
2 tbsp. orange pekoe tea

2 cups water
1 teasp. whole cloves
1/2 teasp. whole cardamom

Boil all ingredients except tea together for 5 mins. Add tea, cover and remove from heat. Steep 5 additional mins. Strain and serve hot. Serves 4.

Hot Coffee with Egg

Old recipe used in place of milk for nourishment when no refrigeration.

1 egg yolk, 1 teasp. sugar and 1 cup strong, hot coffee

Whip egg yolk with sugar until thickened and light yellow in color. Slowly stir hot coffee into egg mixture until well-blended.

Spiced Rhubarb Cooler

2 lbs. rhubarb
1-inch stick cinnamon
1/8 teasp. mace
2 tbsp. lemon juice
1 pint ginger ale

3 cups water
4 whole cloves
1/2 cup orange juice
1 cup sugar syrup (see below)

Cut rhubarb in small pieces; do not peel. Add water and spices; simmer over low heat until tender; strain. Add cooled sugar syrup and fruit juices. Chill. Pour over ice in pitcher or tall glasses; add ginger ale. Serves 6.

Sugar Syrup: Combine 1 cup sugar and 1 cup water in saucepan; stirring over low heat until sugar is dissolved. Bring to boiling point, let boil without stirring about 7 mins. Cool. Pour into jar, cover and keep in refrigerator if not using immediately. Makes 1 cup.

OLD-FASHIONED LEMONADE

1 CUP SUGAR
RIND OF 2 LEMONS, GRATED OR
OR CUT INTO SMALL PIECES

1 CUP WATER
1 CUP LEMON JUICE

COMBINE SUGAR, WATER AND LEMON RIND* IN SAUCEPAN; STIR OVER LOW HEAT UNTIL SUGAR IS DISSOLVED. BOIL ABOUT 7 MINS. AND COOL. ADD LEMON JUICE AND 4 CUPS WATER. IF A SWEETER LEMONADE IS PREFERRED, USE LESS LEMON JUICE IN PROPORTION TO SUGAR SYRUP. POUR OVER ICE IN PITCHER OR TALL GLASSES. SERVES 6-8.

*USE OF THE RIND AS WELL AS THE JUICE NOT ONLY ADDS FLAVOR BUT IS AN ECONOMY AS FEWER LEMONS ARE NEEDED TO GET THE DESIRED STRENGTH.

MINTED LEMONADE: PLACE SOME BRUISED MINT LEAVES IN THE BOTTOM OF THE PITCHER BEFORE ADDING LEMONADE; GARNISH WITH A SPRIG OF MINT.

RASPBERRY LEMONADE: ADD 1 PINT OF CRUSHED RASPBERRIES TO BOILED SUGAR-WATER MIXTURE; STRAIN. ADD LEMON JUICE AND PROCEED AS DIRECTED.

ORANGEADE: INSTEAD OF LEMON JUICE; SUBSTITUTE 2 CUPS OF ORANGE JUICE, THEN ADD 1/4 CUP LEMON JUICE.

CONDIMENTS

CREAM CHEESE -WATERCRESS DIP

8 OZ. CREAM CHEESE, SOFTENED
1/3 TO 1/2 CUP CHOPPED WATERCRESS
   LEAVES
SALT AND PEPPER

GRATED HORSERADISH TO TASTE
   (DRAIN BOTTLED HORSERADISH WELL)
2 TBSP. MILK

BEAT CREAM CHEESE AND MILK WITH ELECTRIC MIXER UNTIL SMOOTH. STIR IN WATERCRESS AND HORSERADISH, BLENDING WELL. SEASON WITH SALT AND PEPPER TO TASTE. SERVE ON CRACKERS OR MELBA TOAST. MAKES ABOUT 1-1/3 CUPS.

HOT SAUCE*

1/2 CUP FLOUR
1 CUP KETCHUP
1/2 CUP LEMON JUICE
1/2 TEASP. ONION SALT
2 TEASP. CHILI POWDER
1/2 BOTTLE TABASCO SAUCE
1/2 STICK BUTTER

2 TBSP. MUSTARD
1/2 CUP VINEGAR
1/2 TEASP. GARLIC SALT
3 TEASP. BROWN SUGAR
3 TEASP. RED PEPPER
1 QUART WATER

MIX ALL INGREDIENTS WELL AND SIMMER ON LOW HEAT UNTIL THICKENED. MAKES APPROXIMATELY 1 QUART OF SAUCE. MAY REFRIGERATE FOR SEVERAL WEEKS AND USE AS NEEDED.

*THIS SAUCE HAS MANY USES INCLUDING THAT WEST VIRGINIA FAVORITE SANDWICH, "HOT BOLOGNA" WHICH CONSISTS OF BOLOGNA SLICED THICK (ABOUT 1/2-INCH) SATURATED IN HOT SAUCE, LIGHTLY FRIED IN BUTTER, PUT ON A BUN WITH ADDITIONAL HOT SAUCE ADDED.

OLD-FASHIONED BREAD & BUTTER PICKLES

PLACE ABOUT 25 LARGE CUCUMBERS IN COLD WATER UNTIL CRISP, THEN WIPE DRY AND SLICE. ADD 12 ONIONS SLICED AND 1/2 CUP SALT. LET STAND FOR ONE HOUR. DO NOT DRAIN. ADD 1 QUART VINEGAR, A LITTLE WATER, 2-12 CUPS SUGAR, 2 TBSP. MUSTARD SEED, 2 TBSP. GINGER ROOT AND 2 TBSP. CELERY SEED. BOIL ALL TOGETHER FOR ABOUT 5 MINS. WHILE HOT, FILL JARS AND SEAL.

FOR MANY GENERATIONS, EARLY SETTLERS DEPENDED ON THEIR HOMEMADE PICKLES FOR THE ONLY GREEN VEGETABLE THEY COULD PRESERVE THROUGH THE WINTER. TODAY THEY'RE STILL A POPULAR ITEM IN STATE AND COUNTY FAIR JUDGINGS.

Cole Slaw Dressing

3 WELL-BEATEN EGGS
1/4 CUP SUGAR

1/4 CUP VINEGAR
SALT AND PEPPER

BEAT ALL INGREDIENTS WELL AND PLACE OVER BOILING WATER IN A DOUBLE-BOILER. STIR CONSTANTLY UNTIL THICK. IF LUMPY, BEAT WITH EGGBEATER UNTIL CREAMY AND SMOOTH. MAY ADD A LITTLE MAYONNAISE.

Honey Cream Fruit Sauce

1 PINT SOUR CREAM
1/4 CUP ORANGE JUICE

1/2 CUP HONEY

MIX ALL INGREDIENTS THOROUGHLY. CHILL. SERVE OVER FRESH FRUIT. MAKES 3 CUPS.

Mint Sauce

STRIP LEAVES FROM FRESH MINT TO MAKE ABOUT 1/2 CUP FIRMLY PACKED. CHOP FINE AND PLACE IN SMALL, STURDY JAR OR MORTAR AND PESTLE. ADD 2 TBSP. SUGAR AND 1/4 TEASP. SALT. POUND UNTIL LEAVES ARE BRUISED THOROUGHLY. STIR IN 1/3 CUP CIDER VINEGAR AND SAME AMOUNT OF WATER. KEEPS WELL IN REFRIGERATOR. SERVE WITH COLD MEAT, ESPECIALLY LAMB.

Pickled Eggs

THE TIME WAS THAT EVERY LOCAL TAVERN IN WEST VIRGINIA WOULD HAVE A BIG JAR OF PICKLED EGGS ON THE BAR TO PROVIDE SOME NOURISHMENT FOR THE BEER DRINKERS.

8 EGGS
2 TBSP. SUGAR
3 TO 4 WHOLE CLOVES
2 TEASP. CARAWAY SEEDS
ENOUGH BEET JUICE TO COLOR EGGS A ROSY PINK

1 TEASP. SALT
2 CUPS CIDER VINEGAR
8 PEPPERCORNS
1 BUD GARLIC

HARD BOIL THE EGGS, CHILL. PEEL AND CHILL AGAIN. PUT EGGS IN A LARGE GLASS JAR WITH A TIGHT LID. IN A SAUCEPAN COMBINE REMAINING INGREDIENTS AND BRING TO A BOIL. REDUCE HEAT AND COOK SLOWLY FOR ABOUT 1/2 AN HOUR. POUR HEATED MIXTURE THROUGH A SIEVE ONTO EGGS IN JAR. COVER TIGHTLY AND LET SET FOR AT LEAST THREE DAYS BEFORE SERVING. MAKES A PRETTY GARNISH FOR SALAD PLATES.

Hot Peppers in Russian Dressing

6 QUARTS HOT PEPPERS
RUSSIAN DRESSING
COOKING OIL
GARLIC

1/2 CUP SALT
1/4 CUP SUGAR
8 CUPS VINEGAR
4 CUPS WATER

REMOVE SEEDS FROM PEPPERS* AND CUT INTO DESIRED SIZE. PACK INTO JAR. ADD 3 TBSP. RUSSIAN DRESSING, 2 TBSP. OIL AND 1 CLOVE GARLIC TO EACH PINT. COMBINE WATER, VINEGAR, SALT AND SUGAR. BRING TO A BOIL. POUR OVER PEPPERS AND SEAL. PROCESS IN WATER BATH 10 MINS. MAKES 8 PINTS.

*USE RUBBER/PLASTIC GLOVES TO PREVENT SKIN IRRITATION.

Russian Dressing

1 CUP MAYONNAISE
1 TBSP. GRATED HORSERADISH
1 TEASP. WORCESTERSHIRE SAUCE

1/4 CUP CHILI SAUCE OR KETCHUP
1 TEASP. GRATED ONION

MAKES ABOUT 1-3/4 CUPS

Piccalilli

EVERY WEST VIRGINIA COUNTRY HOMEMAKER HAS THEIR OWN SPECIAL RECIPE FOR THIS DELICIOUS RELISH.

6 CUPS CHOPPED GREEN TOMATOES
1-1/2 CUPS CHOPPED GREEN PEPPERS
7-1/2 CUPS CHOPPED CABBAGE
3 TBSP. WHOLE MIXED PICKLING SPICES
4-1/2 CUPS 5% VINEGAR

1-1/2 CUPS CHOPPED SWEET RED PEPPERS
2-1/4 CUPS CHOPPED ONIONS
1/2 CUP CANNING OR PICKLING SALT
3 CUPS BROWN SUGAR

WASH, CHOP AND COMBINE VEGETABLES WITH SALT. COVER WITH HOT WATER. LET STAND 12 HOURS. DRAIN AND PRESS IN A CLEAN, WHITE CLOTH TO REMOVE ALL LIQUID. TIE PICKLING SPICES LOOSELY IN SPICE BAG AND ADD TO COMBINED VINEGAR AND BROWN SUGAR. HEAT TO BOILING. PLACE VEGETABLES IN SAUCEPAN. BOIL GENTLY 30 MINS. OR UNTIL VOLUME OF MIXTURE IS REDUCED BY HALF. REMOVE SPICE BAG. FILL HOT, STERILE JARS WITH HOT MIXTURE, LEAVING 1/2-INCH HEADSPACE. ADJUST LIDS. PROCESS PINTS 10 MINS. IN BOILING WATER BATH. MAKES 9 HALF-PINT JARS.

PICKLED PEPPER/ONION RELISH

6 CUPS FINELY CHOPPED ONIONS
3 CUPS FINELY CHOPPED GREEN PEPPERS
1-1/2 CUPS SUGAR
2 TBSP. CANNING OR PICKLING SALT

3 CUPS FINELY CHOPPED SWEET RED
  PEPPERS
6 CUPS 5% WHITE VINEGAR

COMBINE ALL INGREDIENTS. BOIL GENTLY FOR 30 MINS. OR UNTIL MIXTURE THICKENS AND VOLUME IS REDUCED BY ONE-HALF. FILL STERILE JARS WITH HOT RELISH, LEAVING 1/2-INCH HEADSPACE; SEAL TIGHTLY. STORE IN REFRIGERATOR AND USE WITHIN ONE MONTH. IF EXTENDED STORAGE IS DESIRED PROCESS IN BOILING WATER BATH FOR 10 MINS., PACKED IN PINT OR HALF-PINT JARS. MAKES 9 HALF-PINTS.

DEVILED EGGS

6 HARD COOKED EGGS
1 TEASP. VINEGAR
1/2 TEASP. SALT
1/4 CUP MAYONNAISE OR SALAD DRESSING

1 TEASP. PREPARED MUSTARD
2 TBSP. MELTED BUTTER OR
  MARGARINE
1/8 TEASP. PEPPER

CUT EGGS IN HALF, LENGTHWISE. REMOVE YOLKS AND MASH WITH A FORK. ADD REMAINING INGREDIENTS TO YOLKS, WHIPPING UNTIL SMOOTH AND CREAMY. HEAP INTO WHITE HALVES. SPRINKLE WITH PAPRIKA AND REFRIGERATE.

GRANDMA'S CHOW-CHOW

4 QUARTS OF GREEN TOMATOES
2 QUARTS SMALL WHITE ONIONS
6 SWEET RED PEPPERS
WATER
1 JAR OF LITTLE SOUR GHERKIN PICKLES

12 GREEN BELL PEPPERS
SEVERAL SMALL HOT RED PEPPERS
  (TO TASTE)
1 HEAD CAULIFLOWER
2 CUPS PICKLING SALT

CUT UP ALL VEGETABLES; COVER WITH WATER AND SALT AND LET SIT OVERNIGHT. NEXT MORNING BOIL FOR 3 MINS. AND DRAIN UNTIL COMPLETELY FREE OF LIQUID. COMBINE DRESSING INGREDIENTS. BOIL UNTIL CREAMY, POUR OVER VEGETABLES AND ADD GHERKINS. SEAL IN QUART JARS. MAKES 8 QUARTS.

DRESSING

2 QUARTS VINEGAR
5 TBSP. TURMERIC
5 CUPS GRANULATED SUGAR
1 TBSP. MUSTARD SEED

5 TBSP. GROUND MUSTARD
6 TBSP. FLOUR
1 TBSP. CELERY SEED
1 PINT WATER

Rhubarb Spread

10 cups rhubarb
8 cups sugar

2 (3-oz.) boxes wild strawberry
and 1 box red raspberry Jell-O

Wash and dry rhubarb. Cut into 1-inch pieces. Put rhubarb in saucepan with sugar. (Do not add water.) Cook over low heat. When it starts to boil, cook 10 mins. Remove from stove and add dry Jell-O. Fill jars and seal. Refrigerate. May also be kept in plastic containers in the freezer until ready to use. Makes 12 half-pints. Recipe can be halved.

Harvest Applesauce

1/3 cup margarine
1/2 cup maple syrup
2 tbsp. lemon juice
1/8 teasp. ground ginger

1-1/2 lbs. tart cooking apples,
pared, cored and sliced
1/4 teasp. ground cardamom

Melt margarine in medium saucepan. Add apples, syrup and lemon juice. Cook, uncovered over medium heat, stirring frequently, until apples are very soft and almost all the moisture is gone (about 20 mins.). Cool slightly then put into food processor and process until finely chopped. Add remaining ingredients and serve hot or cold. Makes 2 cups.

Pickled Peaches

2 lbs. sugar
2 sticks cinnamon
4 quarts fresh peaches, pared, whole or halved

2 cups vinegar
2 tbsp. whole cloves

Boil sugar, vinegar and spices for 20 mins. Drop fruit, a few at a time into syrup and cook until tender. Pack in hot sterilized jars, adding syrup to 1/2-inch from top. Seal. Makes 4 quarts.

Thick Barbecue Sauce

2 medium onions, chopped fine
3/4 cup Coca-Cola Classic
3/4 cup ketchup
2 tbsp. vinegar

2 tbsp. Worcestershire sauce
1/2 teasp. chili powder
1/2 teasp. salt

Combine ingredients in a saucepan and bring to a boil. Reduce heat and simmer, covered, for about 45 mins. or until the sauce is very thick. Stir occasionally. Makes 2 cups.

Hot Dog Chili

In a large saucepan, put 1 quart water. Crumble in 2 lbs. of hamburger and beat with a fork to break the meat into very small pieces. Add:

1 teasp. Worcestershire sauce
6 oz. can tomato paste
1-1/2 teasp. ground allspice
2 large onions, chopped
2 tbsp. chili powder
1 teasp. black pepper
1/2 teasp. red pepper

1-1/2 tbsp. vinegar
1 large bay leaf
1 teasp. cinnamon
1/2 teasp. cumin
1 clove garlic
1 teasp. salt

Simmer 3 or 4 hours. Remove garlic clove and bay leaf. Serve on hot dogs or spaghetti. Makes about 3-1/2 pints.

Ginger Pears*

9 lbs. fresh pears
6 lbs. sugar

3 oz. crystallized ginger
4 lemons

Pare and core pears; cut into thin slices. Mix pears and sugar, and place over low heat in large kettle. Stir until sugar is melted and syrup forms. Simmer until fruit is clear, stirring occasionally. Add grated rind of 2 lemons and the juice of all 4 lemons. Add ginger, cut into small pieces and simmer until syrup is thick. Put into sterilized jelly glasses and cover with paraffin wax, or seal in sterlized pint jars while hot. Approximately 18 jelly glasses.

*Makes interesting and unusual Christmas present.

Hot Pepper Jelly*

1/2 cup hot peppers (may use dried
   cayenne from garden, or
   canned Jalapenos), seeded, chopped
1 cup chopped bell peppers

1-1/4 cups cider vinegar
6 cups sugar
2 (3-oz.) packages of Certo

In blender/food processor blend everything together, except sugar. Pour into large saucepan and add sugar. Stir constantly over high heat to rolling boil point and boil 1 min. Add few drops of green food coloring and mix well. Put into sterilized jars and seal with wax. Makes about 10 baby food jars.

*I always make this for friends at Christmas with the suggestions
that it is good with pork or lamb and delicious on
crackers spread with cream cheese.

Spiced Pickled Cantaloupe

2 QUARTS CANATALOUPE, CUT INTO
  1-INCH SQUARES
1 QUART COLD WATER
3 CUPS BOILING WATER
1 CUP WHITE VINEGAR

1-1/2 TBSP. WHOLE ALLSPICE
4 TBSP. PICKLING SALT
4 CUPS SUGAR
2-3 STICKS CINNAMON
1-1/2 TBSP. WHOLE CLOVES

SELECT FIRM, SLIGHTLY UNDERRIPE CANTALOUPE. CUT IN HALF, REMOVE SEEDS AND RIND AND CUT INTO SQUARES. COMBINE COLD WATER AND SALT STIRRING UNTIL DISSOLVED. POUR OVER CANTALOUPE, COVER AND LET STAND FOR 3 HOURS. DRAIN. COMBINE BOILIG WATER, SUGAR, VINEGAR AND SPICES. BRING TO A BOIL, STIRRING UNTIL SUGAR IS DISSOLVED. ADD DRAINED CANTALOUPE. BRING TO A BOIL AND BOIL FOR 10 MINS. COOL. COVER AND LET STAND OVERNIGHT. DRAIN SYRUP FROM CANTALOUPE. BRING SYRUP TO A BOIL; COOK 10 MINS. ADD CANTALOUPE AND BOIL AGAIN. REDUCE HEAT AND SIMMER ABOUT 45 MINS. OR UNTIL CANTALOUPE IS CLEAR AND TRANSPARENT. POUR IMMEDIATELY INTO HOT STERILIZED JARS. SEAL AT ONCE. MAKES ABOUT 2-1/2 QUARTS. MAKES NICE CHRISTMAS GIFT.

Zucchini Marmalade

2 LBS. YOUNG ZUCCHINI
JUICE OF 2 LEMONS
1 TEASP. GRATED LEMON PEEL
1 (13.5 OZ.) CAN CRUSHED PINEAPPLE,
  DRAINED

1 (1-3/4 OZ.) PACKAGE FRUIT PECTIN
5 CUPS SUGAR
2 TBSP. FINELY CRUSHED CRYSTAL
  LIZED GINGER

PEEL ZUCCHINI AND SLICE VERY THINLY AND PUT IN LARGE KETTLE. ADD LEMON JUICE, LEMON RIND AND PINEAPPLE. BRING TO A BOIL, THEN LOWER HEAT AND SIMMER UNCOVERED UNTIL TENDER, ABOUT 10 MINS. ADD PECTIN AND BRING TO BOIL OVER HIGH HEAT. ADD SUGAR AND GINGER. BRING TO A FULL ROLLING BOIL FOR 1 MIN., STIRRING CONSTANTLY. MAKES 5 HALF-PINT JARS.

INDEX